"In this remarkable new collection (again, the impact of St Teresa's writin; today as they were 500 years ago. Julien had the privilege to know this past quarter century, approaches St Teresa's mystical texts from her own training, and practice, of Jungian depth psychology. She has been a Jungian analyst, supervisor and teacher at the Association of Jungian Analysts in London for many years. She brings her deep knowledge of the healing of the psyche to these mystical texts, recognizing what she describes as 'the unprecedented spiritual longing and emergency of our own times.'

"Julienne takes the 'bull by the horns' and presents the fusion of the Jungian path with the transcendent mysteries in a refreshingly unembarrassed fashion. She states that one of the consequences of the deep spiritual hunger of our generation is to foster 'an overwhelming need for the depth dimension of the Christian tradition.' Those looking for this depth dimension need look no further, they will find it in this set of priceless essays—indeed, a 'diamond of great price.'"

Professor Peter Tyler, Professor of Pastoral Theology and Spirituality, St Mary's University, London

"Julienne McLean, in *The Diamond Heart: Jungian Psychology and the Christian Mystical Tradition*, has accomplished a remarkable task. She articulates the heart of Christian contemplative and mystical experience in a manner possible only to one who is, herself, a devoted practitioner of that tradition—bringing it into dialogue with depth psychology, which is uniquely able to attest to the importance of such traditions for individual and collective well-being in the twenty-first century. In this collection of essays, depth psychology achieves its potential to articulate the threshold at which human psychological experience implies and invites participation in what is divinely transcendent. While focusing on Teresa of Avila's *The Interior Castle*, McLean's narrative veritably dances in affectionate familiarity with exemplars of spiritual practice from across time and space, including Pseudo-Dionysius, Gregory Palamas, and John of the Cross. Analysts, therapists, and spiritual directors whose work often takes place at the psychological-spiritual threshold will recognize the sagacity of McLean's treatment. For others, this book might be their first experience of how depth psychology and genuine spirituality can complement and mutually illuminate each other, and how stimulating of personal reflection and insight the conversation between them can be."

-Robert Isaac Skidmore, PhD, MDiv, Orthodox Priest, Professor in School of Clinical Mental Health Counseling, Southern Oregon University. Author of *Edge of the Abyss: The Usefulness of Antichrist Terminology in the Era of Donald Trump*

THE DIAMOND HEART

Jungian Psychology and the
Christian Mystical Tradition

JULIENNE MCLEAN

 CHIRON PUBLICATIONS • ASHEVILLE, NORTH CAROLINA

www.ChironPublications.com

Interior and cover design by Danijela Mijailovic
Printed primarily in the United States of America.

ISBN 978-1-68503-095-7 paperback
ISBN 978-1-68503-096-4 hardcover
ISBN 978-1-68503-097-1 electronic
ISBN 978-1-68503-098-8 limited edition paperback

Library of Congress Cataloging-in-Publication Data

Names: McLean, Julienne, author.
Title: The diamond heart : Jungian psychology and the Christian mystical tradition / Julienne McLean.
Description: Asheville : Chiron Publications, 2023. | Includes bibliographical references and index. | Summary: "Two towering figures thread their way through this book: St Teresa of Avila, the sixteenth century Spanish Carmelite saint, writer and reformer and C. G. Jung, the founder of modern depth psychology. Through sharing fifteen key papers, chapters and talks written over nearly twenty-five years, the author draws on their writings to focus on, and explore, the interface and relationship between the Christian mystical tradition and Jungian, depth psychology. Jung saw the human psyche as "by nature religious" and made this insight a principal focus of his explorations. In this regard, the book aims to explore an essentially depth approach to spirituality and numinosity relevant for todays' largely post-religious situation. Jungian depth psychology, with all its own richness, can serve as an essential psychological foundation for, and bridge to, the Christian mystical tradition. Over the past 1500 years, the Christian tradition of theologia mystica, or mystical theology, has flourished in particular communities and individuals with great transformative beauty, vitality and strength - like a mysterious, hidden river of Love overflowing into society, such as in sixteenth century Spain. Key to understanding the transmission of this tradition down the centuries has been the sixth century writings known as the Dionysian Corpus, written by Pseudo Dionysius the Areopagite. These writings have evolved over more than 1000 years of interpretation and translation, being closely identified with the tradition of theologia mystica. The author looks forward with enthusiasm, hope and optimism to renewed, creative and invigorated approaches to understanding the nature of our inner life that characterize the essential writings of St Teresa of Avila and C.G. Jung. St Teresa of Avila's writings assure us our life journey can be graced by divine presence - describing various stages of transformation of the soul, in God's Love, in her classic book on prayer, the Interior Castle. Living symbols were a major preoccupation in the life and writings of C.G. Jung, where he explored the psychological foundation of religion, particularly the Christian tradition - what he termed the path of individuation. The author believes, under different guises, we are in the midst of another flowering of theologia mystica in our own secular time. The unprecedented spiritual longing and emergency of our own times is fuelling a strong need for the depth psychological tradition of Jungian psychology and the ancient tradition of theologia mystica to become more widely known, understood, practiced and lived. There is a wider evolutionary shift happening in our times - in the diamond heart of individuals, groups, nations and the global community. Something new and unprecedented is being born in our world today - we are not only in a new time, but a new era"-- Provided by publisher.
Identifiers: LCCN 2023003189 (print) | LCCN 2023003190 (ebook) | ISBN 9781685030957 (paperback) | ISBN 9781685030964 (hardcover) | ISBN 9781685030971 (ebook)
Subjects: LCSH: Teresa, of Avila, Saint, 1515-1582. | Jung, C. G. (Carl Gustav), 1875-1961. | Psychology--Religious aspects--Christianity. | Psychology and religion. | Mystical union.
Classification: LCC BF51 .M35 2023 (print) | LCC BF51 (ebook) | DDC 200.1/9--dc23/eng/20230202
LC record available at https://lccn.loc.gov/2023003189
LC ebook record available at https://lccn.loc.gov/2023003190

Acknowledgements

This book is a collection of my published papers, talks and three chapters from my book, *Towards Mystical Union* over the past twenty-five years, which have now been newly woven together in this edition of fifteen chapters. This book aims to present a larger, woven matrix of golden, deeply interconnected threads, themes and insights, within an emerging "diamond heart" mandala, of new meaning, understanding, links and connections. This ongoing work, of course, is continually being formed, informed and reformed by the great living traditions of knowledge, texts, study and personal/clinical experience of Jungian psychology and the Christian mystical tradition.

The origin of each chapter is:

- *Chapter One appeared in the Association of Jungian Analysts 21st Anniversary Feschrift, 1977 – 1998, published 1st September, 1998, London, UK.*

- *Chapter Two was a talk to the Association of Jungian Analysts, London, UK, 2005*

- *Chapter Three appeared in Vinayasadana journal, Vol 11, No. 1, 2011, reproduced with kind permission.*

- *Chapter Four was a paper presented at the Orthodox Psychotherapy conference, London, UK, 2010.*

- *Chapter Five was printed as pamphlet Number 299 by the Guild of Pastoral Psychology, London, UK, 2007.*

- *Chapter Six was published in the Mount Carmel journal, Vol 53, 1, Jan-March, 2005, reproduced with kind permission.*

- *Chapter Seven published in the Mount Carmel journal, Vol 53, 4, Oct-Dec, 2005, reproduced with kind permission.*

- *Chapter Eight was presented at the Orthodox Psychotherapy Conference, London, UK, 2011.*

- *Chapter Nine was presented at the 2019 Summer School of the Association of Jungian Analysts, Oxford, UK.*

- *Chapter Ten is a chapter in "Towards Mystical Union," Julienne McLean (St Pauls, 2003, 2013, 2017).*

- *Chapter Eleven is a chapter in "Towards Mystical Union," Julienne McLean (St Pauls, 2003, 2013, 2017).*

- *Chapter Twelve was published in the Mount Carmel journal, Vol 62, 4, Oct-Dec, 2014, reproduced with kind permission.*

- *Chapter Thirteen was published in the Mount Carmel Journal, Vol 63, 1, Jan-March, 2015, reproduced with kind permission.*

- *Chapter Fourteen is a chapter in "Towards Mystical Union," Julienne McLean (St Pauls, 2003, 2013, 2017).*

- *Chapter Fifteen was co-authored with Professor C.H. Cook, as chapter 7 in Mystical Theology and Contemporary Spiritual Practice, Cook, McLean and Tyler, Routledge, 2018. Reproduced with kind permission of the C.H. Cook, as co-author.*

Acknowledgements

I want to thank many colleagues, friends, teachers and mentors over more than thirty years for their loyalty, patience, support, wisdom, assistance, friendship, colleagueship and encouragement. In particular, I owe a great debt of gratitude and thanks to Professor Peter Tyler, Professor of Pastoral Theology and Spirituality at St Mary's University, Twickenham, London for his wisdom, friendship and guidance over more than twenty five years. Also, my sincere thanks for the loyal support, help, colleagueship and strong professional community with my Jungian colleagues at the Association of Jungian Analysts, London. And, especially, deepest gratitude and thanks to the Carmelite Friars at the Discalced Carmelite Friary, at Boars Hill, Oxford, UK.

Table of Contents

Section One

Jungian Psychology and the Christian Mystical Tradition

Section Two

Reflections on the Christian Mystical Tradition

Introduction

The vast successes of science and technology of the past two centuries have in no way altered what Julienne McLean identifies as the main challenge of human life: that when lived at its deepest, life confronts us with conundrums which neither science nor contemporary secular psychology can solve, namely mystery, paradox, ambiguity and contradiction. Scientific and technological advances have improved life materially to an extent unimaginable to our recent ancestors but the human condition, the human tragedy, remain essentially unchanged and perhaps unchangeable. This book is not a sentimental appeal to the wisdom of the past but a serious and urgent attempt to identify the true nature of the current dilemma of Western mankind and to point in the direction of remedy.

Two towering figures thread their way through the book: St Teresa of Avila and C. G. Jung. The author is not attempting an academic compare-and-contrast of the Carmelite mystic and the depth psychologist, but rather draws on their writings to focus on her own approach to the contemporary human problems of disenchantment and meaninglessness. She takes the reader into the terrain left empty by the widespread collapse of formal Christian religious belief and practice. Rather than attempt to reanimate this, she raises pertinent questions about an approach to spirituality and numinosity that is now made possible by a largely post-religious situation; in other words, not lamenting that which has been lost but looking at the possibilities for a renewed and invigorated approach to spirit in a landscape no longer dominated by church hegemony. Everything in the author's essays looks forward with enthusiasm and hope, not backwards in nostalgia. The vigour and optimism that characterise the work of Teresa and Jung run through her texts.

"Modern secular psychology," the author suggests, "is generally unable to contain, and relate to, mystery, paradox, ambiguity and contradiction," yet it is our inevitable experience of these that, sooner or later, challenge us most deeply in life. It is quite probable that the reader of this book will be, or will have been, so challenged and looking for sources of help and guidance in the face of difficulties that knowledge alone cannot resolve. In the author's view, the stymying of the ruling contemporary scientific approach in the face of these is not an end-point but potentially a portal, a threshold which, if crossed with care and a degree of healthy trepidation, can lead beyond the improbable phantasy that all problems in life can be solved and thus lead into a world in which resolve replaces resolution, the resolve which Paul Tillich called, "the courage to be."

It is in the face of such challenge that some seek the help of a psychotherapist only to discover that much of psychotherapy has also been colonised by the approach of secular science. Some of the essays in this book are addressed specifically to McLean's professional analytic colleagues and take the form of a carefully argued plea for the psychotherapist to look beyond the finitude and verifiable but limited facts of science. Rather than the scientific psychological approach of trying to replace the unknown by the known she argues for a more respectful approach to the unknown (and, indeed, the unknowable) in which the technique of investigation is augmented by approaches closer to the techniques of prayer and meditation. She draws on the approach both of Jung and of Teresa to flesh out what this way of engaging with that which is beyond our current knowledge might look like it in practice.

A crisis of language currently bedevils the field to which McLean contributes. For example, the reification of the term "the unconscious" in depth psychology improperly suggests that it is a natural object for scientific scrutiny in the contemporary sense, to be researched as a physician might research the liver. Against such misleading reification, McLean describes the unconscious as "the unknown as it immediately affects us," thus gently nudging the reader away from the world of scientific investigation to a starting point of one's own experience. It is worth noting that Jung, when claiming to be an empiricist, was primarily referring to the empirical data of his own considered experience.

This is also the point to which McLean directs the reader in the quest for engagement with experiences whose origin and nature is unknown. The term "mysticism" has in contemporary speech slipped into near-pejorative use, suggesting an escapist, equivocal or even evasive attitude to what "hard" science should be able to verify or dismiss. By referring to its root etymology in the concept of "hiddenness," the author clarifies the way she uses term and renders it fit for purpose in a contemporary discussion of that which we cannot directly measure or investigate. "Spirituality" is a term used so broadly that any author is obliged to explain their use of it and again, McLean's essays helpfully indicate a viable working use of the term.

It seems to me no accident that so many of the important terms in the field explored in these essays should carry pejorative tones. The rational scientific mind of the post-Enlightenment era is not comfortable with that which it cannot investigate in its own terms of measurement and verification. The fact that so much of human experience is not susceptible to such investigation leaves the contemporary scientific mind with a major problem of how to handle such material. Mystical theology (Teresa) and depth psychology (Jung) offer different paradigms and practices to approach what science necessarily leaves to one side. Each has created its own language in this enterprise and McLean's essays offer a helpful lexicon for those who are uncertain what, for example, Jung means by "symbol" or "individuation process" or Teresa by "union with Christ." Once mastered, these technical languages enable the reader to enter with confidence what may hitherto have seemed a field too specialised for the general reader. McLean addresses those of us who are in the grip of the dilemmas of human life. Few of those so engaged will have the expertise to read Jung or Teresa without some help with the terminology they use.

This brings me to what I regard as the crux of McLean's work. Both Teresa's Carmelite mysticism and Jung's analytical psychology are traditions. By this I mean that they can only be fully transmitted experientially, not merely through texts. In the former case, transmission has been from spiritual director to directee, both being held in the practice of the Christian religion. In analytical psychology, the tradition has been handed down over a much shorter time-span from analyst to analysand and from analyst to clinical supervisee. Neither could be learned merely from reading texts, the nature of the material precludes this. McLean's essays explain why this must be so. Both disciplines deal with that which is hidden, not accessible to scientific investigation, measurement and scrutiny. This hidden material includes most of that which is most fundamental in the human condition, notably the areas McLean pin-points of the paradoxical, ambiguous or contradictory nature of human problems at their most profound and troublesome. McLean notes that, in the approach of contemporary science, the emphasis is on remembering, whereas in the traditions she sets forth, forgetting is more important. In the former, one gathers, re-collects information; in the second, the task is letting go, the "lysis" or loosening and unbinding which is written into the very term "analysis." Re-membering science is juxtaposed to dis-membering mysticism and analysis.

Transmission of scientific knowledge, so defined as "remembering," is essential exoteric, it can be written down and transmitted with perfect accuracy. The knowledge base of mysticism and analytical psychology, however, can only be transmitted esoterically. Because much of its material defies any clear setting-forth, is ineffable and therefore cannot fully be grasped; it can only be transmitted within an apprenticeship model of the passing on of a craft. "Esoteric" is another term which attracts disapproval in the milieu of scientific rationalism, with implication of a defensive evasion of proper scrutiny. McLean explains at key points in her essays why the most important aspects of human life cannot be done justice without a degree of hiddenness in our approach to them. Because the material with which we are dealing is so profoundly ambiguous and volatile (analogous to spirit in its chemical sense) the teaching of how to handle it requires a degree of protection from over-defining scrutiny. I doubt that many psychotherapists would warm to a description of our practice as "occult" but that is exactly what it is, in the sense that the sites of analysis and supervision are both occluded in the sense of being protected from scrutiny by a third party.

The author gratefully pays homage to the analyst through whom this esoteric craft was passed to her, Dr Gerhard Adler. McLean is fortunate in that Adler was one of Jung's inner circle, hence the chain of transmission from its origin to her is a very short chain indeed. The freshness, excitement, vibrancy and authenticity of Jung's circle in Zurich characterises these essays.

McLean's essays make it clear that the goal envisaged justifies the high price, to the scientific mind, of the sacrifice of clarity, the capacity for certainty, verifiable data and knowledge. The goal is nothing less than transformation, the subject of her penultimate chapter. Only by letting go of certainties and re-valorising that which is by its nature both uncertain and hidden can transformation take place. Such transformation, in McLean's view, does not originate in some personal self-development project managed by the conscious subject but rather originates in serious wounds. It is the pain of the wounds which life inflicts on us that drive us to the depths, to spirit, to that which science cannot engage or can only engage peripherally. This book is primarily addressed to the walking wounded whose pain is beyond the reach of contemporary science. Put more simply, in Jung's own words which serve as the epigraph for Chapter 2:

"... the fact is that the approach to the numinous is the real therapy and inasmuch as you attain to the numinous experiences, you are released from the curse of pathology."
(letter to PW Martin, 1945)

George Bright
Supervising Analyst of The Society of Analytical Psychology
London, Easter 2022

Section One

JUNGIAN PSYCHOLOGY
AND THE
CHRISTIAN MYSTICAL TRADITION

Chapter One

WALKING TOWARDS JERUSALEM

Tribute to Dr Gerhard Adler (1904 - 1988)

This paper is intended to be a brief tribute to some aspects of the work and approach of Gerhard Adler. I want to discuss two seminal principles which held particular importance for Gerhard throughout his career, alongside certain reflections from my personal analysis with him and my subsequent analytical work. These principles relate, firstly, to the fundamental importance of the quest for, and role of, meaning as central to psychological health and wellbeing, and secondly, to aspects of the dynamics and processes of "remembering" and "forgetting."

I would like to say, at the outset, that my thoughts and reflections in this paper are not intended to address or discuss major theoretical or clinical issues concerning what a Jungian analysis "should" or "should not" be and that, perhaps, I would not necessarily share or agree with all of Gerhard's ideas and thoughts today. This paper essentially is a grateful tribute to the perspective and approach of a profoundly religious man who saw the world and the psyche in a very particular way, and reflections from my personal analysis between 1985 -1988 (when he died), which had a particular transformative effect on my whole life and vocation as a Jungian analyst.

At the heart of Jung's work, which was faithfully continued by Gerhard, was his lifelong exploration of the psychology of the *homo religiosus*. One of his important contributions was the recognition and value that he accorded the "religious function" of the psyche—the innate and autochthonous religious urge of our deeper self, or soul—which he regarded as an inborn need of the Self, which he firmly believed could not be neglected or violated without grave injury to psychic health and well being, particularly in the second half of life.

His particular interest and emphasis in this regard lay in what he regarded as the central role of experience, encounter, or *unio mystica*, with the numinous, or the sacred, as the main authentic way to a renewed belief and faith in God for many modern individual—*"Theology does not help those who are looking for the key, because theology demands faith, and faith cannot be made; it is in the truest sense a gift of grace. We moderns are faced with the necessity of rediscovering the life of the Spirit; we must experience it anew for ourselves."*[1] One of his primary concerns was to investigate the religious nature of the psyche and its central function and role in the development and unfolding of psychic wholeness and integration. Jung was particularly aware that, in the main, he was not addressing those who felt secure within their religious beliefs, but was primarily addressing those who could no longer rely exclusively on their faith and belief, and wished to know and understand more, those for whom the traditional Judeo-Christian concepts of God and spirituality were no longer meaningful and significant, yet who had a strong sense of the sacred and the numinous in their lives.

It is in this tradition that Gerhard was deeply rooted and committed and made his own significant contributions. He furthered some of Jung's original pioneering work by exploring certain aspects of the nature and dynamics of the Self[2] as well as contributing to our psychological understanding relating to the use and function of symbols[3] and the approach and attitude to the numinous within analytic work.

Quest for meaning

One dominant concern of Gerhard's work was his overriding interest to cultivate and investigate individual's quest for meaning, psychic integration and synthesis. He lectured on the subject to the Jung Institute in Zurich in 1962, which was subsequently published as a paper "On the Question of Meaning in Psychotherapy," appearing in English in 1979 in his anthology The Dynamics of the Self[4]. This book is an important contribution to literature on Jung's understanding of the self and the journey of individuation, as Gerhard reflects on, and summarises, forty years of his own analytic practice concerning individuals' quest for meaning and purpose within their own personal analysis, and comments on broader issues, tensions and paradoxes concerning related collective, social and existential questions and realities.

For Gerhard, facilitating and enabling individuals search for, and intimate relating to, their own inner psychic reality, through "the struggle for an inner point of vantage, for knowledge of an inner reality in which the fragmentation of the other reality could find synthesis and new meaning"[5] was of paramount importance. Equally so was his particular love and passion for the wider creative milieu of the arts, music and literature. He understood the work of many of the 20th centuries leading artists, such as Kandinsky, Klee and Franz Marc as similarly reflecting an "orientation inward, a turning toward the psychic centre and universal ground of all reality," and viewed their artistic formulations as representing their affinity with the "prophetic knowledge of the eternally, valid, archetypal world of the psyche—the Greater reality of the inner mystical construction."[6]

Most of our own major life transitions, changes and transformations are usually within particular contexts and milieux of meaning. My own positive memories of, and lifelong gratitude to, Gerhard falls within a particular personal context and life story, as my own quest for meaning and purpose had a particular intensity and poignancy at the beginning of my analysis with Gerhard. I started the analysis in my late twenties, in 1985, which continued for three and a half years up to the time of his death in December, 1988. Following two degrees in psychology, professional publication of several requisite academic journal articles, I had continued to experience a pervasive sense of inner atrophy and disconnection—a type of existential alienation that was affecting most areas of my life and work. It was a state of profound suffering of the soul, where I could not connect to, or find, sufficient purpose or meaning. Jung comments in his biography on the severe effects of meaning and purpose—*"meaninglessness inhibits fullness of life and is therefore equivalent of illness. Meaning makes a great deal endurable—perhaps everything."*[7]

Much of my childhood and adolescence in Sydney, Australia, had centred on my interest in religion and the local Christian church and community, and from a very young age I had always felt a strong connection and fascination with the deeper religious life. I attended church from a young age, being the only member of my family to have even the remotest interest in such things. There had been many moments as a child—either in church, on retreat, or in the wild Australian "bush"—which I would describe as religious or numinous experience, where a presence of something quite beyond me, which I recognised as a sense or touch of God, or something quite Other and Mysterious, had been unquestionably real and strong.

Through my adolescence, this "awareness or fundamental connection" was almost totally buried and repressed, and by the time of my early adulthood, I felt very lost and disorientated, living in a state of existential alienation and looking back, real suffering of soul. By the time I was 26, I had two degrees in psychology with distinction, was a qualified psychologist working hard in research and clinical work—yet, I felt as if I was dying on the "inside" of hunger and thirst for the real things of the soul and Spirit. So, as my life had taken its prescribed course, my spiritual and religious side had been buried and repressed, reinforced by many years of study and work in predominantly cognitive/behavioural psychology and research orientated psychological disciplines and specialties.

So I entered Jungian analysis with Gerhard in 1985 when I was 28. In this context and background, you can, perhaps, understand why the therapeutic relationship, and analytical work, with Gerhard began to change my life, as, for me, it was real "soul food," which was gradually beginning to forge the beginning of the way "home" to an essential re-connection with my own soul and the reality of the Holy Spirit. Most individual's first analysis or analytic experience carries a particular quality of archetypal transference and intensity about it, which I believe, is different to subsequent analyses. This was certainly true for me. As my own analysis began to unfold and psychic layer upon layer was uncovered, "seen" and related to within the analysis, much that had made "no-sense" to me slowly and painfully, with a certain sense of suspicion and awe, began to make more and more meaningful sense.

Ariadne's invisible thread slowly, but very surely, began to unravel the all too often confusing, dark and disorientating labyrinth of psychic enquiry, observation and exploration. Through the continuous sense of slow, arduous psychological relatedness to, and recollection of, the many fragmented and disparate parts of myself, I became more and more recollected and alive through my Jungian analysis and subsequent analytical training. I only worked with him for the last three years of his life, but it was enough for the real "birth of my soul" to be initiated, and enough to instill faith and hope in the ongoing, lifelong, real transformative possibility of the deeper psychological and spiritual life.

This continuous sense of slow psychological relatedness to, and recollection of, the fragmented parts of myself slowly gained an increasing sense of reality and gravitas. My rather classical "initial dream," in June 1985, of the analysis symbolised some of the important processes and qualities which were dominant in the analysis:

> "I am moving with my family to a large, new house on the island of Crete. I do not recognise the island, but I remember the location from a conversation with the people moving out of the house. It is a very large, modern three story house on the side of a hill, overlooking the harbour. I walk through the house to the kitchen and see through the window a large, moored container ship waiting to depart. It looks very strange and mysterious, as it is completely sealed in what looks like think, black stocky tape. I walk down to the next story, and feel overwhelmed by the beautiful gardens that are in full bloom within the enclosure of the house. There are all different kinds and colours of flowers which are carefully arranged in straight rows, with paths separating the rows. I am surprised and pleased at the prospect of moving into this new house, and being able to enjoy such a beautiful garden between working and studying upstairs in the house."

I came to understand the sealed container ship ready to depart as representing the beginning of the long interior journey that lay ahead within the analysis and beyond. Gerhard notes that "for most people the question of meaning becomes the starting point for a long and hazardous night sea journey. That is why at the beginning of an analysis we often find dreams of journeys and of dangerous expeditions."[8] Somehow, I felt both very reassured, and quite anxious about this dream at the time. It certainly was the beginning of a long and difficult inner exploration of my own soul story and sense of uniqueness and destiny. The symbol of the enclosed garden in full bloom, however, was very reassuring— somehow reinforcing my strong sense of propitious timing, of *kairos*, of the "right moment" to embark on such a challenging and rigorous analysis.

Meaning is powerfully conferred and created when psychological and subjective connection is developed, and related to, as *"an organic part of an ordered whole, when it gives rise to the incontrovertible feeling of a suprapersonal order, of being directed towards a goal, of fulfilling a pattern—or to put it in personal terms, numinosity."*[9] Through my first analysis with Gerhard, I was able to make conscious, and attempt to embody, a particular interior logic, psychic order and vocation, which has conferred a depth of meaning and purpose that has remained and continued to grow over the years. And yet, of course, such an experience and sense of interconnectedness is never for the sake of the individual alone— *"in the numinous, transpersonal character of the experience resides more than subjective experience. There is an archetype of meaning as such, and even when meaning seems to be highly subjective, the experience still remains a general human possibility and a constituent element of all humanity."*[10]

Dynamics of Remembering and Forgetting

An important feature of analytical psychology is the continuing theoretical and clinical reflections and contributions relating to the nature and dynamics of the self. The central goal of transformation in relationship to the self in the analytic endeavour which, teleologically, moves psychological development and change towards increasing individuated and integrated states of being and awareness, is of major interest and concern. In this light, Gerhard's paper *Remembering and Forgetting*[11] was an important contribution to this field of enquiry.

The paper was originally a lecture in California in 1976, which also appeared in his 1979 anthology, "Dynamics of the Self." In it, he discoursed on a range of psychological, philosophical, mythical and religious aspects relating to dynamics and processes of memory, with particular reference to the "contrapuntal" motif of remembering and forgetting. In this essay, he discussed the role of memory, both ego psychology and psychopathology, as well as an analysis of memory contained in archetypal images of the collective unconscious, what Yeats described as the "Great memory passing on from generation to generation."[12]

Gerhard noted that the essence of memory is to "recollect, to collect what one once knew, to collect together into a new whole" and the literal meaning of recollection is to "refine within."[13] He discussed the theme of remembrance and recollection "as the task of the soul"[14] from the perspective of the platonic/neoplatonic tradition, Kabbalah and the Upanishads. He emphasised the predominance of the self in the dynamics and processes of remembering, and that "*memory is memory of the archetypal foundations; true memory is relating to the transpersonal and suprapersonal centre of the psyche—to the self.*"[15]

Gerhard continued his discourse on the motif of forgetting, and gave a commentary on the experiences and writings of well-known contemplatives and mystics throughout the centuries who emphasised, in certain circumstances, and at certain times, the necessity and purpose of a temporary relinquishment of ego-control and perspective, of an abandonment of the will, of a surrender to the Divine, of a particular type of letting go. He noted the same archetypal pattern, expressed in the forgetting of the ego's concern with the world was "*to be found not only in the Far East, but also in our western culture, among the great mystics of Germany, England, Spain, or Italy, or of Jewish Hasidim and in the near East amount the devotees of Islam.*"[16] He discussed many of the similarities relating to the theme of forgetting, letting go, surrender and abandonment which have been expressed by different individuals and mystical traditions over the centuries— by the Hesychasts of the Greek Orthodox tradition, in the writings of Mechthild von Madgeburg, the thirteenth century German mystic, in the English Mystical treatise, the Cloud of Unknowing, and particularly the mystics of Judaism and Islam.

Gerhard's work and focus in these areas was of particular lifelong relevance and inspiration to me. In the past few years, I have made an in-depth study of the Christian mystics in this regard, particularly St Teresa of Avila and St John of the Cross, the well-known mystics and saints of sixteenth century Spain. I have recently published an article entitled *"Towards Sacred Union – the Mystical Journey of the Soul,"* where I discuss her writings regarding the seven mansions of the soul contained in her classic, *The Interior Castle.* I also attempt to place her writings and experiences within a broader spiritual and historical context, in order to demonstrate connections and interrelationships between the Christian, Sufi and Jewish mystical traditions.[17]

Walking towards Jerusalem

"I wake up in a friend's house, and there are many hurried preparations going on in order to leave the house. I was going to be leaving with them. Then, I find myself on the outskirts of Jerusalem, and there is a huge march in front of me, with people walking six abreast in a very disciplined way, like a spiritual army, towards the city of Jerusalem. I am inappropriately dressed in city clothes. I go to change into more appropriate clothes in a small hut nearby, and hurriedly run to join the end of the marchers going past."

This was the last dream of my personal analysis, in December 1988, and in fact, occurred a week before Gerhard passed away. I knew he had been a deeply religious man and somehow, had been able to assist my psychic relatedness and integration to a point where I could embrace, more fully and consciously, my own deeper religious questions and experiences, and indeed, to join a symbolic, interior journey to Jerusalem. My analysis had been saturated with my ongoing aim and attempt to relate to, discuss and understand the many personal and religious themes, symbols, issues and conflicts that were continually bubbling and churning away within. If anything could sum up my first analytic encounter, it would be as a critical introduction phase in an ongoing lifelong quest and journey of realising and integrating the transpersonal archetypal factor of inner order and significance, as this continually relates to the integration and wholeness of who "I am" in constant relationship with the Other.

What I was always struck by, and what deeply impressed me was, I suppose, like the many reports of analysands of Jung, how profoundly real, and indeed central, he regarded the numinous and individuals relationship to it. Indeed, he regarded this as the core of his own work, where Andrew Samuels wrote that he put his main emphasis on symbolic transformation and reiterated what Jung had earlier written in a 1945 letter that the main interest of his work was with the approach to the numinous…"the fact is that the numinous is the real therapy."[18]

Acknowledging, and consciously attempting to relate to the reality of the spiritual dimension, that works *on us* and *in us*, that is continually changing and transforming our sense and perception of ourselves, others and the world is a particular vocation to which I believe Gerhard was dedicated. He was someone who deeply understood and served as a unique gatekeeper and facilitator to the powerful sense of order and meaningfulness which lies more often than not beyond our conscious knowledge or awareness.

His lifelong vocation to facilitate individual's conscious return to themselves, to the unconscious, and to the wider community continued to the day of his death. I remain deeply grateful for the psychological help, support and assistance he gave to me in my own quest and pilgrimage towards Jerusalem.

Endnotes

[1] C. G. Jung, *The Collected Works of C. G. Jung, Volume 4,* "Freud and Psychoanalysis," p. 339.

[2] G. Adler, *Dynamics of the Self.*

[3] G. Adler, *The Living Symbol.*

[4] G. Adler, *Dynamics of the Self,* pp. 62-87.

[5] Ibid., p. 65.

[6] Ibid.

[7] C. G. Jung, *Memories, Dreams and Reflections,* p. 371.

[8] G. Adler, *Dynamics of the Self,* p. 74.

[9] Ibid., p. 78.

[10] Ibid.

[11] Ibid., pp. 118-164.

[12] Ibid., p. 165.

[13] Ibid., p. 121.

[14] Ibid., p. 131.

[15] Ibid.

[16] Ibid., p. 158.

[17] J. McLean, *Toward Sacred Union – The Mystical Journey of the Soul,* pp. 35-41.

[18] A. Samuels, *Jung and the Post Jungians,* p. 16.

Chapter Two

OPENING THE HEART, APPROACHING THE NUMINOUS

The main interest of my work is not concerned with the treatment of neurosis but rather with the approach to the numinous. But the fact is that the approach to the numinous is the real therapy and inasmuch as you attain to the numinous experiences, you are released from the curse of pathology.

Jung, 1945[1]

Over the past two decades, there has been resurgence of interest and exploration into all matters relating to spirituality and mysticism, alongside an increasing interfaith dialogue between the different religious traditions. Whilst there has been a decrease in attendance at traditional religious services, there has been a huge increase in the number of individuals seeking to incorporate and integrate the sacred or spiritual dimension into every aspect and dimension of living and life—from their intimate, personal and family relationships, to their working life, to the wider relationships in their local and national communities to the growing global community that the internet revolution is creating.

With the entrance into the twenty first century, there appears to be a general sense of spiritual crisis or emergency. Polly Young Eisendrath recently commented in her new book, *The Psychology of Mature Spirituality*[2], that enlightened secularism and humanism no longer seem adequate for living an ethical life for the vast majority, yet many are also increasingly wary of traditional religious dogmas, creeds and politics that, more often than not, require adults to behave intellectually and emotionally like children or adolescents. It is as though our religious paradigm, understanding and sense of the sacred or spiritual, often needs to forge new language and new modes of communication in each new generation—for those areas of life when the old can be too fraught, too laden, too rich with nuances, preconditioned associations and, sometimes, which have become rather mechanical or dead, lifeless concepts.

I see that more and more people increasingly sensing that their spiritual development is a vital and necessary component of a living a healthy and effective life. By spiritual development, I would mean a lifetime of engagement with a transcendent source that is both intimate and Other. For many people, and for many clients that we see in our consulting rooms, the source of their pain and suffering can often be spiritual and theological, as well as deeply emotional and psychological. Many, of course, do not frame their traumas, conflicts and anxieties in traditional religious language, but they indeed know that they are experiencing themselves as unconnected and alienated to a larger meaning, purpose or reason for living, and unconnected to work that is worthy and valuable, which gives opportunities to express authenticity, integrity and creativity.

Intimately bound up with these collective factors, there is now a significant rekindling of interest in spirituality, and this can often include a desire for, a hunger towards a more personally direct encounter with, or more immediate knowledge and understanding, of spiritual realities, of the transcendent Other, of the numinosity of life. This was, of course, at the very heart of Jung's lifelong work.

Jung wrote: *"Theology does not help those who are looking for the key, because theology demands faith, and faith cannot be made; it is in the truest sense a gift of grace. We moderns are faced with the necessity of rediscovering the life of the Spirit; we must experience it anew for ourselves."* If Jung wrote this more than fifty years ago, it appears that it is even more true and relevant in our own day. What does this critical aspect of Jung's work mean to us today—personally, clinically, professionally—in the wider social milieu, in some of the important decisions that individuals, groups and society are in the midst of at present? Where is the Jungian community in addressing and continuing to explore these most basic and vital issues and questions of life?

Is Jung's embrace of spirituality and encounter with the numinous, as a vibrant, essential part of the individuation process, in danger of being forgotten, deemed irrelevant, embarrassing or even lost by subsequent generations? Where other schools of psychology may dismiss this aspect of Jung's work, the acceptance of, and central value accorded, the numinosity of the unconscious, and the religious, or spiritual, character of the therapeutic endeavor was, in reality, one of the most unique contributions of his psychology.

Adler carried on this tradition, where he refers to the importance of the religious dignity, and the relevance of the individual, as the receiver and carrier of numinous revelation in his 1974 IAAP Congress address. This was, in part, reproduced in his 1983 statement regarding the founding of our Society, the Association of Jungian Analysts, here in London in 1977. Dr Adler spoke of, in his 1974 address, of:

> ". . .the truth of archetypal images, the dominant influence which they exert on the fate of mankind, the reality of the inner Olympus with its gods and goddesses... and the religious dignity and the relevance of the individual as the receiver, and carrier of numinous revelation. At the centre of all of Jung's research we can put the search for the numinosum. All the other areas of Analytical Psychology have to be looked at from this angle."[3]

But what does this *really* mean for us today, in a different time and generation more than twenty years on? I would like to inject a little more life, interest and sense of urgency to exploring these fundamental questions. The exploration of the deep and important relationship between spirituality, mysticism and Jungian psychology is a field of increasing importance and relevance, even more so that many of us are three or four generations apart from Jung. We have to explore and investigate these issues in our own time, cultural milieu and generation. It is a whole dimension of life and living which I feel has been traditionally neglected and underemphasized in analytical psychology and the psychotherapy community in general.

There even appears to be an increasing trend for depth psychology, and psychotherapy in general, to be reluctant to explore these vital areas now, even to denying the importance of the spiritual life and the reality of the Transcendent dimension. This *could* be construed as a necessary pendulum swing from an overemphasis, in this area, in earlier Jungian and post Jungian generations or the ongoing need to refine and reform our linguistic clinical inheritance, that needs to be constantly reviewing and reconstructing over the time and generations. This is always a difficult, but essentially a creative process, and is vitally necessary if core ideas, principles and realities are to stay alive and relevant across time and generations. This paper is a small contribution in this evolutionary process.

Most individuals have moments of awakening to a different dimension of being, of living, than their ordinary waking consciousness throughout their lives. This dimension of reality, call it archetypal, spiritual, mystical or *fourth dimensional* is much more commonly experienced and sensed than most like to think. These moments—or experiences—call them ego transcendent moments, religious experiences, mystical experiences, or encounters with the numinous - belong to some of the most intimate and personal of what it means to be human, yet they are of a universal validity and anyone can share in them, as they are rooted in the collective unconscious and in collective archetypes. It was Jung's exploration and study of the religious function of the psyche that showed, in his view, that the soul is religious by nature, and in psychological terms, mystical experiences are exceptional only in regard to their intensity or degree, not in their essence.

What are the signs of our direct encounter with the Transcendent, with the Numinous—with the mystical—there can be a sense of being absolutely alive, a tremendous vitality, a direct, immediate basis of credal statements, a sense of a great treasure, beauty, splendour. There can be an overwhelming sense of dread, of tremendous fear, of encountering the *mysterium tremendum.* This is the place of the real experience of the dark night of the soul, encountering profound spiritual darkness and suffering, even in Job-like ways. There is a sense of breaking through to something other, something is shown to us that is very different, it is not mediated by symbols, ideas or thoughts.

It exceeds all the usual ways of apprehending reality, it is an atypical unique experience, it can be like fire within, an immense calm, limitless peace, a sense of profound well being and blessing, a sense of coming home or belonging, waves of endless Love or a sense of entering nothingness from which all things come. Alternatively, it can be experienced as rhythmic surges of energy, incredible joy, of transcendent ecstasy, water gushing, my breath

17

is the breath of God, absolute freedom, energy like electricity and being plugged into a Source, a markedly increased sense of Presence or that life and existence seems to be in this very moment Now, a sense of the eternal. There can be a change in our sense of time and space, a sense of the holy, or holiness.

Some traditions speak about the non-physical sense of the sweet smell, or perfume, of the Holy Spirit, which Jung himself spoke about in his autobiography. Another tradition speaks about these ego transcendent experiences in terms of "taste"—as if we are guests invited to a special banquet—where there are particular flavours, sounds, scents, textures and colours which is like nothing that has been tasted before, which is difficult to describe to those to have not been to such a banquet.

In the famous text written more than 100 years ago, *The Varieties of Religious Experience*,[4] which strongly influenced Jung, William James explored some of the basic characteristics of encounters with the numinous, or fourth dimension, which I will quickly summarise. These sorts of ego transcendent experiences have a quality of *ineffability*—they defy expression in logical rational terms, and are often only fully intelligible to those who have already experienced some analogous experience. Neither the smell of a rose, nor the sensation of being in love, nor the pleasure which comes while listening to a great symphony, are amenable to adequate logical or intellectual description. Most utterances of such dimensions are really rather inadequate, but for those it has touched it leaves a certainty of the reality of that dimension. The attempt to express the *inexpressible* is, of course, where psychology and theology go hand in hand.

Secondly, James pointed to the *noetic quality* of this dimension by defining these states as "states of insight into depths of truth unplumbed by the discursive intellect, insights which carry with them a tremendous sense of authority," which is related to Jung's famous utterance—I don't just believe, I know. We actually know something different in this dimension. It tends to break the subject/object dualism, and purely intellectual thinking, and introduces us into a transcendent reality.

Somehow, there can be a sense of insight, of knowing, touching, tasting, seeing the wholeness of things and life, of seeing and being within the profound interconnectedness of things which defies the mind, reason and the intellect alone. More importantly, our faculty for intuitively penetrating the veil of temporal reality seems to be activated by a source beyond ourselves. There can appear a consciousness of the Oneness of everything—a sense of unitive being, or non-duality. There can be a change in the sense of time and space, a sense of the eternal.

Thirdly, these states generally transcend the ego, and can often feel, or be experienced as much more real and awake than our ordinary waking consciousness. We are much more alive, awake so to speak. These experiences represent another level, or dimension, of reality which is deeper than the previous one. Each new dimension constitutes an awakening from its predecessor. Often these transcendent states can seldom be sustained for long, and have the quality of *transiency*, if there is not further inner work to make the state more permanent. The following of a particular way of life can increase their frequency and make the states more permanent.

Fourthly, the sense of inner stillness, quietness, surrender is vital. James called this *passivity*, which is a term that can be misunderstood. The implication of this characteristic is that ego-transcendent states almost always bring with them the feeling of something which is given. It is the preparation, the conscious surrender, in order to be receptive to the numinous—it is not possible to create or manipulate this state. There is a distinct quality of otherness. The essential quality of stillness, of the body, mind, emotions, has the capacity to restore our ability to remember, to recollect, remaining ourselves and not be distracting or identifying with the outside. That is why prayer, meditation and contemplation are some of the more traditional ways of connecting to, and living within, this deeper dimension.[5]

So, how does all this relate to our analytic endeavour? The idea of the transformation of the self is central to our depth analytic endeavour. Indeed, Jung's volume 5 – *Symbols of Transformation* —written in 1912 and revised in 1952—[6] was the seminal text that designated Jung's break with Freud and the beginning of the development of Jung's own school of thought, where he first addressed his ideas on the nature of the transformation of psychic energy and the conditions under which transformation can occur within the self.

Jung demonstrated that mental events could be understood as taking place along a continuum, or spectrum of consciousness, which he compared to the light spectrum—at the infrared end of the spectrum, psychic functions change into physiological processes that relate to the earliest instinctual body based drives through to the ultraviolet end of the scale as archetypes, psychic structures that precondition fantasies and ideas by producing symbolic images. At the heart of the idea of transformation of libido is the nature of the self, which he imaged as a mandala, representing the organising, integrating function of the personality, which possesses and holds purpose and meaning through all the stages of development and transformation.

I would like to build on and discuss Jung's core concept of the transformation of the self along a spectrum of consciousness, and incorporate many important clinical ideas and concepts from other analytic schools of thought. In this regard, the author and analyst Nathan Field, in his book *Breakdown and Breakthrough*[7] and several other recent articles, have made important contributions to this area by discussing, at some length, this notion of a multidimensional continuum, or spectrum, in terms of *four major dimensions* of being, or states of mind, or consciousness.

In this spectrum, *one dimensional functioning* relates to autistic states of mind, and the autistic/contiguous position, popularised by the work of Thomas Ogden, which can develop into *two dimensional functioning*, the paranoid-schizoid position of Klein. Each new dimension constitutes an awakening, a major psychic shift, as well as entailing tremendous fear and resistance, from its predecessor, and the development to *three dimensional functioning*, to symbolic perception, and the symbolic life, is a major transformation of the self, which, of course, was much of Jung's own emphasis. Within this spectrum of consciousness, there can be the natural transformative movement towards *fourth dimensional reality*, which relates to ego transcendent experiences, or encounter with the numinosum, or the Transcendent, which I have highlighted earlier in this paper and will further amplify.

In his description of autistic children, Donald Meltzer refers to a *"one-dimensional world,"* which is characterised as *"substantially mindless, consisting of series of events not available for memory or thought.... Gratification and fusion with the object is undifferentiated."*[8] Jung called this state *participation mystique*, the state of non differentiation where subject and object are fused. In this dimension the self remains deeply entrenched within an archaic identity, which is kept in place by the major defences of splitting, primitive idealisation and projective identification. In this dimension, there is a close analogy between mental and physical digestive processes, where identification is the psychic equivalent of ingestion, projection is the psychic equivalent of excretion and projective identification is the psychic equivalent of fusion.

Ogden, in his classic book, *The Primitive Edge of Experience*, described this one-dimensional state of mind as the autistic contiguous position. From a developmental perspective, it is an attempt to describe the most primitive, elemental, presymbolic, mode of psychological organisation. It is a sensory dominated mode in which the most inchoate sense of self is built upon the rhythm of physical sensations, particularly the sensations at the skin surface.[9]

Ogden summarises this state is where –

> ..."the relationship to the object in this mode is certainly not a relationship between subjects, as in the depressive mode; nor is it a relationship between objects, as in the paranoid – schizoid mode. Rather, It is a relationship of shape to the feeling of enclosure, of beat to the feeling of rhythm, of hardness to the feeling of edgedness. . . the experience of self at this point is simply that of a nonreflective state of sensory 'going on being' derived from bodily needs. . . there is practically no sense of inside or outside or self or other."[10]

More often than not, in our analytic work we will encounter this more primitive psychological organisation in terms of the autistic capsule, or hidden, unconscious encapsulated pockets within the personality of our clients. This is usually experienced as a terror stricken frozen bit which, developmentally, has been left behind and covered over, which usually hides enormous suffering, psychic pain, tears and heartbrokenness.

The shift from *one to two dimensional functioning* involves the crucial move into discrimination and thence to language. At this stage two dimensional thoughts and feelings are often only of the polarised kind, with clear-cut distinctions between good and bad, right and wrong. Sensations, thoughts, feelings and impressions are divided into positive and negative, useful or harmful, necessary or unnecessary, pleasant and unpleasant, where love can readily turn to hatred, bliss to boredom, desire to revulsion.

The two-dimensional state is either omnipotent or impotent, bully or victim, manic or depressed, gullible or paranoid. Each state, while it has possession of consciousness, imposes its own reality and excludes its opposite. In this mode, the rapid alternation of opposite, polarised or contrasting states of mind evoke a powerful sense of instability, as if there is no centre, very little sense of Self as yet.

Hester Solomon described the two dimensional mode in graphic terms[11] –

"In the two dimensional environment inner and outer processes and interactions are highly controlled, leaving only enough space for the self to exist—but nothing and no-one else—existence in a void. I use the image of two dimensions to denote a plane with no depth or contour, and no space for another—solitary confinement of the self in the two dimensional claustrum.[12]

Essentially, at a deep level of psychic functioning, in this mode there is a fundamental foreclosure on object relatedness in preference for an existence in a two dimensional solitary confinement, where all that can really be known about are the conditions necessary for the survival of the self, fuelled by the conviction that to risk being open to experiencing the reality of another, an existence in three dimensions, is to risk psychological annihilation. Transformation of the self is precluded in the rigid, two-dimensional oppositional world because any change is anticipated as threatening the self's survival.

The defensive splitting mechanisms that occur in unconscious phantasy in this paranoid schizoid mode *maintain the foreclosure on object relatedness. This early defence system prior to the formation of the ego ensures that the self remains intact—which develops into the completely self reliant, self sufficient ego—rather than disintegrated, even in the face of catastrophic deprivation, but at the same time has the negative outcome of ensuring that processes of relating to, and reintrojecting encounters with the external world, are rendered null and void."*[13]

I would like to make a comment about the two dimensional mode of functioning from a more political, collective and institutional level, which, of course, translates as a more fundamentalist point of view, or ideology, or policy. In a very interesting chapter in Polly Young Eisendrath's recent book *The Psychology of Mature Spirituality*, called "Emissaries from the Underworld – Psychotherapy's challenge to Christian Fundamentalism," the author discusses the "fundamentalist" state of mind which is akin to the two dimensional mode:

"Fundamentalism offers a vision of divine judgement rather than love. It is a conservative moral stance that tends to hypostatise ethical sensibility into moral law, and radically to split the world into two; Christian and non-Christian, God and the devil etc.". . .Fundamentalism is a state of mind that touches all of us, no matter our beliefs, when we fear difference and become dogmatic, and is a style of thinking that is evident in all religions.[14]

For the fundamentalist, transcendence is not a capacity to pass through anxiety, but an other worldly refuge from it. . .in this form, transcendence is a spiritual clarity which divides the human world into those who are saved and those who remain in darkness, which involves an identification with the transcendent order and a continual effort to overcome the downward pull of the body's sexuality, aggression, sickness and death. Such identification forecloses our capacity of intimate empathy, as well as the aesthetic and embodied foundations of compassionate ethics.[15]

Fundamentalist beliefs are used defensively to support ego functioning, particularly its distortions through splitting and projection. . .The way fundamentalist experience is organised is familiar to us as a way of coping with extreme anxiety and unmanageable psychic pain. . .for the fundamentalist the shadow side of life is split off, disowned and projected into the world and the devil. . .instead of taking responsibility for the darker aspects of themselves, they shroud the world in darkness through projection."[16]

Fundamentalism is not characteristic of any one religion, but is a state of mind, a particular psychological attitude that occurs in every field of life. As I have said earlier, the fundamentalist state of mind is in essence a psychological defence mechanism that reflects a deep internal schism—the paranoid/schizoid mode. From a Jungian perspective, the possibility of real interior transformation essentially resides in moving towards, and being in, a three dimensional symbolic mind—which means struggling with the opposites, or our very different states of mind, to a third position, or new attitude, through the creation of symbolic thinking, that unites and transcends opposites, leading to new syntheses and integration. Symbolic thinking becomes the synthesis of new understandings and new perspectives, where, simultaneously, different aspects and points of view which were not accessible in the two dimensional mode can now be held internally and reflected on.

Often, the passage from a two-dimensional to a three dimensional existence is possible only under the most grueling conditions of sacrifice, surrender, and psychic pain and suffering. Jung called it the transcendent function, which is a natural developmental process where our opposite attitudes, goals, affects and impulses conflict, collide and coincide—our constant, conscious struggle, self-reflection and deepening understanding going back and forth, constantly washing the conflicts, pain and opposites, and slowly circumambulating around a deeper sense of self. Gradually, a third alternative, position or attitude builds up, that includes both sides and also something new within begins to grow. . .something is building up, slowing transcending the conflict and two-dimensional functioning to resolve our conflict, seeing it differently from a new, transcendent source, or attitude.

So, the transcendent function slowly moves our ego out of our assumption we are in charge, in control of our life, and through becoming aware of our unconscious life and processes, a bigger centre, our self or soul, grows. Through our disorientation, darkness, confusion, suffering and pain, something new is birthing within, a new image, symbol, a breakthrough, a new perception that brings new life, insights, relief and some peace. As Jung explains, *"the psychological 'transcendent function' arises from the union of conscious and unconscious contents. . .the unconscious is not this thing or that; it is the Unknown as it immediately affects us."*[17]

Three dimensional represents all that civilised society holds dear—rationality, balance, adulthood, fairness, flexibility, restraint, the ability to listen and to respect the integrity of another. Three dimensional is searching, reflective and ambivalent, where the creative capacity for imagination, metaphor and symbolisation is central. In this dimension, opposite states of mind and positions have changed and combined into something new, that is much more than the sum of the constituent parts—there is now much more space inside and outside for thought, reflection and an enhanced sense of inner freedom to respond in different ways to life situations.

This dimension relates to a sober sense of reality, which recognises that nothing can be perfect, that nothing is permanent, and that the past cannot be magically changed or undone. It is the state of deep hope where impotence and imperfection can be lived with, loss mourned, damage repaired and sorrow learnt from. It is the state where we learn and experience how all of our life experiences can carry a great deal of meaning.

Three dimensions is that interactive space created by our readiness and openness to relate with another, which primarily allows for mutuality, change and exchange. This state can be experienced as a revolution and a dramatic transformation, through the often very painful and difficult sacrifice of profoundly held, unconscious core beliefs in the omnipotence and total self sufficiency of the self to the three dimensional state of interdependency, mutuality and relationship with another.

It can be experienced as a quantum leap to a different level of being—a leap from the two dimensional world of mirroring, imitation, artifice and control to a world of creative activity in a shared three dimensional space where trust, hope, gratitude, generosity and mature love are possible. Analytically, this is tantamount to the client discovering and acknowledging the existence and importance of the analyst, evidenced by repeated experiences of the analyst being reliably available and present, and able to impart to the patient a sense of being understood, thought about and responded to.

Like sensing a three dimensional space, or world, from the two dimensional mode, moving from *three dimensional to four dimensional* can be similar—as if a chink of something new, a small sense of light that we had not seen, or sensed before, is more present—and often challenges and disrupts our usual mode of consciousness. It is as if it is a different dimension of what we sense is *real* is more present and alive.

In his book Nathan Field describes ways in which a four dimensional state can be experienced:

> "*It is, as if, there is a simultaneous union and separation of self and other. I have in mind those moments where two people feel profoundly united with one another yet each retains a singularly enriched sense of themselves.*
>
> *We are not lost in the other as in fusion, but found— there seems to be a transpersonal, autonomous, directing intelligence, mutual to the two partners, somehow constituted by their union, and yet not reducible to either nor directly manipulable. . .it is to acknowledge a relationship beyond the therapeutic alliance, beyond the depressive position, beyond object relationship, beyond secondary process into something, which incorporates, underlies and transcends the ego.*"[18]

The four-dimensional state is by all means not uncommon, which many have tried to convey in art, music, poetry. The main point here I would like to elucidate is that this dimension, I believe, can strongly relate to the spiritual and mystical, and many of the characteristics of our human encounter with the Transcendent which I outlined earlier on in the paper relates to this fourth dimension. Although the four-dimensional state often occurs spontaneously, certain structured situations, such as *prayer, meditation and therapy* can certainly facilitate it.

In the most favourable circumstances, these situations are characterised by *stillness, silence, a sense of presence and intense mutuality.* When the four-dimensional state occurs in the one to one therapeutic setting, it carries the conviction that healing is taking place. I would like to stimulate your own reflection—what is your own sense, or experience, either in the consulting room or personally of the fourth dimensional state, or mode?

I think that this dimension is also something to do with sensing, or knowing, however dimly or distantly, that reality where there is profound unity and interconnectedness of life. Somehow there is sense of being able to *see life* more and more clearly—a sense of being connected to, in a real and living way— the larger archetypal patterns, designs and meaning of our life. There is definitely a sense of becoming a part of a larger whole that is always there. I think it is beginning to apprehend, or touch, or taste the level of reality that Jung described as the *undus mundus,* or latent unitary reality.

I would like to share a recent dream, which could be seen, symbolically, as move from three to fourth dimensional sight:

> "I am in a large lift which on the outside of a tall building. I become aware that we are slowly ascending. There is an increasingly panoramic view that is visible over the whole landscape. I look down and see that we are overlooking a large harbour. Then, I see that hundreds of small individual boats and sailcraft are beginning to enter the harbour. By this time, we are so far away that I can't see the small details of the boats, but they are all painted white, as if they were sparks of light, which appears very distinctive. Then I begin to see the boats arrange themselves into a large moving flotilla as they enter the harbour precincts. As I am intently watching the unfolding spectacle before me, all of a sudden, as if in a flash, all the boats seem to disappear.
>
> I am shocked and taken aback at their apparent disappearance. I begin to focus on the scene even more closely, with the strange feeling that something very strange,

almost miraculous seems to be happening. As I begin to focus with different eyes, I observe that all the boats have rearranged themselves underwater, on the bottom of the harbour floor, into a very intricate mandala shape. All the individual boats have now become intimately, seamlessly, interconnected and interweaved together into a rather large and beautiful mandala of light that has arranged itself underwater. It is only visible from the greater height."

It is an interesting symbol—the mandala of light which appears spontaneously underwater. When I was reflecting on it, I thought of the internet, and what that may be symbolising for us in our generation. Is it a new collective symbol which is emerging for this fourth dimension—communication and relationship via cyberspace, or network of light signals, which is irrespective of time, space, nationality, geography?

Finally, I would like to make a few brief comments about individuation and beyond. Jacobi made a very interesting comment in her book *The Way of Individuation*:

> "The experience of God in the form of an encounter or 'unio mystica' is the only possible and authentic way to a genuine belief in God for modern man. The individuation process can 'prepare' a man for such an experience. It can open him or her to the influence of a world beyond his rational consciousness. . .one might say that in the course of the individuation process, a man arrives at the entrance to the house of God. When he or she opens the door and penetrates to the inner sanctuary where the divine images are, this last step is left to him or her alone."[19]

So, in conclusion, I hope this paper can inject a more life, interest and sense of urgency to exploring these fundamental questions.

Is Jung's embrace of the spirituality and mysticism in danger of being forgotten, deemed irrelevant, embarrassing or even lost by subsequent generations? What does this critical aspect of Jung's work mean to us today—personally, clinically, professionally—in the wider social milieu, in some of the important decisions that we as a group are in the midst of at present? Where is the Jungian community in addressing and continuing to explore these most basic and vital issues and questions of life?

Endnotes

[1] C. G. Jung in a Letter to P.W. Martin.

[2] P. Young –Eisendrath and M. Miller (Editors), *The Psychology of Mature Spirituality.*

[3] Association of Jungian Analysts Feschrift, 1977-1998, p. 7.

[4] W. James, *The Varieties of Religious Experience.*

[5] J. McLean, *Towards Mystical Union*, pp. 30-32.

[6] C. G. Jung, *The Collected Works of C. G. Jung, Volume 5.*

[7] N. Field, *Breakdown and Breakthrough: Psychotherapy in a New Dimension.*

[8] D. Meltzer, *Explorations in Autism.*

[9] T. Ogden, *The Primitive Edge of Experience*, p. 30.

[10] Ibid, p. 32.

[11] H.M. Solomon, *The Self in Transformation: The Passage from a Two to a Three-Dimensional Internal World*, pp. 225-238.

[12] Ibid, p. 228.

[13] Ibid, p. 230.

[14] P. Young –Eisendrath and M. Miller (Editors), *The Psychology of Mature Spirituality*, p. 147.

[15] Ibid, p. 148.

[16] Ibid, p. 149.

[17] C. G. Jung, *The Collected Works of C. G. Jung, Volume 8*, pp. 68-69.

[18] N. Field, *Breakdown and Breakthrough: Psychotherapy in a New Dimension.*

[19] J. Jacobi, *The Way of Individuation.*

Chapter Three

JUNG AND THE CHRISTIAN WAY

Introduction

Several contemporary Christian authors regard Jung's most important contribution was his essentially pastoral response to counter the corrosive and personally debilitating effects of modernity on the psyche[1]. As modern secular psychology is generally unable to contain, and relate to, mystery, paradox, ambiguity and contradiction, Jungian psychology tends to value, and respect, these psychological states and integrates them into its theoretical and clinical understanding of psychological growth and maturation. The symbols of religion, particularly the Christian symbols, were a major preoccupation in his life and work where he was attempting to show the psychic roots of religion and the psychological relevance of Christianity, with his epistemology diverse enough to emphasise the existence, and reality, of unseen factors indirectly, via the subjective experience of dreams, symbols of transformation, fantasies, intuitions, hunches, awe and dread.

Homo religiousus: Hardwired for Belief in God

In this brief paper, I want to focus on two particular pastoral ways in which Jung addressed these important modern issues, and how his depth psychology, I believe, is essential in revitalising Christian spirituality today. At the heart of Jung's work was his lifelong exploration of the psychology of the *homo religiousus*. One of his central contributions was the recognition and value that he accorded the "religious function" of the psyche—the innate religious urge which he regarded as an inborn need of the psyche which, he firmly believed, could not be neglected or violated without grave injury to psychic health and well being, particularly in the second half of life.

His main concern was to present a psychology of life integration and wholeness, free from attachments to formal religious language or ideology. He wanted the religious dimension of the psyche—the quest and longing for God, the sacred or holy—to be seen as natural and innate, as a "fact" of the psyche, rather than as supernatural or as an object of "belief." Jung was fairly ambivalent about traditional Christianity, striving to preserve the spirit of religious tradition but throwing many old religious forms into an alchemical fire, as he was certain that religious faith points to the reality of, and authentic, transformative encounters with, the living God—"*I am not addressing myself to the happy possessors of faith, but to those many people for whom the light has gone out, the mystery has faded and God is dead. For most of them there is no going back, and one does not know either whether going back is always the better way. To gain an understanding of religious matters, probably all that is left for us today is the psychological approach. That is why I take these thought-forms that have become historically fixed, try to melt them down again and pour them into moulds of immediate experience.*"[2]

His treatment of religion may look destructive and disrespectful to some, but underneath he saw himself as an alchemist in the laboratory of faith, consisting in creatively exploring new postmodern expressions of the eternal religious spirit.[3] He viewed his depth psychology as providing an essentially modern psychological bridge between traditional Christian dogma and doctrine and authentic and healing human experience and encounter with the holy, the numinous or the Holy Spirit. He was convinced that man's perennial religious impulse would rise again in self and society in new and creative ways, and his explorations took him back to the ancient past and the late medieval period, and forward to the world yet to be born.

Spiritual Revolution in Postmodern World

He knew that profound changes were happening both in society and in the psyche of modern men and women, and that fresh and new expressions of religion were both necessary and in the making. Of course, what Jung was looking forward to and was prophetically writing about in the 1940's and 1950's is now happening in many quarters in our postmodern world, but it is a quiet spirituality revolution.[4] This is not religion in its old forms, but religion in the sense of mythos or sacred story—as a searching for, and re-connection to, all that is holy, and for Christians, how our individual life is part of, and binds, conforms us to the human, and divine, life of Jesus in ever more life giving and transformative ways.

Secondly, I want to emphasise here today the other vital contribution was his vocation as healer of the soul, and his depth psychology is basically a psychology of healing of psychic disturbance, which he states clearly in a late letter—*"I am simply a psychiatrist, for my essential problem, to which all my efforts are directed, is psychic disturbance: its phenomenology, its aetiology, and teleology. Everything else is secondary for me."*[5] The main thrust of his psychology was to articulate, and describe, from his working with thousands of people for over fifty years, the way of healing of human neuroses.

He called it the journey of individuation, the integration of psychological opposites where unconscious material is raised to consciousness and is incorporated by it. Individuation is, in a way, a rounding off of the psyche and is therefore often symbolised, in art and dreams, by mandala patterns—where we can become a separate undivided conscious unity, a distinct whole, first by unifying ego consciousness, and then the whole psychic system of conscious and unconscious, in order to approach wholeness. In his writings, Jung emphasized repeatedly that the process of individuation is mainly a psychological one, and not a spiritual one.

A large thrust of Jung's psychology, was an attempt to offer the Christian tradition in particular (and the other religious traditions in general) psychotherapeutic understanding, and treatment, for its deeply ingrained tendency to split the physical and spiritual aspects of the human psyche. Jung's anguished answer to these modern monumental questions was contained in his last great volume, *Mysterium Coniunctionis*, "An Inquiry into the Separation and Synthesis of Psychic Opposites in Alchemy" (*Collected Works Volume 14*), which is a book about the power of love to heal the conflict between the opposites in the divided self and divided society.[6] It was the culmination of Jung's alchemical studies begun the 1920's, and completed the opus of his lifetimes contribution to modern depth psychology. This volume focuses on the profound healing that can take places when the power of love—God's love—constellates the wholeness latently present in our psyche. This deep psychological healing process brings us to the centre of our being, where the power of God's love, through relationships, is capable of healing all the conflicts between the opposites, healing all the dualities and splits within ourselves.

Individuation, Integration and Spirituality

Usually our psychological journey towards individuation and integration can't really be separated from our spiritual journey of prayer and longing in our heart and soul to be immersed in God's love and real community, and that when we use the term "soul," "true self," "essence," etc., we are including what we would call "psyche." All experienced phenomena can be expected to have at least some connections with unconscious psychodynamics and these connections are neither good nor bad in and of themselves. It is only upon considering their fruits—their effects upon the experienced and lived life of faith—that we can begin to appreciate and appraise their true value.

Since we come to know God through our psyche, we must be prepared to heal and transform all the muck of our own interior stable in which the divine can be born. Inherited with the pure gracious gift of God's self are the unacceptable parts of our lives that get attached to our views of God. In our journey towards the centre of ourselves and beyond, the way deepens and darkens as it progresses, and as soon as we turn towards the interior world of self reflection, self knowledge and prayer, we usually encounter whole dimensions of ourselves that have previously been unconscious, hidden and unknown. In modern psychological terms, these are called the "shadow" parts of the psyche, which encompasses all the psychic contents that have been driven back into the unconscious: all the neglected, undeveloped, unacknowledged parts of our personality which need to be constantly recognised and accepted, so as to be dissolved and transformed—"made new"—by God's love, throughout our psychological, and deeper prayer journey.[7] It is a mysterious paradox that the place of our greatest pain, vulnerability and powerlessness is the door through which our heart can be so broken that it forces us to turn away from the outer world and trace the thread of our own darkness back to our source in God. Unless we can fully participate in life and become relatively differentiated, the wholeness that the individuation process is striving for cannot be reached. Conscious and unconscious stand in a reciprocal, dynamic relationship; out of the unconscious rise contents and images, and they show themselves to the conscious mind as though secretly asking to be grasped and understood, so that "birth" may be accomplished and "being" created.

So, the aim of the individuation process is a synthesis of all partial aspects of the conscious and unconscious. It seems to point to an ultimately unknowable, transcendent "centre" of the personality, which Jung calls the Self, which is always there, as the central, archetypal, structural element of the psyche, operating as the organizer and director of all psychic processes. The symbol of the quaternity, usually in the form of the square, is one of the oldest symbols, besides the circle, of the self, which symbolizes all the parts, qualities, and aspects of unity.[8] These "uniting symbols" most vividly represent the fundamental order of the psyche, the union of its polaristic qualities, and are the prime symbols of the self and of psychic wholeness. Jung called them the "*atomic nuclei*" *of the psyche,* representing the *coincidentia oppositorum,* or union of opposites, in particular of conscious and unconscious contents, and transcend rational understanding.

All these symbols are the vehicles and at the same time the product of what Jung called the transcendent function, that is, of the psyche's symbol making capacity, of its creative power, the process of transformation to new attitudes and perspectives and paths to psychic renewal—"*The raw material shaped by thesis and antithesis, and in the shaping of which the opposites are united, is the living symbol*".[9] The transcendent function is one of the central tenets of Jung's model of psychological growth through dialogue with the unconscious with application both as a vital clinical tool, understanding the workings and dynamics of everyday life with profound spiritual implications.[10]

Towards the Unknown Within

With this notion of the self, Jung was reaching to describe, intuitively and theoretically, a psychological dimension that was far exceeding the limits of individual's usual conscious self awareness and identity. Jung's notion of the self stretches our psychological and ontological understanding *towards* the unknown within, *towards* the personal relation to, and encounters with, a transcendent reality, which is normally hidden from our everyday consciousness. Jung's writings contain much of the psychological teaching of the ancient Christian contemplative tradition transposed into the idiom of twentieth century psychology. In his concept of the self, Jung shares the belief that God's presence lies within the centre of the soul, expressed from a psychological, rather than a mystical, perspective, and his writings on the psyche contain much of the teaching of Christian spiritual direction and guidance from past centuries, in the idiom of modern depth psychology.

The mystical writers down the centuries, and indeed the Christian contemplative tradition in general, suggests that there are even deeper dimensions of experience that are able to be awakened and engaged, and that the individuation process is but a threshold, a transition, to another way of knowing. This deeper spiritual journey in essence, is regarded as a continuation of the Jungian integration/individuation process, but on a deeper, or higher octave, so to speak. From this wider spiritual perspective, individuation is not an end point in itself, but the completion of one journey and an arrival, a preparation for another, as yet unknown journey.

Jung movingly writes of the beginning of this cusp between two ways of knowing, or the entrance to another way of knowing. Mystical knowledge, Jung claims, differs from ordinary knowledge in that it effects a transformation, and it is found not in the succession of images which pass across the imagination and from which we abstract our concepts, but by a penetration of the mind into the centre of its own being—in mystical experience that transforms. Jung writes, *"it is not that something different is seen, but that one sees differently. It is as though the spatial act of seeing were changed by a new dimension."*[11] And, Jung writes, this new way of seeing, this new dimension, is dependent on the birth of a new centre, which he called the Self.

Here, Jung is referring to that important cusp, or transformation, between two ways of knowing or being, towards a more mystical or contemplative consciousness, towards union in the centre of the soul. The 14th century text the *Cloud of Unknowing* speaks of the *"the sovereign point of the spirit,"* called the *apex mentis* or the "substance of the soul," or "the centre of the soul."[12] St John of the Cross often speaks of the "centre of the soul" e.g. In Canticle, I, 6: *And it is to be observed, if one would learn how to find this Spouse (as far as may be in this life), that the Word, together with the Father and the Holy Spirit, is hidden essentially in the inmost centre of the soul.*[13] Mystical union or the spiritual marriage was the primary metaphor of St Teresa to describe this mystical dimension. Among other major mystical categories are those of contemplation and the vision of God, deification, the birth of the Word in the soul, ecstasy, or radical obedience to Divine Will.

Horizontal and Vertical Thinking

Whereas ordinarily we think horizontally, one image or concept being replaced by another, the language of the contemplatives indicates that mystical thought is vertical: it does not entail the acquisition of new ideas and concepts but is a descent into the darkness of one's own mind, void of images and conceptual thinking. This world of perpetual solitude found by the descent into oneself is the sovereign point of the spirit, the centre of one's being: it is the world in which reigns silence and union. In short, mystical knowledge does not move in successive images but spirals down into the depth of the soul to encounter God in the obscurity of silence.[14]

St Teresa and St John of the Cross use ways of speaking which have been employed by numerous mystics from St Augustine to Ruysbroeck—a way of speaking reminiscent of depth psychology—that view mental activity not horizontally but vertically, not in space but in silence, not in motion but in rest, not in time but in timelessness. This distinction between two ways of knowing, two ways of being or different forms of awareness has been described by Christian saints and mystics throughout the centuries.

In personal terms, the fruit of this deeper journey is that we come to know our self in new ways, this knowledge coming from the Divine, and not from our ego-centric, perspective. So, it is really describing that cusp, or transition, when the integration of the natural personality, or the process of individuation, has generally occurred, and a deeper process of spiritual transformation is underway. It is arguable whether depth psychology has yet evolved to the point where it can speak meaningfully about these deeper contemplative states of mind—that dimension of experience which lies beyond the familiar polarity of consciousness and unconsciousness.

The Christian contemplative tradition teaches us that the centre of the soul may be trusted, a centre which reveals itself as life giving, not annihilating, pointing not to our personal life alone but to the image of the crucified, and resurrected, Christ as the symbol and reality that contains our whole life. Our Christian journey is graced by divine presence accompanied by emergence of the figure of Christ, where the movement towards the innermost chambers of the human heart in prayer, relationship and community is a response to His divine call of Love. This divine image not only expresses the growing intimacy with God, but also, as a psychological symbol, signals the emergence of a more completely individuated personality, a fuller realization of our true self.

41

This longing for union with the love of God remains as a permanent feature of the psyche, despite this longing not always fitting in with traditional religious forms. Modern Christian people long for relationship with the transformational healing love of God, through Jesus, enabling them to live in truly authentic, life giving ways. Jung was explicit in saying in a 1945 letter that this was what his work was all about: *The main interest of my work is not concerned with the treatment of neuroses but rather with the approach to the numinous. The fact is that the approach to the numinous is the real therapy and inasmuch as you attain to the numinous experiences you are released from the curse of pathology.*[15] He was describing the psychological healing path towards direct authentic encounters with the living God and it is this that postmodern people want, not only doctrinal or creedal religion. Part of Jung's contribution was to show that such experiences are not reserved for an elite, but belong to the normal range of human life and what might have once seemed rarefied, remote and reserved for saints and monastics is now in great demand and longed for by many ordinary people.

Conclusion

I would like to finish with Ann Ulanov's helpful wisdom of the psyche:

"We live in the psychological century, where explorations of inner space probe as far as those that go into outer space. Theology and the church hobble themselves when they fail to recognize the broad, deep, rich life of the unconscious already there in religious ritual, symbol, doctrine and sacrament. It is a failure to take seriously the transcendent in its persistent immanence, in and among us. Within the system of the psyche, we experience unconscious contents as transcendent to our egos. Theology's failure to take the unconscious

seriously leaves the immanence of God unreceived, incarnated. Consciousness of the psyche's reception of God is essential if we are to perform the ministry of the ego in housing all that we are given to be."[16]

Endnotes

[1] A. Bedford Ulanov and A. Dueck, *The Living God and the Living Psyche*, p. 8.

[2] C. G. Jung, *The Collected Works of C. G. Jung, Volume 11, Psychology and Religion – East and West*, para 148.

[3] D. Tacey, "After Tradition: Closer Encounters with the Sacred." *Guild of Pastoral Psychology* Paper Number 300.

[4] D. Tacey, *The Spirituality Revolution*.

[5] C. G. Jung, *The Collected Works of C. G. Jung, Volume 2*, para 70-71.

[6] C. G. Jung, T*he Collected Works of C. G. Jung: Volume 14. Mysterium Coniunctionis*.

[7] J. McLean, *Towards Mystical Union*, pp. 130-144.

[8] C. G. Jung, *The Collected Works of C. G. Jung, Volume 11*, para 98-102.

[9] C. G. Jung, *The Collected Works of C. G. Jung, Volume 6, Psychological Types*, para 828.

[10] J.C. Miller, *The Transcendent Function*.

[11] C. G. Jung, *The Collected Works of C. G. Jung, Volume 11*, para 891.

[12] A. C. Spearing, *The Cloud of Unknowing and Other Works*.

[13] K. Kavanaugh & O. Rodriguez, O. (Trans.) *The Collected Works of St John of the Cross*, p. 480.

[14] J. McLean, *Teresa of Avila and Depth Psychology*, p. 16.

[15] C. G. Jung in a Letter to P.W. Martin.

[16] A. Bedford Ulanov, *The Wisdom of the Psyche*, pp. 118-119.

Chapter Four

C. G. JUNG and PRAYER

Exploring the interface between Depth Psychology and the Christian Contemplative Tradition

I would like to start with a quote that speaks of the essence of our subject from Thomas Merton:

"In the 'prayer of the heart' we seek first of all the deepest ground of our identity in God. We do not reason about dogmas of faith, or "the mysteries." We seek rather to gain a direct existential grasp, a personal experience of the deepest truths of life and faith, finding ourselves in God's truth. Inner certainty depends on purification. The dark night rectifies our deepest intentions. In the silence of this 'night of faith' we return to simplicity and sincerity of heart. We learn recollection which consists in listening for God's will, in direct and simple attention to reality. Recollection is awareness of the unconditional. Prayer then means yearning for the simple presence of God, for a personal understanding

of his word, for knowledge of his will and for capacity to hear and obey him."[1]

One of the basic ideas in the western Christian contemplative, or mystical, tradition is that spiritual life moves through stages in an ascending or descending order. This triple way or threefold path is the traditional Christian way of referring to the stages of spiritual development or transformation. Although not as widely used today, this threefold concept has had considerable influence on the development of the Christian spiritual tradition. The term is most often used to refer to the stages of *awakening, purification or purgation, illumination and union.* This classical division into purgative, illuminative and unitive stages was established in the early Christian centuries and has survived most of the transitional differences and school polemics in the following centuries.

This ancient classical map of the spiritual journey towards mystical union was slowly developed over years of inner experimentation by the early Christians and the Desert Fathers and Mothers. It became crystallized through medieval mystics such as Hugh of St Victor, Blessed Jan van Ruysbroec and St Catherine of Siena, and reached a height of refinement with St Teresa and St John of the Cross. Variations and subdivisions multiplied, but the core of the doctrine has remained the same for more than a thousand years.

The tradition can be seen though the mystical writings of the high Middle Ages and into the modern period. St Ignatius of Loyola (1491-1556), St Teresa and St John all make use of this threefold path in their writings. Ignatius relates the first week of his spiritual exercises to the way of purification, while weeks two and three correspond to that of illumination. Likewise, in Teresa's mystical text *The Interior Castle*, the first mansions refer to the state of purification, those in the middle to that of illumination and the final mansions to that of union. John's masterful exposition of the purgative way in his *Dark Night of the Soul* and A*scent of Mount Carmel* are justly celebrated, while his *Spiritual canticle* and *Living Flame of Love* related more to the other two stages of illumination and union.[2]

What I am exploring here is the interface between Jungian psychology and the Christian mystical, or contemplative, tradition, as highlighted by the life and writings of the Spanish mystics, St Teresa of Avila and St John of the Cross. This interface is not a simple one—whereas key theses such as search, journey, transformation, self-knowledge can be seen as mutually endorsed in both traditions—we could say that the vision of the end, or the *telos*, of the final goal, varies.

The *telos* of the psyche, according to analytical, or Jungian, psychology, is to achieve individuation, which can be summarised as a process by which the integration of psychological opposites is attained, and by which unconscious material is raised to consciousness and is incorporated by it. Individuation is the name for the ongoing maturation process by which a person becomes a psychological individual, which is to say, a separate undivided conscious unity, a distinct whole —by first the process of unifying ego consciousness, and then the whole psychic system of conscious and unconscious— in order to approach psychological wholeness.

In his writings, C. G. Jung emphasized repeatedly that the process of individuation is mainly a psychological one, and not a spiritual one. I think Thomas Merton also succinctly described the purpose of the individuation journey:[3]

"The first thing you have to do, before you even start thinking about such a thing as contemplation, is to try to recover your basic natural unity, to reintegrate your

compartmentalized being into a co-ordinated and simple whole and learn to live as a unified human person. This means that you have to bring back together the fragments of your distracted existence so that when you say 'I.' there is really someone present to support the pronoun you have uttered. The worst thing that can happen to a man who is already divided up into a dozen different compartments is to seal off yet another compartment and tell him that this one is more important than all the others, and that he must henceforth exercise a special care in keeping it separate from them. That is what tends to happen when contemplation is unwisely thrust without warning upon the bewilderment and distraction of western man."

Whereas individuation can be seen as the stage at which the hidden circular movement of the soul around its centre emerges in full flowering into the daylight of mature consciousness, the goal, or telos, of the contemplative, is to be drawn into, absorbed within the ineffable abyss of this centre point within our heart, within that "*nothing consisting of nothing*" that is "*incomprehensible by thought.*" There are countless illustrations of the telos of the contemplative journey throughout the writings of the Christian mystics and saints across the centuries, Meister Eckhart, the Cloud of Unknowing, John of the Cross and Teresa of Avila, which I am exploring more fully.

So, in our journey towards individuation and psychological maturation, Jungian psychology describes the way into our unconscious processes lies initially through emotion and affect. An active complex usually makes itself known through disrupting the ego with affect, and this compensation from the unconscious offers potential for growth—these are our crises, suffering, woundedness, pain, longing and desire for God. Eventually, Jung goes on, these affective disturbances can be traced to primordial roots in instinct, and can also lead to symbols that anticipate the future. In order to approach wholeness, the conscious/unconscious systems must be brought into relationship with each other, as our psyche consists of two incongruous halves which together form a whole, and our course of development arising out of the conflict between the two fundamental psychic facts of conscious and unconscious.

Jung's anguished answer to these modern monumental questions is contained in his last great volume, *Mysterium Coniuntionis, "An Inquiry into the Separation and Synthesis of Psychic Opposites in Alchemy,"* which is a book about the power of love to heal the conflict between the opposites paired off in the Self.[4] It was the culmination of Jung's alchemical studies begun the 1920's, and *Mysterium Coniunctionis* is the completion of the opus of his lifetime contribution to modern depth psychology. This volume focuses on the deep healing that takes places when the power of love constellates the wholeness latently present in the Self, implying that individuation and reconciliation of opposites typically takes place through relationships, not alone in isolation.

This deep psychological healing process brings us to the centre of our being, where the power of God's love is able, is capable of healing all the conflicts between the opposites, healing all the dualities and splits within ourselves. As such, this individuation process, the way of development and maturation of the psyche, does not follow a straight line, nor does it always lead onwards and upwards. The course it follows is rather "stadial" or "spiral," consisting of progress and regress, flux and stagnation in alternating sequence—usually only when we glance back over a long stretch of the way can we notice the development.

It has also been described an interior Odyssey, deepening "centroversion," Jung spoke of it as a "labyrinthine" path. There are various ways of describing this way—either as the progressive differentiation of our attitudinal and functional modes of being, or in terms of the symbolism of the most important figures that manifest themselves along this way, or as a systematic confrontation, step by step, between the ego and the contents of the unconscious.

Self Knowledge

So, at the early stages of the psychological journey, of the growing remembering and recollection of our soul and awakening to the presence of love and the Holy Spirit, the journey of self-knowledge and the transformation of our shadow are central. Usually our psychological journey towards individuation and integration can't really be separated, in my view, from our spiritual journey of prayer and longing in our heart and soul, our burning desire, to be immersed in God's love, and that when we use the term "soul," "true self," "essence" we are including what we would call "psyche."

My basic assumption throughout is that spiritual growth is *generally* accompanied by psychological growth and maturity. From a spiritual perspective, real psychological self-knowledge is necessary for true compassion, because a deeper self-understanding brings true humility, and that true self-knowledge is the essential psychological foundation on which the love journey to the deeper chambers of the heart is based. This is because the process of spiritual growth involves continually looking in both directions: towards greater self-knowledge and humility, and greater knowledge of God.

So, truly knowing ourselves is about growing familiar with, and accepting, our fallibility and our needs, those open or concealed; also, our relationship with ourselves and with others which constantly and vigilantly requires an honest, totally sincere, transparent awareness of our motivations, intentions and drives, both conscious and, importantly, unconscious.

It entails opening up our deepest traumas, anxieties and fears so that they may be healed—which, from the perspective of the deeper spiritual way, is indispensable work. It also means allowing a full and loving integration of the many places where we are most vulnerable and unloved; of our blocks and of our psychic and emotional pain; also, of the limitations of what we can do on our own, without God's love and the action of grace in our life. Ultimately, it is about knowing our total dependence on God who, in his love, holds and heals us.

Alongside discerning the movement of the Holy Spirit in our lives, and inviting him into the depths of our heart, we need to be constantly acquainted with our own nature and origin, both conscious and unconscious. The desire to move towards deepening states of contemplative prayer must be augmented by an ongoing struggle to develop an in-depth understanding of ourselves.

Real self-knowledge does not mean an intellectual knowledge of human nature, but true "heart" knowledge of ourselves from the perspective of prayer and of a growing union with God. We need an increasing ability to sense, articulate and respond adequately to what is going on within our psyche. There is a wealth of areas in play: intellectual capacities; feelings and emotions, both negative and positive; sensation and intuition; conscious and unconscious motives; primitive instincts and the rational (and irrational) nature. Through purification and purgation, we gradually learn to become dispassionate and to attain to a *peaceful condition of the soul*.

If we are truly open to the Holy Spirit's potential in our lives, we will be able to acknowledge that pain and pleasure, joy and sadness, success and failure may either work for, or against, our growth in life in the Spirit. All experienced phenomena can be expected to have at least some connections with unconscious psychodynamics and these connections are neither good nor bad in and of themselves. It is only upon considering their fruits—their effects upon the experienced and lived life of faith—that we can begin to appreciate and appraise their true value. In the innermost dwelling places of the heart, there is precisely a state of peace and spiritual rest, a gentle control of our feelings and passions, a deep living of fruits of the Spirit: compassion and goodness, long-suffering and gentleness, faithfulness and temperance, together with the good works which is the natural active outflow of a contemplative "resting in union with God."

Transformation of our Shadow

In our journey towards individuation and beyond, the way deepens and darkens as it progresses as we become more conscious of our pre-verbal, pre-rational fantasies, instinctive drives and bodily passions and impulses, as well as, of course, touching transcendent realms. As soon as we turn towards the interior world of self-reflection, self-knowledge and prayer, we usually encounter whole dimensions of ourselves that have previously been unconscious, hidden and unknown. This dimension of our growing self-knowledge is particularly vital in regard to our spiritual journey and deepening life of prayer; it can never be denied or neglected without, I believe, psychological and spiritual injury to the individual. All the neglected and dark sides of ourselves are usually encountered fairly quickly.

In modern psychological terms, these are called the "shadow" parts of the psyche, or our inferior function, which Jung as the *"negative side of the personality, the sum of all those unpleasant qualities we like to hide, together with the insufficiently developed functions and the content of the personal unconscious."*[5] The shadow, as it were, is the mirror image of our conscious identity, or ego, and is compounded partly of repressed, partly of unlived psychic features which, for moral, social, educational or other reasons, were from the outset excluded from our consciousness and from active participation in life and were therefore repressed or split off.

Accordingly, the shadow can be marked by both positive and negative qualities. Besides the personal shadow there is, in Jung's view, also the "collective shadow" in which the general evil is contained. It gives expression not to the contents belonging to the personal life history of the individual, but to everything negative, everything that opposes the spirit of the time in the Christian middle ages, it was represented by witches and sorcerers. So, the "shadow" encompasses all the psychic contents that have been driven back into the unconscious: all the neglected, undeveloped, unacknowledged parts of our personality which need to be constantly recognised and accepted, so as to be dissolved and transformed—"made new"—by God's love, throughout our psychological, and deeper prayer journey.

This is the inner transformation of unconscious psychological wounds that takes place when the heart and mind are open to God. From a spiritual perspective, these are the early stages of our spiritual life, which are often fraught with distractions and obstacles that seem to pull us away constantly from the ever deepening contemplative journey towards God.

St Teresa symbolises these negative and broken parts of ourselves as the "poisonous creatures": the lizards and snakes in the moat outside the castle, that represent all the dynamic forces that attack, block and distract us from without, and hinder and disturb us from within, the shadow parts of the psyche, encompassing all those psychic contents that have been driven back into the unconscious: all the neglected and undeveloped parts of our personality which, however, need to be constantly recognised, accepted and transformed.

Another common description of our shadow side is the *wounded inner child*, where parts of ourselves have been relegated to the unconscious after childhood trauma. If psychological wounds from childhood are not tended and healed, and especially if they are sustained and reinforced into adulthood, then they feed the repressed, shadow side of our personality. There are often painful memories and experiences, even personal qualities, which we may have forgotten and denied and concealed from both ourselves and others. Locked in the dark basement of the unconscious, out of sight from the world, our shadow parts often carry great pain and vulnerability, suffering, sadness, deep despair, anger, alienation and resentment, which can become ever bleeding wounds.

The confrontation with our shadow is no easy task, and it is often painful and difficult to become aware of our shadow side, with its pride, shame, guilt, manipulation, hunger for power, jealousy, envy, need for revenge, desire for possession, sexual temptations and the like. In these early stages, the psychological task, with prayer and longing for God, is to "enter within ourselves," and not to become over-identified with and over-attached to these parts of ourselves. Through deepening self-knowledge and prayer, and our growing contact with the light and truth of God through grace, the "lizards and snakes" dimension of our psyche can slowly be penetrated and reintegrated through growing recollection in order to be finally transformed through love.

As our psychological and spiritual journey grows and matures, we usually need to struggle to face the neglected, unconscious dimensions of our psyche in a deeper and more honest way, and these psychological and spiritual dangers are present throughout our spiritual journey. Unless we are able to accept, and communicate with, our hidden underground depths at these early stages on our journey, these realms will almost certainly disrupt our spiritual progress—if they are not faced, owned and ultimately transformed, our "lizards and snakes" will turn around and bite; they will poison us and generally wreak havoc on our interior life.

It takes a tremendous amount of humility, integrity and self-honesty, together with charity and virtue, to acknowledge our shadow and to allow the long, arduous work of its transformation to begin. The parts of us that have been repressed and hidden now come to full consciousness for recognition, healing and transformation through acceptance and love. To handle the shadow areas of human experience requires particularly sensitive and patient care. It is possible, once the shadow parts have been accepted, for them to be changed and redirected, and so to become positive sources of creativity and talent. Effective strategies for recognising our vulnerable and shadow areas include analysing our dreams, becoming attentive to fantasies and daydreams, examining closely the nature and content of our humour and, most importantly, becoming conscious of what we project onto others and examining it.

Why is working on, and the transformation of our shadow so important? There are many reasons. Working on our repressed and wounded areas is an integral part of knowing ourselves in any depth. Acknowledging and reintegrating these rejected parts enables us to recover them. Much of our individual creativity and capacity to surrender resides here. The shadow contains not only negative and destructive elements, but also tremendous potential for deeper spiritual growth and development. Jung found that the shadow, in metaphorical terms, consists of ninety percent gold, as it contains the seeds of our very *new* potential which has not yet come to consciousness. All this potential could be tapped were it not for pressures, anxieties, or the amount of work it would take to own and integrate these parts.

Another important reason for befriending and integrating our shadow parts is that doing so is fundamental to authentic self-esteem. How can we truly love ourselves or have confidence in ourselves if a part of us is ignored and works against our own best interests? Also, our shadow parts tend to be projected onto different types of relationships if we do not acknowledge and work with them, so this is essential for maintaining healthy social and personal relationships. Often, the root cause of interpersonal conflicts and professional burnout can be found in shadow projections. Vulnerabilities or shortcomings are projected onto other people and situations.

Becoming aware of these projections onto others, and then being able to take them back, vastly improves interpersonal relations. This is reflected in the biblical premise—don't look for the speck in others' eyes, but to the log in one's own. Others may have their faults and corrections may have to be made, but the premise says our primary responsibility for us as individuals is to attend to our own inner journey that will reveal our neglected areas. This is reflected in the wisdom: *The best criticism of the bad is the practice of the better*. And in the meaning of holding the unresolved tension of the cross of opposites until we are able to live in, and usher in something entirely new and healing.

The confrontation with the shadow and its integration must always be achieved first in the individuation process in order to strengthen the ego for further depth in the journey and for the crucial encounter with the Self. That is why the shadow qualities must first be made conscious, even at the risk of neglecting other aspects and other figures presented by the psychic material. We find the same thing in myths and fairytales, where the hero always needs a friend, his own shadow side, as a companion in order to overcome the dangers of his quest. Ego and shadow together form that comprehensive consciousness which alone is able to meet and come to terms with the archetypal powers and the contrasexual figures in particular.

These are hidden interior places where we can only gradually accept ourselves in our most naked and vulnerable human state and offer ourselves up to be healed by God's love. *It is our wounds that take us home to God.* During this journey, we have to accept and integrate what we find within us—all the pain, anger and hurt—and the many forms that our darkness has taken. We may well find the prostitute, the thief and the beggar within us. We will see the hurt we have caused others and the hurt we have caused ourselves.

It is a mysterious paradox that the place of our greatest pain, vulnerability and powerlessness is the door through which our heart can be so broken that it forces us to turn away from the outer world and trace the thread of our own darkness back to our source in God. We need to experience, acknowledge and fully surrender our inner darkness and pain to the light and endless love of God. Then we can journey, from exile, further and further in the interior castle—to that innermost dwelling place where "God and the soul hold their most secret intercourse."[6]

What we are really speaking about, also, is the whole process of repentance, i.e., change of mind or metanioa, where we must consciously face all of our shadow and darkness. As soon as we realise the depth of our darkness and pride, we begin to understand that we can do nothing about it, and we are then on the road of profound metanoia—all the great Christian fathers emphasised this. This is also St Benedict's way—such as in Chapter 20 of Rule of St Benedict, where he emphasises the need for metanoia: "We must know that God regards our purity of heart and tears of compunction, not our many words."[7]

Our unconscious, which has to be cleansed by repentance by the deliberate sorry for our darkness, pride and hatred of oneself and others—only then can the life of the unconscious be set free. What is required is the tremendous need for the purification of the unconscious. The purpose is the purification of the unconscious is to set the soul free from the daemonic powers and allow it to be transformed by the powers of goodness.

Bede Griffiths says:

> "*I believe that it is the love of Christ alone who can set us free from the unconscious. This new life is not simply a transformation of the unconscious. It is a new power of life beyond nature, something divine which enters into the unconscious and transfigures it. This is what should happen in our Christian life—that the Holy Spirit should penetrate to the depths of the unconscious, to the ultimate root of being, and transform us.*
>
> *The secret is humility and repentance. The ego has to be submitted to God—it has to die and this is the real difficulty. When this can happen, then the true Self appears. The Holy Spirit transforms the soul and a new control comes into play. This control does not repress the unconscious, it penetrates and transforms it. It brings about a marriage between conscious and unconscious, male and female, animus and anima, in which the values of each are preserved.*
>
> *This is the reintegration of our being in Christ. Only the grace which comes from above, the free gift of God in Christ, can really transform us. The power of grace is like a seed that has to grow before it can take possession and transform the soul, and this growth depends on our own co-operation and our external circumstances.*"[8]

But how difficult it is. To submit one's conscious being to God, to separate from the unconscious, is incredibly hard. This is repentance in the deepest sense. The power of grace enters the soul, but it meets with a tremendous resistance from the unconscious, particularly as our unconscious is so largely split off from the conscious. The whole problem is how to open the unconscious to the power of grace, which means, of course, also how to bring the unconscious again into vital relation with the conscious. But this seems to be so incredibly hard. Usually, behind all this there is a hard core of pride and self will which we fail to surrender and which prevents the opening of the unconscious.

The Self, or Soul

So, the aim of the individuation process is a synthesis of all partial aspects of the conscious and unconscious. It seems to point to an ultimately unknowable, transcendent "centre" of the personality, which—paradoxically—is at the same time its periphery. This centre and periphery Jung calls the Self, which is always there, as the central, archetypal, structural element of the psyche, operating in us from the beginning as the organizer and director of the psychic processes.

If our true self, or soul, is withdrawn from projection and recognized as something operative in ourselves, if it is understood as an autonomous reality and is differentiated from the other psychic elements, "*then one is truly one's own yay and nay. The self then functions as a union of opposites and thus constitutes the most immediate experience of the Divine which it is psychologically possible to imagine.*"[9] It then represents the unity in which all psychic opposites cancel out.

With this notion of the self, Jung was reaching to describe, intuitively and theoretically, a psychological dimension that was far exceeding the limits of individual's usual conscious self-awareness, identity, sense of self and experience of psychic reality. Jung's notion of the self stretches our psychological and ontological understanding *towards* the unknown within, *towards* the mystery of existence, *towards* the personal relation to, and possible inclusion in, the infinite, *towards* the numinosum.

The mystical writers down the centuries, and indeed the Christian contemplative tradition in general, suggests that there are even deeper dimensions of experience that are able to be awakened and engaged, and that the individuation process is but a threshold, a transition, to another way of knowing. From the mystical perspective, individuation is viewed as not being an end point it itself, but the completion/integration of one phase of the journey, and an opening to another part of the journey.

In the ancient tradition, this is called a transition from, or threshold between, the "*journey towards God*" to the "*journey in God.*" This deeper spiritual journey in essence, is regarded as *a continuation of the Jungian integration/individuation process, but on a deeper, or higher octave, so to speak.*

Mystical experience, then, that transforms cannot be explained in this way; for in it, Jung writes that "*it is not that something different is seen, but that one sees differently. It is as though the spatial act of seeing were changed by a new dimension.*" And, Jung writes, this new way of seeing, this new dimension, is dependent on the birth of a new centre:

"*If the unconscious can be recognized as a codetermining factor along with consciousness, and if we can live in such a way that conscious and unconscious demands are taken into account as far as possible, then the centre of gravity of the total personality shifts its position. It is then no longer in the ego, which is merely the centre of consciousness, but in the hypothetical point between conscious and unconscious. This new centre might be called the self. If the transposition is successful, it does away with the participation mystique and results in a personality that suffers only in the lower stories, as it were.*

But its upper stories are singularly detached from painful as well as from joyful happenings. The production and birth of this superior personality is what is meant when our text speaks of the 'holy fruit,' the 'diamond body' or any other kind of incorruptible body. Psychologically, these expressions symbolize an attitude that is beyond the reach of emotional entanglements and violent shocks—a consciousness detached, or freed, from the world."[10]

Here, Jung is referring to that important cusp, or transformation, between two ways of knowing or being, towards a more mystical or contemplative consciousness, towards union in the centre of the soul. The 14th century text the *Cloud of Unknowing* speaks of the *'the sovereign point of the spirit'*, called the *apex mentis* or the 'substance of the soul,' or 'the centre of the soul.'[11]

St John of the Cross often speaks of the 'centre of the soul' e.g. In Canticle, I, 6: *And it is to be observed, if one would learn how to find this Spouse (as far as may be in this life), that the Word, together with the Father and the Holy Spirit, is hidden essentially in the inmost centre of the soul.*[12] Mystical union or the spiritual marriage was the primary metaphor of St Teresa to describe this mystical dimension. Among other major mystical categories are those of contemplation and the vision of God, deification, the birth of the Word in the soul, ecstasy, or radical obedience to Divine Will.

This new dimension is of vital interest for one who would sympathetically study the mystics. *They do not see different things: they see differently. A new mode of interior activity is brought into play.* Whereas ordinarily we think horizontally, one image or concept being replaced by another, the language of the contemplatives indicates that mystical thought is vertical: it does not entail the acquisition of new ideas and concepts but is a descent into the darkness of one's own mind, void of images and conceptual thinking. This world of perpetual solitude' found by the descent into oneself, is the sovereign point of the spirit, the centre of one's being: it is the world in which there reigns silence and union. In short, mystical knowledge does not move in successive images but spirals down into the depth of the soul to encounter God in the obscurity of silence. St Teresa and St John of the Cross use ways of speaking which have been employed by numerous mystics from Augustine to Ruysbroeck—a way of speaking reminiscent of depth psychology—that view mental activity not horizontally but vertically, not in space but in silence, not in motion but in rest, not in time but in timelessness.

This distinction between two ways of knowing, two ways of being or different forms of awareness has been described by Christian saints and mystics throughout the centuries— St Augustine speaks of a higher part of the mind reserved for the contemplation of God and a lower part of the mind that reasons. Evagrius of Pontus, the fourth century monk and writer, is one of a host of contemplative writers to make an important distinction between the calculating, reasoning mind that makes use of concepts in a process we call discursive thought and that dimension of mind that comes to knowledge directly without the mediation of concepts, which he called *nous,* an intuitive spiritual intelligence.

So when Evagrius defined prayer as '*communion of the mind with God*' he meant a dimension of our consciousness that runs deeper than discursive thought. St Thomas Aquinas took up this same distinction and, speaking for virtually the entire tradition, called the aspect of the mind that thinks and calculates 'lower reason' and the aspect of the mind that communes directly with God in contemplation 'higher reason.'[13]

Within the Christian Orthodox tradition, the contemplative dimension is known as *hesychia*, which is a term describing the quality of stillness and silence.[14] The hesychast tradition describes these two types of knowing or understanding by distinguishing between what they traditionally call the mind and the heart. The term "heart" refers to this nonconceptual form of knowing, what Augustine and Aquinas later call "higher reason." In this tradition, the heart was not the seat of emotions (emotions would be located at roughly the same level as thoughts) but the deep centre of the person. The heart communes with God in a silent and direct way that the conceptual level of our mind does not.

This important cusp is described by St Teresa in *The Interior Castle* as the movement from the prayer of recollection to the prayer of quiet.[15] In her description of the prayer of quiet and its evolution towards the prayer of union, she uses the metaphor of Light, which is reaching out from the deep interior toward all the human faculties—our emotions, imagination, senses and intellect or reason—as a primary way to describe the approach of God toward the human being, when the Divine "arms of love" are reaching out towards the human mind.

The mystical tradition, as exemplified in the writings of St Teresa and St John, believe that there is a form of consciousness which goes beyond sense impressions, beyond the knowledge we can get from touching, smelling, seeing, tasting and handling, which has to do with essences and the inner being of things. This knowledge has to do with the core of our existence, and that is why it is so intensely intimate. It is also why the process of discovering it is so intensely disturbing because it forces us to confront the silent core of our being. Ultimately, it is divine knowledge, and we can participate in it if we are prepared to embark on the journey into stillness, into quiet, through entering an ascetical process of interior detachment and purification from attachments and identifications with sense impressions.

In personal terms, the fruit of this deeper journey is that we come to know our self in new ways, this knowledge coming from the Divine, and not from our ego-centric, perspective. So, it is really describing that cusp, or transition, when the integration of the natural personality, or the process of individuation, has generally occurred, and a deeper process of transformation is underway. It is arguable whether depth psychology has yet evolved to the point where it can speak meaningfully about these deeper contemplative states of mind—that dimension of experience which lies beyond the familiar polarity of consciousness and unconsciousness.

So, for St Teresa, the journey of prayer, and wholeness and union with God, is a deepening journey of the heart to the innermost chambers where God's Divine Love, through Christ, infuses into, and unites with, the life of our soul. This is traditionally known as bridal mysticism, a deepening love affair where the bride is the soul and the bridegroom is Christ. Her experience and expression of contemplative spirituality throughout her writings are suffused with the language of symbols and imagery—describing the soul as a garden, a tree, a castle, a butterfly, and the action of the Holy Spirit through symbols of water and fountains.

Teresa and Christ

Christ then, who is the image of God in the soul, also psychologically refers to the self. He is a divine image and, at the same time, a self-symbol. The symbol of Christ is of the greatest importance for psychology as it is perhaps the most highly differentiated and developed symbol of the self, which Jung was fairly clear about:

"He is in us and we in him. His kingdom is the pearl of great price, the treasure buried in the field, the grain of mustard seed, which will become a great tree, and the heavenly city. As Christ is in us, so also is his heavenly kingdom. These few, familiar references should be sufficient to make the psychological position of the Christ symbol quite clear. Christ exemplifies the archetype of the self."[16]

As a symbol of our deeper self, Christ addresses each of us to the deepest core of our being, showing us that the wider life available to us, but unknown to our ego-consciousness, which finds its fulfilment in union with Christ, this Divine Image in the centre of our soul. He bears our unlived life and we often fail to recognise that his story is also our story. To reflect on the psychological base of the Christ symbol is not to elude Christian mystery but to illumine the conditions which promise greater life, and to allow Christ to put us back in touch with our deeper self.

Both St John and St Teresa experienced and taught that giving oneself to Christ results in Christ giving us back our self, our self-in-God. As the journey to the centre of our interior castle progresses, Teresa more frequently refers to Christ. The development of a relationship with God naturally heightens ones consciousness of Christ. She writes: *"So that you may see more clearly, Sisters, that what I have told you is true, and that the greater the progress of a soul, the more closely is she accompanied by this good Jesus, it will be well for us to consider how, when his Majesty wills it, we cannot but be always with him."*[17]

In a striking manner, Christ even became more manifest to Teresa through visions in the 6th and 7th dwelling places. These visions represent the Lord in a manner which engages the imagination of the individual, where she writes: *"Though I say 'image,' you understand it is not a painted likeness of him that is seen, but he is truly alive, and sometimes he speaks to the soul, and even shows her great secrets.*[18] Teresa explains that this image is not merely a painting but it is truly alive, and is not seen with her physical sight—*it is the inner eye that sees all of this.*[19] She says that she has never seen a vision with her exterior sense of sight—this inner vision, an alive image of the Lord, had a particular brilliance which she compares to the light of the sun shining through a diamond like cover.

The Imitation of Christ

Teresa is constantly stressing the importance of the imitation of Christ, and affirms that Christ accompanies our journey— Christ is our true life, our final goal, He is the model whom we are to imitate. That imitation will principally be in his suffering: *"fix your eyes on the crucified and everything will become small for you. . . the imitation of Christ that is the effect of this union is an imitation in his great sufferings…"*[20]

Here Jung agrees with St Teresa: *"the demand made by the imitatio Christi—that we should follow the ideal and seek to become like it—ought logically to have the result of developing and exalting the inner man."*[21] The imitation of Christ means that we are to live our individual lives as fully, as responsibly, and as authentically as Christ lived his life, trying to enter into our individual existences with the same obedience and integrity which characterised the life of Christ.

Teresa's journey through the castle teaches us that the centre of the soul may be trusted, a centre which reveals itself as life giving, not annihilating, pointing not to her life but to the image of the crucified Christ as the symbol that contains our life. Teresa assures us that the spiritual journey can be graced by divine presence accompanied by the emergence of the figure of Christ, where the movement towards the innermost chambers of the human heart is a response to a divine call of Love. This divine image not only expresses the growing intimacy with God, but also, as a psychological symbol, signals the emergence of a more completely individuated personality, a fuller realization of the self.

Not only is union with Christ a goal of Teresa's journey through the castle, but Christ and the symbols of religion were a major preoccupation in the life and work of Jung, where he was attempting to show the psychic roots of religion and the psychological relevance of Christianity. Beginning with his childhood dream of a phallic divinity and continuing through reflections on God by an elderly Jung in his autobiography, religious questions were never far from his concerns: *I find that all my thoughts circle around God like the planets around the sun, and are as irresistibly attracted by Him. I would feel it to be the grossest sin if I were to oppose any resistance to this force.*[22]

Teresa tells us that the radical foundation on which we build our lives is a divine presence in those lives. Jung describes flesh and blood developments we may expect as we move toward the self.[23] In a time of shifting consciousness and the disappearance of Christendom as a cultural package, the traditions of Christianity need to be re-examined in the light of our present experience and understanding. In particular, the mystical tradition, as exemplified by Teresa, is a rich source for a deeper appreciation of human interiority. Both Jung and St Teresa offer us the example of courageous pilgrims who trustingly gave themselves over to the journey to the sacred in life.

Endnotes

[1] T. Merton, *Contemplative Prayer*, p. 67.

[2] K. Kavanaugh & O. Rodriguez, (Trans.) *The Collected Works of St John of the Cross*.

[3] T. Merton, *New Seeds of Contemplation*, p. 34.

[4] C. G. Jung, *The Collected Works of C. G. Jung: Volume 14. Mysterium Coniunctionis*.

[5] C. G. Jung, *The Collected Works of C. G. Jung, Volume 7*, para 66.

[6] St Teresa of Avila, *The Interior Castle*, p. 6.

[7] T. Fry, OSB (trans), *Rule of St Benedict*, Chapter 20.

[8] B. Griffiths, *The Golden String: An Autobiography*, p. 71.

[9] C. G. Jung, *The Collected Works of C. G. Jung, Volume 11*, para 262.

[10] C. G. Jung, *The Collected Works of C. G. Jung, Volume 13*, para 67.

[11] A. C. Spearing, *The Cloud of Unknowing and Other Works*.

[12] K. Kavanaugh & O. Rodriguez, (Trans.), *The Collected Works of St John of the Cross*, p. 480.

[13] M. Laird, *Into the Silent Land: the Practice of Contemplation*, p. 26.

[14] K. Ware, *The Inner Kingdom*, p. 89.

[15] J. McLean, *Towards Mystical Union*, pp. 201-211.

[16] C. G. Jung, *The Collected Works of C. G. Jung, Volume 9ii*, para 69-70.

[17] St Teresa of Avila, *The Interior Castle*.

[18] Ibid.

[19] Ibid.

[20] Ibid.

[21] C. G. Jung, *The Collected Works of C. G. Jung, Volume 12*, para 7.

[22] C. G. Jung, *Memories, Dreams, Reflections*, p. 13.

[23] J. Welch, *Spiritual Pilgrims: Carl Jung and Teresa of Avila*, pp. 210-214.

Chapter Five

ST TERESA OF AVILA
AND DEPTH PSYCHOLOGY

I would like to introduce my paper with two relevant quotes from Teresa of Avila's autobiography:

"How what is called union takes place and what it is, I cannot tell. It is explained in mystical theology, but I cannot use the proper terms; I cannot understand what mind is, or how it differs from soul or spirit. They all seem one to me, though the soul sometimes leaps out of itself like a burning fire that has become one whole flame and increases with great force. The flame leaps very high above the fire. Nevertheless, it is not a different thing, but the same flame which is in the fire. What I want to explain is the soul's feelings when it is in this divine union. It is plain enough what union is; in union two separate things become one."[1]

"I used at times, as I have said, to experience the very fleeting beginnings of something which I am now going to describe. When I made that inward picture in which I

threw myself at Christ's feet, and sometimes also when I was reading, there would come to me unexpectedly such a feeling of the presence of God as made it impossible for me to doubt that He was within me, or that I was totally engulfed in Him. This was in no type of vision; I believe it is called mystical theology."[2]

St Teresa, like other saints and masters of the Christian spiritual life, maintained that it is possible, in a real sense, for the human soul to attain union with God. In her extraordinary autobiography, Teresa's pen flowed spontaneously and creatively, expressing many of the most important events, encounters, and spiritual transformations that God worked in her heart and soul in her journey towards divine union. Her detailed writings chronicle her long love affair with Jesus Christ, and the constant action of the Holy Spirit in her soul, that finally took her towards "the highest state of intimacy with God—the spiritual marriage."

Teresa of Avila was a truly remarkable woman. Born in the early sixteenth century into a noble Castilian family, with direct Jewish descent, she showed marked interest in spiritual matters as a child, and took up the religious vocation at the age of twenty-one. She was an acknowledged mystic in her own lifetime, and underwent a staggering range of supernatural graces. She was a prolific writer—writings that were initially intended as spiritual direction texts for her nuns—and ever since, countless generations of pilgrims down the centuries have been guided and directed by the wisdom and holiness of the saint.

Teresa was popularly known during her lifetime as the "Holy Mother" and was canonized as a saint forty years after her death. In 1970, Paul VI gave Teresa's gifts of sanctity and wisdom their due and proclaimed her a Doctor of the Church, the first woman saint to be so recognised. Both St John of the Cross and St Teresa's writings have been hailed as some of the greatest in Christian mystical theology. Their writings are important both historically, coming at the end of the rich medieval development of mystical theology in the west, and theologically, as some of the most profound and significant statements of mystical experience and transformation in the Christian tradition.

Firstly, I need to give some brief details about the Carmelite order in order to put St Teresa's life and work in a wider context for you. "Carmel" is Hebrew and means an orchard or vineyard. From time immemorial Mount Carmel, near Haifa in Israel, has been a holy mountain, known as the sacred mountain of the Holy Land, and is best known as the location of the acts of Elijah, recorded in Old Testament book of 2 Kings, who is regarded as the greatest and holiest of the prophets of the Old Testament. Over the centuries it became a place of veneration and pilgrimage for all the "People of the Book," the Jews, Christians and Muslims.

The Carmelite Order was founded in the twelfth century during the period of the crusades, when a group of Latin crusaders established themselves on Mount Carmel, aiming to live the eremitical life of solitude and contemplation as hermits and ascetics in the grottoes of the sacred mountain, following in the ancient Elijan tradition. Around 1210, St Brocard approached Albert, the Latin Patriarch of Jerusalem, to write a constitution that would serve as the rules for the community then identified as the brothers of the Blessed Virgin Mary of Mount Carmel—this was the community that would become better known as the Carmelites.

Mount Carmel is also known as the mountain of Mary, and even from the earliest times churches dedicated to the Virgin Mary existed on the mountain. Elijah is the main inspiration and founder of the Carmelite order, and, interestingly, several Fathers of the Church—Jerome, John Chrysostom, Basil, Gregory—name both Elijah and Eliseus as patrons and patterns of the contemplative life.

This is the ancient Christian spiritual tradition which Teresa felt called by God to reform and return to its essential spiritual roots of prayer and contemplation in sixteenth century Spain. Teresa definitely felt herself to be the heir to this spiritual patrimony and responsible for the transmission of its values. The significance of the connection with Carmel is not primarily geographical or historical. Carmel, for Teresa, is a family, and above all it represents the people who lived on the biblical mountain of Elijah and who now form the choir of the saints of the Carmelite Order in Glory.

So, now a brief outline of her life. Teresa de Cepeda y Ahumada was born on March 28, 1515, into a noble Castilian family. Spain, at the beginning of the sixteenth century, was newly triumphant, as the country had been recently united under the reign of Ferdinand and Isabella, the new Catholic Monarchs, and across the Atlantic, the wars and triumphs of the conquistadors in the New World was beginning to amass untold wealth for Spain. In 1948, the Jewish ancestry of Teresa was discovered when documents came to light in Valladolid concerning her grandfather, Juan Sanchez, who had been a *judeo-converso*, a Spanish Jew forced by the Inquisition to convert on pain of death or expulsion.

Teresa entered the Carmelite Convent of the Incarnation in Avila in November 1536 at the age of 21, where she was to live for the next twenty-two years of her life, which were filled with incident. There was a great disparity in wealth and living conditions of the women entering the religious life at that time. She writes in her *Life* that she was only half converted during this phase of her life, and it was not until she was about forty-two years of age that the beginnings of sanctity appear in her. To use a favourite image of her own, she was a plant of slow growth, and needed a great deal of watering.

Just after her profession of vows in 1538, Teresa's health totally collapsed, soon after she fell into a serious decline and was even pronounced dead, with her requiem mass being celebrated and a grave dug for her! Thankfully she recovered, remaining in a greatly debilitated state for almost eight months, and for several more years her paralysis, though gradually improving, continued to disable her. Not until her fortieth year did the effects of it entirely leave her. During this time she began to turn back to a deeper life of prayer and forsook the diversions she had previously indulged in with such gusto.

It is by the late 1550's, when she was in her forties, that we begin to get accounts of "Teresa the Mystic." There are many eye-witness accounts of the extraordinary graces that God was granting to her; the locutions, visions, levitations and ecstasies. The quickening of Teresa's spiritual life is often described as her "second conversion," which began about 1555, where she describes the return of a sense of God's presence more vividly than anything she had known before. Teresa, herself, became matter of fact about the visions, ecstasies and unusual experiences which God was granting her, as we read in her autobiography, and regarded the supernatural graces as primarily having meaning and value within the context of her life of prayer and good works.

Through a deepening contemplative call from Christ, Teresa was soon to embark on her destiny to reform the Carmelite Order, which forced her to withdraw from the Incarnation to form a new community, much simpler and smaller, based around the austerity of the original Rule of St Albert. Amidst the greatest secrecy, Teresa's first foundation was made on St Bartholomew's Day, August 24, 1562, known as the Discalced (literally shoeless) reform. She called the next four and a half years "the most restful years of my life," devoting herself to the establishment of her new convent, and beginning her writing career in earnest, completing her first two works—*The Life* and *the Way of Perfection*.[3]

From then until the end of her life, she was concerned with the establishment and spread of the reform that she had begun. In 1567, a new house was founded at Medina del Campo and foundations at Valladolid, Malagon, Toledo, Salamanca, Segovia and elsewhere followed. The remarkable stories of all these foundations are contained in her *Book of Foundations*.[4] 1567 was also significant as the year of Teresa's first encounter with one of the most influential people in her life, the mystic and St John of the Cross Although only twenty-five when they met in Medina, Teresa, at fifty two, immediately recognized his great spiritual gifts and proposed that he help her in establishing a male branch of her Reform—which he duly did. The two of them got on famously, yet sadly their correspondence has not been preserved.

Further troubles were ahead, and moves were afoot to have the Reform suppressed. In April 1575, a General Chapter of the Carmelites was held in Spain, which decided to suppress her 12 convents, prohibit her from founding new ones and recommending that she should "retire" indefinitely to a convent of her choice in Castile—effectively becoming a prisoner. She obeyed her superiors but continued to battle from behind the walls of the Toledo convent. John of the Cross was spared even that luxury, being kidnapped by fellow monks in December 1577 and held prisoner in a cell at the Discalced monastery in Toledo for nine months. Yet as this reign of terror and persecution towards her Reform was at its height, these two mystics, separately and intensely, turned within themselves to their spiritual resources and produced some of the greatest works of mystical literature—*The Interior Castle and the Spiritual Canticle*.[5]

By 1580, peace was declared and Teresa, sixty-five by now and calling herself "an old crone," set off on the road to continue founding more convents. John, having escaped, began to write and preach in earnest, which had by now taken a heavy toll on his health, and he died at the age of 49 in 1591. Teresa struggled on, making the thirteenth of her foundations, and in 1581 she heard that the conflict within the Carmelite Order had ended in partition. By the 1580's, however, it was clear that she was coming to the end of the road and in 1582, was asked by the Duchess of Alba to attend the labour of her daughter-in-law so that the delivery would be blessed by the presence of the saint. When she arrived, she was told the child had already been born and she was no longer required. Exhausted and totally worn out, she retired to the convent at Alba de Tormes and there sank quickly. She died at nine o'clock on October 4, 1582, exactly four hundred and twenty five years to the day today.

She had reformed the Carmel, giving it the possibility to start again upon its original foundation, the one still present in our day. She had founded seventeen monasteries, not counting the eleven Carmel's for men which had been established during her lifetime. The religious living in these monasteries numbered more than five hundred brothers and sisters. She had travelled over four thousand miles on the terrible roads of the two Castiles, Estremadura, and Andalusia and had written ten books and twelve thousand letters.[6]

So, what is Christian mysticism and what is mystical theology attempting to describe? Essentially, mysticism is describing the sort of knowledge of God that is obscure to the mind or the intellect. The meaning of "mystical" lies in the Greek root "*mu-*," which has to do with hiddenness, that which is closed or concealed to ordinary human consciousness. In his book *The Origins of the Christian Mystical Tradition*, Professor Andrew Louth succinctly describes mysticism as:

> "*characterized as a search for, and experience of, immediacy with God. The mystic is not content to know about God, he longs for union with God. Union with God can mean different things, from literal identity, where the mystic loses all sense of himself and is absorbed into God, to the union that is experienced as the consummation of love, in which the lover and the beloved remain intensely aware both of themselves and of the other.*

> *How the mystics interpret the way and the goal of their quest depends on what they think about God, and that itself is influenced by what they experience: it is a mistake to try to make out that all mysticism is the same. Yet the search for God, or the ultimate, for His own sake, and an unwillingness to be satisfied with anything less than Him; the search for immediacy with this object of the soul's longing; this would seem to be the heart of mysticism."[7]*

What I am exploring in this paper are the clear similarities and analogies between Jungian psychology and the Christian mystical tradition, as highlighted by the life and writings of St Teresa of Avila, as well as key divergences and differences. For both traditions, the immediate experience of the numinous, of the Holy Spirit, of the presence of God, or the perceiving of an originally hidden transcendent reality imminently in the soul, plays a pivotal role. This experience was central in Jung's approach to analytical psychology, which was clearly expressed in a 1945 letter – *"the main interest of my work is not concerned with the treatment of neurosis, but rather with the approach to the numinous...the fact is that the approach to the numinous is the real therapy, and inasmuch as you attain to the numinous experience, you are released from the curse of pathology.*[8]

However, in general, Jung did not like to be regarded as a mystic: he preferred to be recognized as an empiricist, and thought of himself as a natural scientist. As a scientist and empiricist, he confined himself to the investigation of *human assertions* about the religious, about God, and grounded his psychology of religion on the interpretation and comparison of these facts. The metaphysical God, "God Himself" remained untouched.

Jung's language and his scientific ideas also differed profoundly from the language of the mystical tradition—the mystics tend to concentrate on direct encounters with God, whereas these experiences were subjected by Jung to a critical examination. Analytical psychology tends to be limited to the observation and study of accessible archetypal images and contents that is, to our human, or psychological, assertions.

Jung restricted his research to the human-psychic realm, the "psychic facts," so to speak, and generally refused to make any statement about the transcendental background, except to say that it exists. For example, in a 1952 letter he writes—"*When I say God I mean an anthropomorphic (archetypal) God image and do not imagine I have said anything about God,*" and in a 1957 letter— "*One must always remember that God is a mystery, and everything we say on the subject is said and believed by human beings. We make images and concepts, and when I speak of God I always mean the image man has made of Him. But no one knows what He is like or he would be a God himself.*"[9]

That this background remains hidden does not, of course, reduce its significance. Quite the contrary—for Jung, precisely the inability to "know" in this connection signified, in his own words, richness and a treasure that he sought always to preserve, and appeared to acknowledge when he reached the end of his empirical psychological knowledge, and the possible beginning of another deeper wisdom.

For analytical psychology, the main goal is individuation, which is that ongoing process by which a person becomes a psychological individual, which is to say, a separate undivided conscious unity, a distinct whole—by first the process of unifying ego consciousness, and then the whole psychic system of conscious and unconscious, in order to approach wholeness, the master term describing the goal of the individuation process. In his writings, Jung emphasized repeatedly that the process of individuation is mainly a psychological one, and not a spiritual one.

The way into the unconscious, Jung pointed out, lies initially through emotion and affect. An active complex makes itself known through disrupting the ego with affect, and this compensation from the unconscious offers potential for growth. Eventually, he goes on, these affective disturbances can be traced to primordial roots in instinct, and can also lead to symbols that anticipate the future. In order to approach wholeness, the conscious/ unconscious systems must be brought into relationship with each other: *The psyche consists of two incongruous halves which together form a whole.* This is roughly what Jung means by the individuation process – it is a process or course of development arising out of the conflict between the two fundamental psychic facts of conscious and unconscious.

In this regard, there are tremendous similarities and analogies with the Christian mystical, or contemplative, tradition. In fact, Jung's writings contain much of the psychological teaching of this ancient tradition transposed into the idiom of twentieth century psychology. In his concept of the Self, Jung shares the belief that God's presence lies within the centre of the soul, expressed from a psychological, rather than a mystical, perspective. His writings on the psyche contain much of the teaching of Christian spiritual direction and guidance from past centuries, in the idiom of modern depth psychology. Not only does Jung's account of the structure of the psyche match very closely the teaching in the mystical tradition, but the general depth psychotherapeutic method is similar too.

So, there are significant overlaps—both lay great emphasis on increased consciousness, on increased self-knowledge—so that we can relate more objectively towards the world around us. In both traditions, what is going on below the level of our conscious thinking and agenda is explored and analysed, and instead of ignoring the signs and signals from the unconscious, we are encouraged to pay serious attention to our dreams, to waking fantasies and daydreams, and to our thoughts and impulses. We are encouraged to look at them consciously, to try to understand the unconscious wishes, drives, impulses and unknown parts of ourselves, to become aware of ourselves in depth. This very closely resembles the ancient injunction of spiritual direction in the Christian contemplative tradition to dwell in the cell of self-knowledge, in order to direct our surface attention constantly to the hidden motives underlying our conscious aims and actions, what is called "dwelling in the room of self-knowledge."

In referring to the God-archetype, Jung was suggesting that the psychological reality which wields the greatest power in the psyche functions as a God – *"It is always the overwhelming psychic factor that is called God"* and because the referent of this God archetype is *"unknown and incomprehensible,"* Jung gave it the psychological name of the self, a term *"on one hand definite enough to convey the essence of human wholeness and on the other hand indefinite enough to express the indescribable and indeterminable nature of wholeness."*[10]

Mystical experience, then, that transforms cannot be explained in this way; for in it, Jung writes that *"it is not that something different is seen, but that one sees differently. It is as though the spatial act of seeing were changed by a new dimension."*

> *"This new state of consciousness born of religious practice is distinguished by the fact that outward things no longer affect an ego-bound consciousness, thus giving rise to mutual attachment, but that an empty consciousness stands open to another influence. This 'other' influence is no longer felt as one's own activity, but as that of a non-ego which has the conscious mind as its object. It is as if the subject-character of the ego had been overrun, or taken over, by another subject, which appears in place of the ego. This is a well know religious experience, already formulated by St Paul in Galatians 2:20: It is no longer I who live, but Christ who lives in me. Undoubtedly a new state of consciousness is*

described here, separated from the earlier state by an incisive process of religious transformation.

It could be objected that consciousness in itself has not changed, only the consciousness of something, just as though one had turned over the page of a book and now saw a different picture with the same eyes. I am afraid this is no more than an arbitrary interpretation, for it does not fit the facts. The fact is that in the texts it is not merely a different picture or object that is described, but rather an experience of transformation, often occurring amid the most violent psychic convulsions. The blotting out of one picture and its replacement by another is an everyday occurrence, which has none of the attributes of a transformation experience. It is not that something different is seen, but that one sees differently. It is as though the spatial act of seeing were changed by a new dimension."[11]

And, as mentioned earlier, Jung writes, this new way of seeing, this new dimension, is dependent on the birth of a new centre:

"If the unconscious can be recognized as a codetermining factor along with consciousness, and if we can live in such a way that conscious and unconscious demands are taken into account as far as possible, then the centre of gravity of the total personality shifts its position. It is then no longer in the ego, which is merely the centre of consciousness, but in the hypothetical point between conscious and unconscious. This new centre might be called the self. If the transposition is successful, it does away with the participation mystique and results in a personality that suffers only in the lower stories, as it were.

But its upper stories are singularly detached from painful as well as from joyful happenings. The production and birth of this superior personality is what is meant when our text speaks of the 'holy fruit,' the 'diamond body' or any other kind of incorruptible body. Psychologically, these expressions symbolize an attitude that is beyond the reach of emotional entanglements and violent shocks – a consciousness detached, or freed, from the world."[12]

This new dimension is of vital interest for one who would sympathetically study the mystics. *They do not see different things: they see differently. A new mode of interior activity is brought into play.* Whereas ordinarily we think horizontally, one image or concept being replaced by another, the language of the contemplatives indicates that mystical thought is vertical: it does not entail the acquisition of new ideas and concepts but is a descent into the darkness of one's own mind, void of images and conceptual thinking.

This world of perpetual solitude found by the descent into oneself, is the sovereign point of the spirit, the centre of ones being: it is the world in which reigns silence and union. In short, mystical knowledge does not move in successive images but spirals down into the depth of the soul to encounter God in the obscurity of silence. St Teresa and St John of the Cross use ways of speaking which have been employed by numerous mystics from Augustine to Ruysbroeck – a way of speaking reminiscent of depth psychology- that view mental activity not horizontally but vertically, not in space but in silence, not in motion but in rest, not in time but in timelessness.

This distinction between two ways of knowing, two ways of being or different forms of awareness has been described by Christian saints and mystics throughout the centuries—St Augustine speaks of a higher part of the mind reserved for the contemplation of God and a lower part of the mind that reasons. Evagrius of Pontus, the fourth century monk and writer, is one of a host of contemplative writers to make an important distinction between the calculating, reasoning mind that makes use of concepts in a process we call discursive thought and that dimension of mind that comes to knowledge directly without the mediation of concepts, which he called nous, an intuitive spiritual intelligence. So when Evagrius defined prayer as "communion of the mind with God" he meant a dimension of our consciousness that runs deeper than discursive thought. St Thomas Aquinas took up this same distinction and, speaking for virtually the entire tradition, called the aspect of the mind that thinks and calculates "lower reason" and the aspect of the mind that communes directly with God in contemplation "higher reason."[13]

Writing in the eighteenth century from the Orthodox tradition, a remarkably gentle and insightful Russian monk, Theophan the Recluse, who says *you must descend from your head to your heart. At present your thoughts of God are in your head. And God Himself is, as it were, outside you, and so your prayer and other spiritual exercises remain exterior. Whilst you are still in your head, thoughts will not easily be subdued but will always be whirling about, like snow in winter or clouds of mosquitoes in the summer.*[14]

This important cusp is described by St Teresa in *The Interior Castle* as the movement from the prayer of recollection to the prayer of quiet. In her description of the prayer of quiet and its evolution towards the prayer of union, she uses the metaphor of Light, which is reaching out from the deep interior toward all the human faculties—our emotions, imagination, senses and intellect or reason, as a primary way to describe the approach of God toward the human being, when the Divine "arms of love" are reaching out towards the human mind:

"*When His Majesty wishes the mind to rest from working He employs it in another manner, giving it a light and knowledge far above any obtainable by its own efforts and absorbing it entirely into Himself. Then, though it knows not how, it is filled with wisdom such, as it could never gain for itself by striving to suspend the thoughts.*

In this prayer of quiet, when the water flows from the spring itself and not through the conduits, the mind ceases to act; it is forced to do so, although it does not understand what is happening, and so wanders hither and thither in bewilderment, finding no place for rest.. . . Let the spirit ignore these distractions and abandon itself in the arms of Divine Love; His Majesty will teach it how best to act, which chiefly consists in its recognizing its unworthiness of so great a good and occupying itself in thanking Him for it."[15]

The mystical tradition, as exemplified in the writings of St Teresa and St John, believe that there is a form of consciousness which goes beyond sense impressions, beyond the knowledge we can get from touching, smelling, seeing, tasting and handling, which has to do with essences and the inner being of things. This knowledge has to do with the core of our existence, and that is why it is so intensely intimate. It is also why the process of discovering it is so intensely disturbing because it forces us to confront the *silent core of our being.* Ultimately, it is divine knowledge, and we can participate in it if we are prepared to embark on the journey into stillness, into quiet, through entering an ascetical process of interior detachment and purification from attachments and identifications with sense impressions.

In personal terms, the fruit of this deeper journey is that we come to know our self in new ways, this knowledge coming from the Divine, and not from our ego-centric, perspective. So, it is really describing that cusp, or transition, when the integration of the natural personality, or the process of individuation, has generally occurred, and a deeper process of transformation is underway. It is arguable whether depth psychology has yet evolved to the point where it can speak meaningfully about these deeper contemplative states of mind—that dimension of experience which lies beyond the familiar polarity of consciousness and unconsciousness.

It is important to clarify that for St Teresa (and St John), their beginners are those souls who have already entered into a state of serving God, and so the realm of grace must be taken into account, the supernatural realm. They are mainly writing for those further along the way. There is a well known theological principle that *grace builds on nature*—if nature is in a mess then grace, as a rule, waits, for nature to be put in order before acting in a strong and paramount manner.

So, for Teresa, the journey of prayer, and wholeness and union with God, is a deepening journey of the heart to the innermost chambers where God's Divine Love, through Christ, infuses into, and unites with, the life of our soul. This is traditionally known as bridal mysticism, a deepening love affair where the bride is the soul and the bridegroom is Christ. Her experience and expression of contemplative spirituality throughout her writings are suffused with the language of symbols and imagery—describing the soul as a garden, a tree, a castle, a butterfly, and the action of the Holy Spirit through symbols of water and fountains.[16]

In Teresa's anthropology of the soul in the text, *The Interior Castle*, in order to distinguish mystical knowing from ordinary knowing, she separated the interior part of the soul, where supernatural objects are "felt" and "understood" from the exterior part, where merely natural sensation and knowing occurs. Teresa bases her anthropology on an interior/exterior division of the soul which she uses to show which operations are to be considered natural, and which, beyond that, are supernatural and mystical, using this division to differentiate ordinary knowing of the world from mystical knowing, as pertaining to different regions of the soul, called the exterior and the interior respectively.[17]

Teresa goes a long way towards developing a formal doctrine of the spiritual senses, in a tradition going back to Origen, and takes the view that there are two sets of senses in the soul, by which the soul "feels" natural things and supernatural things separately, between what the soul feels in the interior and what it feels materially in the bodily senses. For example, what the soul feels in the interior are "spiritual impulses" which "wound" the soul "*as* though an arrow is thrust into the heart," feelings of pain, she says, which have no resemblance to bodily pain.

When the soul "withdraws" within itself, which Teresa calls *interior recollection,* it uses "other senses" as distinct from the "exterior senses." It is through these other senses "within itself" that the soul attains "communication with God in solitude." Thus, the soul possesses two sets of senses, with two separate epistemological abilities associated with each of these sets—there is the ordinary sensory knowing ability through the exterior senses, and a parallel spiritual knowing ability through the interior senses. Just as the soul comes to feel and know things through the exterior senses, so it attains communication with God through a similar but distinct set of interior senses and operations.[18]

She makes her own distinctions to show how the two kinds of knowing are related, introducing the symbolic figures of Mary and Martha to refer to this division in the soul. She explores the relationship between Mary and Martha as the analogy for the two parts of the soul—firstly, to emphasise the division in the soul caused by mystical transformation, and also looking forward to the final unity of the soul, in a unity patterned on Christ's union of natures and the distinction-within-unity of the persons of the Trinity.

In speaking about Martha and Mary, her aim is to show the two types of operations, relating to the interior and exterior of the soul respectively, are distinct, but *also pointing to the possibility of their reconciliation: where the worldly-directed activity of Martha becomes fully consistent with the interior life of Mary, so that there is one unified operation of the soul in union, in which Mary and Martha "work together."* This is the gradual development of division in the soul to unification, *where the virtuous activity of Martha becomes completely unified with the interior life of Mary.*[19]

Teresa assures us that the spiritual journey can be graced by divine presence, where the movement towards the innermost chambers of the human heart is a response to a divine call of Love. In this journey of Christian contemplative prayer, the deepening relationship with God is accompanied by the emergence of the figure of Christ in the deepest dwelling places of the heart. This divine image not only expresses the growing intimacy with God, but also, as a psychological symbol, signals the emergence of a more completely individuated personality, a fuller realization of the self. From this perspective, her writings, in particular *The Interior Castle*, are regarded as important documents of Christian individuation.

Not only is union with Christ a goal of Teresa's journey through the castle, but Christ and the symbols of religion were a major preoccupation in the life and work of Jung, where he was attempting to show the psychic roots of religion and the psychological relevance of Christianity. Beginning with his childhood dream of a phallic divinity and continuing through reflections on God by an elderly Jung in his autobiography, religious questions were never far from his concerns: *I find that all my thoughts circle around God like the planets around the sun, and are as irresistibly attracted by Him. I would feel it to be the grossest sin if I were to oppose any resistance to this force.*[20]

Both Jung and St Teresa offer us the example of courageous pilgrims who trustingly gave themselves over to the journey to the sacred in life. Teresa tells us that the radical foundation on which we build our lives is a divine presence in those lives. Jung describes flesh and blood developments we may expect as we move toward the self.[21]

I would like to end with highlighting the remarkable similarities between St Teresa's seminal vision of the soul, and one of Jung's most important dreams, which was seminal regarding the evolution of his understanding of the self. In his autobiography, Jung writes:

"Some years later, in 1927, I obtained confirmation of my ideas about the centre and the self by way of a dream—in the dream, I found myself in a dirty, sooty city. It was night, and winter, and dark, and raining. I was in Liverpool. With a number of Swiss—say, half a dozen—I walked through the dark streets. I had the feeling that there we were coming from the harbour, and that the real city was actually up above, on the cliffs. We climbed up there. It reminded me of Basel, where the market is down below and then you go up through Totengasschen (Alley of the Dead) which leads to a plateau above and so to the Peterplatz and the Peterskirche.

When we reached the plateau, we found a broad square dimly illuminated by street lights, into which many streets converged. The individual quarters of the city were themselves arranged radially around a central point. This point formed a small open square illuminated by a larger street lamp and constituted a small replica of an island. In the centre was a round pool, and in the middle of it was the small island. While everything around about was obscured by rain, fog, smoke and dimly lit darkness, the little island blazed with sunlight. On it stood a single tree, a magnolia, in a shower of reddish blossoms. It was as though the tree stood in the sunlight and was at the same time the source of light. My companions commented on the abominable weather, and obviously did not see the tree. They spoke of another Swiss who was living in Liverpool, and expressed surprise that he should have settled here. I was carried away by the beauty of the flowering tree and the sunlit island, and thought, 'I know very well why he has settled here.'[22]

In the latter months of 1579, whilst travelling with three of her nuns through a heavy snowstorm, Teresa sought refuge in an inn, where she met her old friend and former confessor, Fray Diego. This gentleman wrote in a letter many years later how they—he and Teresa—had been in conversation *"about their Divine Master a very great part of the night,"* and how the next evening, Teresa had *"recounted to him the story of how she came to write The Interior Castle."* Nine years later he wrote what Teresa had recounted to him that evening in a letter:

"*This holy mother had been desirous of obtaining some insight into the beauty of a soul in grace. Just at that time she was commanded to write a treatise of prayer, about which she knew a great deal from experience. On the eve of the festival of the Most Holy Trinity she was thinking what subject she should choose for this treatise, when God, who disposes all things in due form and order, granted this desire of hers, and gave her a subject.*

He showed her a most beautiful crystal globe, made in the shape of a castle, and containing seven mansions, in the seventh and innermost of which was the King of glory, in the greatest splendour, illumining and beautifying them all. The nearer one got to the centre, the stronger was the Light, outside the palace limits everything was foul, dark and infested with toads, adders, vipers and other venomous creatures.

While she was wondering at this beauty, which by God's grace can dwell in the human soul, the light suddenly vanished. Although the King of Glory did not leave the mansions, the crystal globe was plunged into darkness, became as black as coal and emitted an insufferable colour, and the venomous creatures outside the palace boundaries were permitted to enter the castle."[23]

Endnotes

[1] St Teresa of Avila, *The Life of Saint Teresa by Herself*, p. 122.

[2] Ibid, p. 71.

[3] K. Kavanagh & O. Rodriguez (trans), *The Collected Works of St Teresa of Avila*, 3 Volumes.

[4] Ibid.

[5] Ibid.

[6] J-J Antier, *Teresa of Avila – God Alone Suffices*, p. 287.

[7] A. Louth, *The Origins of the Christian Mystical Tradition*, p. xv.

[8] C. G. Jung, *Letters I and II*.

[9] Ibid.

[10] C. G. Jung, *Collected Works, Volume 12*, para 20.

[11] Ibid.

[12] C. G. Jung, *Collected Works, Volume 13*, para 67.

[13] M. Laird, *Into the Silent Land: the Practice of Contemplation*, p. 26.

[14] I. Chariton, *The Art of Prayer: An Orthodox Anthology*, p. 183.

[15] St Teresa of Avila, *The Interior Castle*, pp. 60-61.

[16] J. McLean, *Towards Mystical Union*, p. 74.

[17] E. Howells, *John of the Cross and Teresa of Avila: Mystical Knowing and Selfhood*, p. 71.

[18] Ibid, p. 74.

[19] Ibid, p. 79.

[20] C. G. Jung, *Memories, Dreams, Reflections*, p. 13.

[21] J. Welch, *Spiritual Pilgrims: Carl Jung and Teresa of Avila*, pp. 210-214.

[22] C. G. Jung, *Memories, Dreams, Reflections*, p. 223.

[23] E.A. Peers, (trans) *The Complete Works of Saint Teresa of Jesus, Volume 2*, p. 187.

Chapter Six

ST TERESA OF AVILA AND SELF-KNOWLEDGE:
Psychology and the Spiritual Journey

St Teresa's masterpiece, *The Interior Castle*, is the product of the saint's most mature spiritual reflection, discernment and understanding of the contemplative life.[1] In this work, she portrays the life of prayer as an interior journey through seven dwelling places towards our deepest centre, the seventh mansions, the place where God dwells. But while the journey is one towards union with God, we should not overlook the theme of self-knowledge which is so necessary for our whole spiritual journey. It is a theme emphasised by Teresa in the earliest mansions:

> *"Knowing ourselves is something so important that I wouldn't want any relaxation ever in this regard, however high you may have climbed into the heavens. While we are on this earth nothing is more important to us than humility. So I repeat that it is good, indeed very good, to try to enter first into the room where self-knowledge is dealt with rather than fly off to other rooms." (IC I:2:9; cf. I:2:8)*[2]

Healing and self-knowledge

When, in this profound work, Teresa uses the term "soul," she includes what psychologists today might refer to as "psyche." Her basic assumption throughout is that spiritual growth is *generally* accompanied by psychological growth and maturity. For Teresa, real self-knowledge is necessary for true compassion, because a deeper self-understanding brings true humility. She is underlining the spiritual wisdom that wherever we go in the vast interior regions of our soul in prayer, we always need to go through, and humbly come back to, the rooms of self-knowledge. She knows, too, that without our gaze upon God, we will find ourselves unable to be free "from the mud of fears, faintheartedness, and cowardice" (IC I:2:10).[3] The process of spiritual growth, for Teresa, involves continually looking in both directions: towards greater self-knowledge and humility, and greater knowledge of God.

Interestingly, Teresa's emphasis on the importance of self-knowledge is generally in accord with the approach of modern depth psychology. For Teresa, knowing ourselves is about growing familiar with, and accepting, our fallibility and our needs, those open or concealed; also, our relationship with ourselves and with others. This requires an honest, transparent awareness of our motivations, intentions and drives, both conscious and, importantly, unconscious. It entails opening up our deepest traumas, anxieties and fears so that they may be healed—which, from the perspective of spiritual direction, is indispensable work. It also means allowing a full and loving integration of the many places where we are most vulnerable and unloved; of our blocks and of our psychic and emotional pain; also, of the limitations of what we can do on our own without God's love and the action of grace in our life. Ultimately, it is about knowing our total dependence on God who, in his love, holds and heals us.

Awareness of the unconscious

Alongside discerning the movement of the Holy Spirit in our lives, and inviting him into the depths of our heart, we need to be constantly acquainted with our own nature and origin, both conscious and unconscious. As Teresa writes:

> "*It is a shame and unfortunate that through our own fault we don't understand ourselves or know who we are. Wouldn't it show great ignorance, my daughters, if someone when asked who he was didn't know, and didn't know his father or mother or from what country he came? Well now, if this would be so extremely stupid, we are incomparably more so when we do not strive to know who we are, but limit ourselves to considering only roughly these bodies. Because we have heard and because faith tells us so, we know we have souls. But we seldom consider the precious things that can be found in the soul, or who dwells within it, or its high value.*" *(IC I:1:2)*[4]

The desire to move towards deepening states of contemplative prayer must be augmented by an ongoing struggle to develop an in-depth understanding of ourselves. Real self-knowledge does not mean an intellectual knowledge of human nature, but a true "heart" knowledge of ourselves from the perspective of prayer and of a growing union with God. We need an increasing ability to sense, articulate and respond adequately to what is going on within our psyche. There is a wealth of areas in play: intellectual capacities; feelings and emotions, both negative and positive; sensation and intuition; conscious and unconscious motives; primitive instincts and the rational (and irrational) nature. Through purification and purgation, we gradually learn to become dispassionate and to attain to a *peaceful condition of the soul.*

If we are truly open to the Holy Spirit's potential in our lives, we will be able to acknowledge that pain and pleasure, joy and sadness, success and failure may either work for, or against, our growth in life in the Spirit. All experienced phenomena can be expected to have at least some connections with unconscious psychodynamics and these connections are neither good nor bad in and of themselves. It is only upon considering their fruits— their effects upon the experienced and lived life of faith—that we can begin to appreciate and appraise their true value.[5] In the innermost dwelling places of Teresa's castle, there is precisely a state of peace and spiritual rest, a gentle control of our feelings and passions, a deep living of fruits of the Spirit: compassion and goodness, long-suffering and gentleness, faithfulness and temperance. Together with this is the emphasis on good works, so stressed by Teresa, which are the natural active outflow of a contemplative "resting in union with God."

Lizards and snakes

In *The Interior Castle*, Teresa shows that our spiritual life deepens and darkens as it progresses. It reaches down into our pre-verbal, pre-rational fantasies, instinctive drives and bodily passions and impulses, as well as touching transcendent realms. She describes how, in the first mansions, prayer is fraught with distractions and obstacles that seem constantly to pull us away from God. This is because, as soon as we turn towards the interior world in prayer and reflection, we usually encounter whole dimensions of ourselves that have previously been unconscious, hidden and unknown. This dimension of our growing self-knowledge is particularly vital in regard to our spiritual journey and deepening life of prayer; it can never be denied or neglected without, I believe, psychological and spiritual injury to the individual.

All the neglected and dark sides of ourselves are usually encountered fairly quickly. In modern psychological terms, these are the "shadow" parts of the psyche. The "shadow" encompasses all the psychic contents that have been driven back into the unconscious: all the neglected, undeveloped, unacknowledged parts of our personality. Teresa symbolises these more negative, broken parts as the *lizards and snakes* in the moat outside the castle. They will need to be constantly recognised and accepted, so as to be dissolved and transformed—"made new"—by God's love, throughout our spiritual journey.

Images and symbols

In the process of a person's becoming more self-aware, images and symbols have an important role to play. Teresa's writings on the contemplative life are suffused with them. A living, dynamic mix of many and varied images arose within her in response to her own direct spiritual progress and surrender to God. At different times, the soul is a garden, a tree, a castle, a butterfly; and there is a whole range of other imagery besides, such as fountains and water. Teresa seems to move effortlessly and randomly, between various symbolic representations of the spiritual life, changing and using them to suit her own needs and expression of the life of prayer.

From a modern psychological perspective, various images and symbols, when related to states of recollection, can be vitally important. They can unite and transform the many disparate and unrecollected parts of ourselves in the early dwelling places. They also provide a different way of holding, reflecting on and expressing a spiritual wisdom which could otherwise not be articulated. Jung describes the role of symbols as expressing "an as yet unknown and incomprehensible fact of a mystical or transcendent nature. . .[and] what cannot be characterised in any other way"—as standing for "something that is only divined and not yet clearly conscious."[6]

Here, he is referring to the power of symbols and images to act as mediators between the known, conscious, maybe more rational, parts of ourselves and the unknown, unconscious parts, including our physical instincts and bodily impulses. Working with the images and symbols that arise within us—in our dreams, in the imagination, or in prayer, as Teresa did—can provide a fundamental place for integration and healing.

Teresa's symbolic expression varied as her soul became increasingly transformed towards union with God—which shows that what was happening to her could not be adequately expressed in any other way. She uses the symbol of the outer walls of the interior castle to represent the early stages of prayer where our consciousness is still distant and separate from God, who dwells in the centre of the soul, though there is a sincere longing to be more intimately related to him. She uses this symbol of the castle and its mansions to represent the slow interior processes of protecting, nurturing and purifying the soul in thorough preparation for the very different relationship that God offers in the deeper prayer of quiet and union. Informed by the more radical change in her own experience of God, Teresa describes in the fifth mansions how God "brought her into the inner wine cellar" (IC V:2:12; cf. 1:12)[7] in the prayer of quiet; and in the seventh dwelling place, that of spiritual marriage, she offers equally profound symbols for the union of the soul with God: "Let us say that the union is like the joining of two wax candles to such an extent that the flame coming from them is but one. . .[Or] when rain falls from the sky into a river or fount; all is water" (IC VII:2:4).[8]

Dreams and the spiritual journey

The important symbols that arise in an individual's spiritual journey are, in my experience, most often expressed in dreaming. Dreams present the unknown realm of our interior life through symbol and narrative, and they are an essential modern tool for self-knowledge. Jung emphasised the role of dreaming for understanding the complexity of unconscious processes, and he considered dreams the royal road into exploring and integrating the unconscious, unknown parts of ourselves. This is because dreams bring to a *conscious* attitude or course of action a compensatory emphasis from the *unconscious*, so that the psyche checks its own excesses by providing a balance for our conflicts and tendencies. The real function of dreams is to keep us focusing on the processes of our unconscious and on how it is constantly responding to the demands, decisions and fluctuations of conscious life. They also urge us to be aware of, and responsive to, the presence of other unseen and unknown interior processes.

Teresa notes that for as many entrances as there are to the first mansions, there are just as many self-deceptions to be battled with and conquered: lies, confusion, vanity, cruelty, ignorance and doubts. This is why a genuine, growing self-knowledge is so necessary in the early stages of the spiritual life. Here, we come face to face with how profoundly ignorant we can be of who and what we are; of our real possibilities for a deepening reliance, faith and dependence on God; and of how much we need to let go, in order to enter the "wine cellar of the Lord." Our spiritual journey will open up the depths of our unconscious, in all the darkest and most terrifying places, and dreams and symbols provide meaning and connection to our inmost centre.

What Teresa is emphasising is the ancient injunction of spiritual direction to dwell in the cell of self-knowledge—in order to direct our surface attention to the hidden motives underlying our conscious aims and actions, and so as to grow authentically in our life with God.

Endnotes

[1] St Teresa of Avila, *The Interior Castle*.
[2] All IC quotes are from St Teresa of Avila, *The Interior Castle*.
[3] St Teresa of Avila, *The Interior Castle*, p. 14.
[4] Ibid., p. 6.
[5] G. May, *Care of Mind, Care of Spirit*, p. 62.
[6] C. G. Jung, *The Collected Works of C. G. Jung, Volume 6,* para 815-817.
[7] St Teresa of Avila, *The Interior Castle*, p. 77.
[8] Ibid., p. 176.

Chapter Seven

GOD ENTERS THROUGH OUR WOUNDS:

St Teresa and the "Shadow"

On the eve of Trinity Sunday, 1577, Teresa of Avila received a vision of the beauty of the soul in grace. The next day, she began to write her masterpiece, *The Interior Castle*, describing the soul as a crystal globe containing seven mansions[1]. In this work, the life of prayer is portrayed as an inner journey towards our deepest centre, the seventh mansion, the place where God dwells. Modern depth psychology can give us a better understanding of the inner transformation of unconscious psychological wounds that takes place when the heart and mind are open to God.

This article will focus on what is called our "shadow," described by Carl Jung as the "negative side of the personality, the sum of all those unpleasant qualities we like to hide, together with the insufficiently developed functions and the content of the personal unconscious."[2] For it is the "shadow" that is the source of psychological difficulties which can predominate in the early stages of our spiritual development. Teresa highlights these impediments to spiritual growth in the first mansions.

Introducing lizards and snakes

The early stages of our spiritual life are often fraught with distractions and obstacles that seem to pull us away constantly from the ever deepening contemplative journey towards God. At this point, *"these wild animals or beasts. . .make [the beginner] close his eyes to everything but them"* (IC I:2:14). Some of the main tests in this early phase concern our spiritual sincerity: whether we are *really* turning away from external material pursuits, passions and pleasures, and trying to develop the necessary one-pointed interior concentration in prayer. As soon as we begin to live the life of prayer in earnest, we encounter whole dimensions of ourselves that have, until now, been unconscious, hidden and unknown.

The shadow side of ourselves is usually encountered fairly quickly. Teresa symbolises these negative and broken parts of ourselves as the "poisonous creatures": the lizards and snakes in the moat outside the castle. For her, these symbols represent all the dynamic forces that attack, block and distract us from without, and hinder and disturb us from within. In modern psychological parlance, these venomous creatures are the shadow parts of the psyche, encompassing all those psychic contents that have been driven back into the unconscious: all the neglected and undeveloped parts of our personality which, however, need to be constantly recognised, accepted and transformed.

The wounded inner child

A common description of our shadow side is the *wounded inner child*, where parts of ourselves have been relegated to the unconscious after childhood trauma. If psychological wounds from childhood are not tended and healed, and especially if they are sustained and reinforced into adulthood, then they feed the repressed, shadow side of our personality. The effect of repression is to cut off access to that part of ourselves. We may repress feelings, a character trait, a talent or way of thinking, for fear of disapproval or rejection by a parent, teacher or other authority figure. When any part of ourselves is cut off, much of our potential and creativity is also repressed.

Hidden within the "wounded inner child" are often painful memories and experiences, even personal qualities, which we may have forgotten and denied—and concealed from both ourselves and others. These undeveloped contents of our psyche can be sometimes quite powerful, even overwhelmingly so, if strongly denied or repressed. Locked in the dark basement of the unconscious, out of sight from the world, our shadow parts often carry great pain and vulnerability, suffering, sadness, deep despair, anger, alienation and resentment. They can become ever bleeding wounds, and so for many people confrontation with our shadow is no easy task.

Treading the brink

Spiritual directors affirm how difficult it is for us to become aware of our shadow side, with its pride, shame, guilt, manipulation, hunger for power, jealousy, envy, need for revenge, desire for possession, sexual temptations and the like. In the early stages of our spiritual journey, our shadow side is often just beginning to reveal itself. It can start to gather momentum in the second mansions where confronting, and battling with, the lizards and snakes becomes even more necessary. This process is an important part of interior ascesis or purification, essential in these early mansions if we are to journey further within the castle.

Likewise, Teresa is adamant how hard it is in these early stages to "enter within ourselves," especially if we are accustomed to being preoccupied with the "insects and vermin," external and worldly matters—or our broken and wounded parts, as it were. Her reason is that we have become over-identified with and over-attached to them: "nor does it seem [such souls] can enter within themselves. They are now so used to dealing always with the insects and vermin that are in the wall surrounding the castle that they have become almost like them" (IC I:1:6).[3] It is through prayer, our contact with the light and truth of God, that we will gradually begin to penetrate the "lizards and snakes" dimension of our psyche. Only then will our shadow begin to be slowly reintegrated and transformed in love.

In the second dwelling places where we struggle to face the neglected, unconscious dimensions of our psyche in a deeper and more honest way, she tells us that this is an ongoing battle and that preventing failure is not always possible: "in the midst of such poisonous creatures one cannot help but be bitten at one time or another" (IC I:2:14).[4] As Teresa shows, these psychological and spiritual dangers are present throughout our spiritual journey, even to the seventh and innermost mansions: "sometimes our Lord leaves these individuals in their natural state, and then it seems all the poisonous creatures from the outskirts and other dwelling places of this castle band together to take revenge for the time they were unable to have these souls under their control" (IC VII:4:1).[5] Although it is rare, she says that sometimes the Lord allows such attacks—albeit in more subtle forms—so that we will appreciate the tremendous favours we are receiving, and develop great fortitude in trials and adversity.

As St Teresa wisely advises, unless we are able to accept, and communicate with, our hidden underground depths at these early stages on our journey, these realms will almost certainly disrupt our spiritual progress. If they are not faced, owned and ultimately transformed, our "lizards and snakes" will turn around and bite; they will poison us and generally wreak havoc on our interior life. It takes a tremendous amount of humility, integrity and self-honesty, together with charity and virtue, to acknowledge our shadow and to allow the long, arduous work of its transformation to begin.

The parts of us that have been repressed and hidden now come to full consciousness for recognition, healing and transformation through acceptance and love.

Embracing the shadow

To handle the shadow areas of human experience requires particularly sensitive and patient care. It is possible, once the shadow parts have been accepted, for them to be changed and redirected, and so to become positive sources of creativity and talent. Effective strategies for recognising our vulnerable and shadow areas include analysing our dreams, becoming attentive to fantasies and daydreams, examining closely the nature and content of our humour and, most importantly, becoming conscious of what we project onto others and examining it.

In particular, I would like to highlight the importance of dreams in making us aware of our wounds, pain and traumas. Dreaming is usually one of the main ways in which the unconscious makes human interiority available to itself. It represents unknown and unconscious realms of our inner life through symbol, image and story, usually in its own unique language, meaning and structure. There are various images in dreams that often represent the shadow side of our personality. The most common ones are animals, particularly hostile ones, such as tigers, wolves, crocodiles, snakes and toads. Often, too, shadow figures pursue us in dreams in the form of burglars or dangerous enemies; or they appear, symbolically, as derelict, disused areas in need of repair, restoration or redevelopment. Jung's observations led him to conclude that images of animals, which the psyche produces, refer to instinctual forces at work in the human personality. In fact, eighty per cent of what surfaces in dreams carries much wisdom, representing valuable aspects of our selves.

The gold in the dross

Why is the shadow so important? There are many reasons. Working on our repressed and wounded areas is an integral part of knowing ourselves in any depth. Acknowledging and reintegrating these rejected parts enables us to recover them. Much of our individual creativity and capacity to surrender resides here. The shadow contains not only negative and destructive elements, but also tremendous potential for deeper spiritual growth and development. Jung found that the shadow, in metaphorical terms, consists of ninety percent gold, as it contains the seeds of our very *new* potential which has not yet come to consciousness. All this potential could be tapped were it not for pressures, anxieties, or the amount of work it would take to own and integrate these parts.

Another important reason for befriending and integrating our shadow parts is that doing so is fundamental to authentic self-esteem. How can we truly love ourselves or have confidence in ourselves if a part of us is ignored and works against our own best interests? Also, our shadow parts tend to be projected onto different types of relationships if we do not acknowledge and work with them, so this is essential for maintaining healthy social and personal relationships. Often, the root cause of interpersonal conflicts and professional burnout can be found in shadow projections. Vulnerabilities or shortcomings are projected onto other people and situations. Becoming aware of these projections onto others, and then being able to take them back, vastly improves interpersonal relations.

The mote in the other's eye

Teresa has great insight into the nature of the shadow, and warns against projections onto others. She admits that others may have their faults and that corrections may have to be made, but says that the primary responsibility for us as individuals is to attend to our own inner journey that will reveal our neglected areas. She is particularly sensitive to what can be learned when these projections of the shadow are made:

> "Let us look at our own faults and leave aside those of others, for it is very characteristic of persons with such well-ordered lives to be shocked by everything. Perhaps we could truly learn from the one who shocks us what is most important. . .nor is there any reason to desire that everyone follow at once our own path, or to set about teaching the way of the spirit to someone who perhaps doesn't know what such a thing is." (IC III:2:13)[6]

In the early dwelling places, the very foundations of our interior castle are beginning to be firmly tested for their endurance, perseverance and self-knowledge. We can experience this as an inner war, requiring steadfast discernment and great moral courage. All our attachments, which keep our hearts spiritually chained, are revealed more and more to our consciousness, and are purified and surrendered in the fires of our longing for God.

Endnotes

[1] All IC quotes are from St Teresa of Avila, *The Interior Castle*.
[2] C. G. Jung, *The Collected Works of C. G. Jung, Volume 7*, para 66.
[3] St Teresa of Avila, *The Interior Castle*, p. 8.
[4] Ibid., p. 25.
[5] Ibid., p. 186.
[6] Ibid., pp. 41-42.

Chapter Eight

SYMBOLS OF TRANSFORMATION IN CHRISTIAN SPIRITUALITY

Symbols of transformation are an important part of psychological and spiritual growth, development and maturation, particularly in times of profound transition, threshold, crises and change. Modern depth psychology asserts that mental concepts and processes alone often fail to grasp psychological and spiritual realities as a whole, so our psyche is often driven to use symbols, images and metaphors. This is because they speak to our whole person—to our mind, heart, senses, memories, body, experiences and imagination—and have the capacity to engage us more fully than mental concepts alone.

A symbol can be *"a term, a name, or even a picture"* that we encounter each day in our lives *"yet possesses specific connotations in addition to its conventional and obvious meanings. . .it implies something vague, unknown or hidden from us."*[1] A symbol whispers to us of the unknown, of mystery, and when our mind examines, or encounters, the symbol, it is often led to ideas that lie beyond the grasp of our reason alone. Let us take the example of a lamp, which is an object of everyday life. We know it as something that provides light to a room. However, on contemplation it might easily come to represent ways in which light shines on the pathways of life. In a Christian context, it could pick up on the image of Christ as the light of the world, or the Word as a lamp to our footsteps. Thus, the symbol is open-ended and cannot be pinned down to one specific meaning. It is speaking to us of something that cannot be defined or completely understood. In this respect a symbol is different from a sign, as a sign refers only to the specific object which it names e.g. traffic signs which, through common usage, mean something very specific.

Hence, implicit in the "symbolic mode" of perception is a vital relational aspect towards our whole person—we are able to be touched more fully and can become more recollected through the use of symbols and images rather than words or language alone. Here, there are possibilities of theology being able to incorporate psychological perspectives, in being able to explore and understand more deeply how symbols and images can help us become fully engaged in the totality of our human experience.

I would like to briefly outline two important roles and functions of symbols in our psychological and spiritual life. Firstly, symbols can provide an integrative, healing function, which have the capacity to unite, connect and heal the many disparate, dissociated and unconscious parts of ourselves. In this way, symbols can allow a different way of holding, reflecting on and expressing a spiritual wisdom that often cannot be articulated in words alone.

Thus, symbols, whether present externally in the environment or produced internally by the mind or our imagination, can help to integrate and unify the psyche by providing an essential bridge from the less adapted, more undeveloped and unconscious parts of ourselves to the more adapted, conscious functions and parts of our personality. In this way, symbols are often expressing deeper, unknown levels of ourselves that we are only, slowly, in the process of consciously understanding and integrating into our whole being.

Here, symbols and images can act as mediators—as integrating, unifying agents—between the known and conscious parts of ourselves and the unknown, unconscious parts. Living, dynamic symbols have the power to unite and transcend psychological opposites, which can lead to new syntheses and integration at deeper levels of our being. Thus the development and use of what is called, in psychological terms, "symbolic thinking" or the "symbolic function" can help and assist in the growth, development and synthesis of new understandings and new perspectives, where, simultaneously, different aspects and points of view which were not previously accessible have the possibility of becoming more available and integrated.

Secondly, symbols provide a transformative and transcending function. Symbols are figurative constellations which point beyond themselves to a more objective spiritual reality. C. G. Jung described, in some detail, the dynamic role of living symbols as facilitating fundamental change and transition of attitude and perspective, which he described as *the transcendent function of symbols*. Here, he describes the role of symbols as expressing:

> "*an as yet unknown and incomprehensible fact of a mystical or transcendent nature. . .so long as a symbol is a living thing, it is an expression for something that cannot be characterized in any other or better way. . .a symbol really lives only when it is the best and highest expression for something divined but not yet known to the observer. It then compels his unconscious participation and has a life giving and life enhancing effect.*"[2]

So, a crucial function of symbols is their dynamic effect as transformers and releasers of life energy. C. G. Jung's seminal text

Symbols of Transformation (Volume 5) explored psychological transformation and outlined the processes whereby life energy is able to be transformed from raw natural drives to the possibility of more meaningful, conscious, insights and understanding through the mediation of universal and religious symbols. Conscious relationship to symbols can free life energy that is blocked or stuck on one level and can redirect it along new levels onto a higher, or deeper, levels of meaning. Here, Jung explains:

> *"With the birth of the symbol, the regression of the libido into the unconscious ceases. Regression changes into progression, blockage gives way to flowing, and the pull of the primordial abyss is broken."*[3]

In relation to some of the more familiar and dynamic Christian symbols of transformation, I would like to refer to the writings on contemplative prayer by St Teresa of Avila (1515-1582), the Spanish Carmelite saint of the sixteenth century. In her last and most famous book, *The Interior Castle*, St Teresa used a creative, living and dynamic mix of many and varied symbols and metaphors to convey meaning and understanding of the deeper dimensions of our contemplative journey of prayer towards "union with Christ"—at different times within this text, she describes the soul as a garden, a tree, a castle and a butterfly.

She also used a whole range of other imagery, such as fountains and water, to describe the spiritual journey and the action of the Holy Spirit in the life of the soul. In her writings, she often seemed to move, effortlessly and spontaneously, between various symbolic representations of the dimensions and stages of the spiritual life, using different symbols and metaphors to suit her style of writing and unique expression of the life of prayer and the fruits of contemplation.

I would like to highlight briefly two of the most important symbols of transformation in *The Interior Castle* and explore how St Teresa used these symbols from a psychological and contemplative perspective. The symbol of the castle is, of course, central to this text. St Teresa wrote of her own direct vision of the castle, which, she felt was divinely inspired—*"I began to think of the soul as if it were a castle made of a single diamond or of a very clear crystal, in which there are many rooms, just as in Heaven there are many mansions."*[4]

She also described this interior castle as *"containing many mansions, some above, others below, others at each side; and in the centre and midst of them all is the chief mansion where the most secret things pass between God and the soul."* and makes reference to the relationship between the mansions as being inside each other—*"Think of a palmito, which has many outer rinds surrounding the savoury pith within, all of which must be taken away before the centre can be eaten."*[5]

This symbol of the castle, with many interior mansions, was central to St Teresa's experience and expression of the journey of prayer and Christian contemplative life, and it is interesting that she describes the castle in a very particular and specific way—as made of a single diamond or very clear crystal. This particular symbol of the soul relates to the biblical reference in John's Gospel, 14:2—*"In my father's house are many rooms, or mansions."* The Spanish word for mansions, *moradas*, which is derived from *morar*, which means "to dwell"—I think "dwelling places" rather than "mansions" is a more helpful description of the stations of the heart, or stages of contemplative prayer that St Teresa is writing about in this text.

In essence, it a powerful and dynamic integrative symbol that contains and unifies many of the spiritual and psychological dimensions of the contemplative life that she was attempting to describe—of the many paradoxes in the earlier phases of the life of prayer, such as experiences of both ecstasy and extreme suffering and mortification; of the process and difficulties in the development of spiritual discrimination and discernment, and, ultimately, of total surrender to God in spiritual union with Jesus Christ.

She uses the symbol of the outer walls of the interior castle to represent the early stages of prayer where our consciousness is still distant and separate from God, who dwells in the centre of our soul. She also used this symbol of the castle and its mansions to represent the slow interior processes of protecting, nurturing and purifying the soul in preparation for the very different relationship that God offers in the deeper dwelling places of prayer in the heart. The spiritual ideal and hope of integrating the most difficult trials and conflicts at the start of our Christian journey with union in God's Light, Presence and Silence in the innermost mansions is described, contained and constantly woven throughout the text by the use of the crystal/castle symbol.

By using this symbol of an interior castle St Teresa is saying that the soul is a place of immeasurable beauty, capacity and spiritual depth. She sees spiritual growth as a constant *"journey inwards"* to the depths *"where the most secret things pass between God and the soul."*[6] It is a living, dynamic, multidimensional symbol that carries a great deal of meaning and spiritual teaching. She is trying to convey the meaning that the various "mansions" or dwelling places of prayer, do not *automatically* exist and that, in the earlier mansions of prayer, the more interior dwelling places have not yet come into existence. So, she is trying to describe our great spiritual potentialities and possibilities, and that we are in the constant process of "becoming in God."

The castle symbol that St Teresa used also has a dual aspect—that of a fortress-like space, with strong fortified walls, combined with it being described as made of diamond or crystal. This symbolic welding of castle and crystal attempts to unite different essential aspects of the spiritual journey of the soul as St Teresa understood it—both the need for strong boundaries and containment to protect the delicate and deepening spiritual transformation process—alongside an emphasis on the soul, from Teresa's view, being precious and jewel-like in God's sight, like a crystal or diamond.[7]

Another central symbol used in the text is that of the butterfly. Virtually all of Teresa's references to this symbol, both of the worm (in Spanish, *gusano*), the silkworm (*gusano de seda*), and the butterfly (*mariposa*), which refers to the transformation of the silkworm, are only to be found in *The Interior Castle*. The particular symbol of the butterfly has been in common usage across different cultures and religious traditions and, I believe, appeals universally and broadly as a symbolic representation for change and transformation.

Teresa used this symbol of the metamorphosis of a silkworm into a butterfly to represent the possibility of the interior change and transformation of our being from the natural ordinary condition of human nature into something supernatural, extra-ordinary, by the action of the Holy Spirit. She was quite taken by this symbol and went to some length to make this analogy with the Christian contemplative soul. The silkworm/cocoon/butterfly symbol is used in this text to represent the path of prayer and the action of God on the soul, which, St Teresa wrote, was akin to a silkworm being enclosed in a "dark cocoon" of prayer as it undergoes the transformation of its basic state from "worm" to "butterfly." Symbolically speaking, the silkworm feeds off the natural world of mulberry leaves ("the general helps given to us all by God"), and when full grown it has the capacity to transform this natural substance into silk. So, enclosed within the darkness of a temporarily constructed cocoon it spins the rather extraordinary substance of silk out of sight of the world. The worm itself is released at the end of its work, no longer the same species, but miraculously transformed into another species entirely—the butterfly.

St Teresa used this symbol to describe the contemplative soul being transformed by the Love, and Light, of God:

> "*The silkworm symbolises the soul which begins to live when, kindled by the Holy Spirit, it commences using the ordinary aids given by God to all, and applies the remedies left by Him in His Church, such as regular confession, religious books, and sermons. Then it comes to life and continues nourishing itself on this food and on devout meditation until it has attained full vigour, which is the essential point, for I attach no importance to the rest. When the silkworm is full grown, it begins to spin silk and to build the house where it must die. By this house, when speaking of the soul, I mean Christ. . .our life is hid in Christ, or in God and that Christ is our life.*"[8]

So, in summary, I believe that the understanding, insight and reflections of modern Jungian psychology on symbols of transformation can help to develop, in the hearts of Christians, the life of the Spirit and psychologically prepare, and build up our capacity to encounter, and be transformed by, the living Christ, who is the Source of our being. Symbols of transformation also help us to make space in our lives for the "unknown" and be able to live with "unknowing and uncertainty," which we can often find difficult. Keeping internal "safe spaces" open and flexible allows the psyche, through the tool of the "symbolic function," continually to work with, and process, all the material that comes to us in daily life, helping us stay in the place of honest self-knowledge.

It is clear that Jung's "symbolic function" is both useful and important to Christian spiritual life—it can help build up our interior life of prayer and the life of our spiritual community, and the experience of our communal and liturgical life can be enlivened and enriched. The "symbolic function" can also help to acquire and deepen our self-knowledge, which is so necessary to relieve and free ourselves from the suffering, fears, anxieties and troubles of our lives so that we can reclaim connection to our own self, to others and to God. The "symbolic function" can also give those leading the Christian spiritual life a useful tool to help them value and reflect on their own direct experience in the living of their daily lives and in their journey to the threshold of the heart of God.

Endnotes

[1] C. G. Jung, *Man and His Symbols*, p. 3-4.
[2] C. G. Jung, *The Collected Works of C. G. Jung, Volume 6, Psychological Types*, para 815-817.
[3] Ibid., p. 325.
[4] St Teresa of Avila, *The Interior Castle*, p. 5.
[5] Ibid.
[6] J. McLean, *Towards Mystical Union*, p. 92.
[7] Ibid., p. 93.
[8] St Teresa of Avila, *The Interior Castle*, p. 74.

Chapter Nine

EDGES OF WISDOM, COMPASSION
AND LIVING WATERS

Over the past four decades, there has been resurgence of interest
and exploration into all matters relating to spirituality, prayer
and meditation, with an increasing interfaith dialogue between
religious traditions. There has been a decrease in attendance at
traditional religious services, and a significant increase in people
seeking to incorporate and integrate a contemplative, or spiritual
dimension, into every aspect and dimension of their lives—from
intimate, personal and family relationships, to working life, to
wider relationships in community and nation to the growing
global community.

In professional psychotherapy and Jungian circles, there is also
greater interest in studying the spiritual aspects of psychotherapy
and Jungian analysis. So, what are the edges of the "psychology of
wholeness" and the rising waters, and fires, of the living Spirit, that
Jung extensively wrote about in the 1940's and 1950's, particularly
in *The Red Book*[1] and *Aion*[2] (Vol.9ii) in our times. Here, I want to
explore the meaning and relevance of the new waters of spirituality,

wisdom and compassion rising and flowing today, particularly as it relates to our profession of being Jungian analysts.

As we know, many of these dramatic changes are part of the huge, new transitional time we are now living in, as Jung wrote in *Civilisation in Transition,* with sweeping global changes in technology, communications and travel, migration, economic and political upheavals, religious ideas and ideals and pandemics. Jung foresaw this decades ago, calling it a coming "spiritual transformation."

> "Jung believed we face, today, what the Greeks called 'kairos,' a time of metamorphosis of the gods, a fundamental change in principles and symbols. He noted that human relationship has not kept pace with scientific, technical and social progress, leaving humanity morally backward and out of balance with its own time. Some kind of rebalancing is inevitable, but the direction it takes and the dangers involved are far from certain."[3]

The Australian academic, Prof. David Tacey, also suggests, following on from Jung's earlier, similar reflections, that we are in the midst of what he terms a "spirituality revolution," as the "*emergence of the sacred as a leading force in contemporary society*," which is not to be confused with the rising tide of religious fundamentalism:

> "Spirituality and fundamentalism are at opposite ends of the cultural spectrum. Spirituality seeks a sensitive, contemplative relationship with the sacred, and is able to sustain levels of uncertainty in its quest because respect for mystery is paramount. Fundamentalism seeks certainty, fixed answers and absolutism, as a fearful response to the complexity of the world and to our vulnerability as creative in a mysterious universe."[4]

At various times in history, Tacey suggests, great streams, or hidden rivers, of spirituality have risen and fallen, according to mysterious rhythms of the collective and humanity. We live in one such time when the rising tide of spirituality is emerging on all sides. This affects all of us in society—in our faith traditions, whether it be in the churches, synagogues or mosques—as well as in politics, education, healthcare and throughout the helping professions. As an expression of the increasing interest in spirituality, different spiritual practices of meditation, prayer, mindfulness are becoming more popular.

So, what role, and importance, do these approaches, attitudes and practices play in our everyday personal and professional lives? It seems that many members of our AJA Jungian organisation definitely feel, and regard, that spiritual development is a vital and necessary component of a living a healthy and effective life in modern times. So, I conducted a small confidential online survey about the spiritual and religious beliefs/practices in our AJA Jungian organisation for this paper.

It was an online, anonymous questionnaire, with six questions (see appendix) and twenty four members replied. In the survey, the first question was *"Would you say that you have a religious, or spiritual understanding of your life (please underline one or more),"* with the second and third *"Can you explain briefly what form your religious/spiritual belief has taken? Some people hold strongly to their views and others do not. How strongly do you hold onto your religious/spiritual view of Life?"*

The fourth question asked *"Do you have a specific religion? If so, can you give more detail?"* and the fifth question *"Do any of the following play a part in your belief. . .prayer, ceremony, meditation, reading and study, contact with religious leader or none of the above."* The last question was 'What role, and importance, is the practice of your belief (e.g. private meditation, prayer, study,*

*religious services) in your personal and professional life (on scale of
0 -10, not necessary to essential)."*

For the collated responses to two questions 3 and 6, the average/
mean was between 7-8, which is very high! For question 3, asking
for indications of the strength and importance of religious/spiritual
views of life, the average/mean response was 7.6, which means
that out of 10, the mean of the group was between 7 and 8—quite
high! And for Question 6, where the survey asked about the role,
and importance of the practice of your belief in your personal, and
professional life, it was the same response—approx. 7-8, out of 10.
So very interesting! (See Appendix for written responses)

So, as the survey showed in our small group of professional
Jungian analysts, there is a significant rekindling of interest
in spirituality, and this often includes a desire for, a hunger
towards more immediate encounter, experience, knowledge and
understanding of spiritual realities, of the transcendent Other, of
the numinosity of life.

This was, of course, at the very heart of Jung's lifelong work.
From a depth psychological perspective, we could understand
this as our connection with a transcendent source of life, that is
both intimate and Other. Our sense of the sacred or spiritual, is
often needing to forge new language, new understandings and
new modes of communication—in our times—in those areas of
life when the old is too fraught and too laden with nuances and
preconditioned associations.

For many people, and for many clients that we see in our
consulting rooms, the source of their pain and suffering can
often be spiritual and loss of meaning, they feel themselves as
unconnected to any sense of larger meaning or purpose or reason
for living, and unconnected to work that is worthy and valuable,
which gives us many opportunities to express our authenticity,
integrity and creativity.

One of Jung's central contributions was the recognition and value that he accorded the religious function of the psyche—the innate religious urge which he regarded as an inborn need of the Self, and which, he firmly believed, could not be neglected or violated without grave injury to psychic health and well being, particularly in the second half of life.

Whilst other schools of psychoanalysis and psychology may dismiss this aspect of Jung's work, the acceptance of, and central value accorded, the numinosity of the unconscious, and the religious, or spiritual, character of the therapeutic endevour was, in reality, one of the unique contributions of Jung's psychology. Of course, Adler (one of the founders of the Association of Jungian Analysts in 1977) carried on this tradition, where he refers to the importance of the religious dignity, and the relevance of the individual, as the receiver and carrier of numinous revelation in many of his writings. We are all aware of Gerhard's important writings—I recently found a copy of his Guild paper on this subject which was written in 1936!

Jung's main concern was to present a psychology of life integration and wholeness, free from attachments to formal religious language or ideology. He wanted the religious dimension of the psyche—the quest and longing for the sacred, divine, Transcendent or holy—to be seen as natural and innate, as a "fact" of the psyche, rather than as supernatural or as an object of "belief." He was seeking the growth and development, in individuals, from "religiosity" towards a genuine, and life enhancing "religious attitude."

Jung's treatment of traditional religion may look destructive and disrespectful, but underneath he saw himself as an alchemist in the laboratory of faith, consisting in creatively exploring new postmodern expressions of the eternal religious spirit. In a truly prophetic role, Jung was seeking to turn religion into an experiential pathway for those who want to risk an inner journey and search for God within.

He viewed his depth psychology as providing an essentially modern psychological bridge between traditional religious dogma and doctrine and authentic, healing human experience and encounter with the holy, the numinous or the Holy Spirit. He was convinced that man's perennial religious impulse would rise again in self and society in new and creative ways, and his explorations took him back to the ancient past and the late medieval period, and forward to the world yet to be born. He knew that profound changes were happening both in society and in the psyche of modern men and women, and that fresh and new expressions of religion were both necessary and in the making.

Of course, what Jung was looking forward to and was prophetically writing about in the 1940's and 1950's is now happening in many quarters in our postmodern world, as the spirituality revolution. This is not religion in its old forms, but religion in the sense of mythos or sacred story—as a searching for, and re-connection to, all that is sacred. . .how our individual life is part of, and binds, conforms us to the divine life in ever more life giving and transformative ways.

So, Jung imagined modern man and woman on a journey of exile and homecoming. At present, we are more aware of our exile and rootlessness, but there is an expectation of a future homecoming. . .we are often moving further away from religious habits, forms and structures of the past that may not be life giving or helpful. Our homecoming is clearly not back to the past, but to the spiritual depths of our being. It is a coming home to ourselves, through a process of gradual self-realisation and awareness.

Jung sees us leaving behind a dominant focus on external structures of religious traditions, and as we come to know ourselves in depth, we can also move towards common spiritual understanding, perceptions and compassion found in all religious traditions. Our exile is away from many of the external forms that nurtured our ancestors, and our homecoming is towards the mystical depths of our heart and soul, that can give individuals, and our religious traditions, renewed Spirit and life.

The term "spirituality" is understood differently in the context of depth psychology from what it usually means when used within traditional religious discourse. Jung primarily refers not to God, as generally understood in the theological or metaphysical sense, but focuses more on our human, subjective perception of transcendent mysteries. Spirituality, in the context of depth psychology and psychoanalysis, is a venture into our deep unknowing, into unknown psychological territory, entering into the waters of our unconscious and the opening our heart and soul outside of our usual defensive psychic containment. It can be understood as a journey, a way, a path to discern the great mysteries of human existence and ponder and reflect on its major riddles and paradoxes. So, in Jungian terminology, this journey and path leads to a kind of spiritualty that is grounded in personal experience of the archetypal symbols of the psyche. The type of spirituality that arises in Jungian analysis tends to be more spontaneous, surprising and a type of unknowing—and almost always contrary to the limited attitudes and expectations of our ego.

That's why Jung called our dreams compensatory, as dreams often compensate and regulate our tendencies to extreme one-sidedness. The spirit of the depths within our souls is usually truth telling, guiding our psychological and emotional growth and development, whether or not our conscious attitude is in a cooperative mood. This is another aspect of the spirituality that flows through our Jungian analytic work. The analytic energy field that is generated by the relationship between analyst and analysand is another possible entry point into an apprehension of a spiritual dimension. What Jung called "transformation" in analysis has its central energies in the fertile context of this relationship.[5]

The transcendent function is a natural process where our opposite attitudes, goals or impulses—complex bundles of image, affect and instinct, coincide and conflict. We can feel tossed from one side to the other, like tennis balls in an intense match. Or, more often, we tend to side with one opposite—thinking it is the right, or reasonable, one to follow—only to be up-ended by another, opposite perspective, viewpoint or anxiety seizing us. Jung found that the psyche naturally goes back and forth between opposites, as slowly a third or new, more transcendent perspective begins to emerge.

Something is slowly growing and building in the centre of our being, transcending our conflicts and anxieties, which functions to resolve it. Our unconscious autonomously throws up symbols, as we consciously receive and wrestle with them. If we do not, some symbols may recede and others can arise. If we consciously enter the back-and-forth of our anxieties and conflicts, where symbols, or body symptoms, can indicate the point of view of our opposing side, as well as the one we endorse, this process of exchange, or interior dialogue, can transform into a conversation of the greatest value. We can more deeply engage in the parts of ourselves that claim equal attention, as we endeavour to make greater psychological space and room for them, which then transforms our whole orientation.

Many years of experience shows the fact that when people consciously experience this transcendent function in themselves, it impresses on them something powerful and living, that really transcends their ego control and comprehension. As Jung put it, it feels like the "*unknown as it intimately touches us.*"[6] The transcendent function slowly moves our ego out of our assumptions that we are in charge of our interior life, and builds up a bigger centre he called the self. Hence, we can often feel the beginning of this process as a disease, a disorientation, darkness, confusion, muddle and that is why we fear it so much.

We are suffering, but we can also feel something new growing within, initially as a new image or even symbol, or a breakthrough of feeling, or a perception that is bringing new life, insights, light, relief or peace. This arrival of the new certainly can feel like a gift, even grace. We can understand, from a depth perspective, that it is a way God can be operating within us, just as the mystical traditions describe. Jung said something similar, in that it *"possesses compelling authority not unjustly characterized as the 'voice of God.'"*[7]

Through this journey, we can restate what Jung means by our self, or soul—a bigger centre within ourselves, or an essential interior bridge to a larger reality within our psyche. We feel as if something is looking out for us, what can be understood in theological terms as Providence. It is unmistakably clear to us that we did not produce this new larger centre within. . .it has grown and developed, like a new flower or shining jewel, with its own autonomous, separate, real newness. So, from a Jungian perspective, it is through struggling with the opposites, or struggling to a new position, through the creation of symbolic thinking, that unites and transcends opposites, which leads to a new synthesis and integration. Symbolic thinking becomes the synthesis of new understandings and new perspectives, where, simultaneously, different aspects and points of view which were not accessible in the two dimensional mode can now be held internally and reflected on.

The possibility of real interior transformation essentially resides in moving towards, and being in three dimensional functioning. Often, the passage from a two-dimensional to a three-dimensional existence is possible only under the most grueling conditions of sacrifice, surrender, and emotional pain and suffering. Three dimensional functioning is searching, reflective and ambivalent, where the creative capacity for imagination, metaphor and symbolisation is central. In this dimension, opposite states of mind and positions have changed and combined into something new, that is much more than the sum of the constituent parts—there is now much more space inside and outside for thought, reflection and an enhanced sense of inner freedom to respond in different ways to life situations.

Three dimensions is that interactive space created by our readiness and openness to relate with another, which primarily allows for mutuality, change and exchange. This state can be experienced as a revolution and a dramatic transformation, through the often very painful and difficult sacrifice of profoundly held, unconscious core beliefs in the omnipotence and total self sufficiency of the self to the three dimensional state of interdependency, mutuality and relationship with another.

It can be experienced as a quantum leap to a different level of being—a leap from the two dimensional world of mirroring, imitation, artifice and control to a world of creative activity in a shared three dimensional space where trust, hope, gratitude, generosity and mature love are possible. Analytically, this is tantamount to the client discovering and acknowledging the existence and importance of the analyst, evidenced by repeated experiences of the analyst being reliably available and present, and able to impart to the patient a sense of being understood, thought about and responded to.

Like sensing a three dimensional space, or world, from the two dimensional mode, moving from *three dimensional to four dimensional* can be similar—as if a chink of something new, a small sense of light that we had not seen, or sensed before, is more present—and often challenges and disrupts our usual mode of consciousness. It is as if it is a different dimension of what we sense is *real* is more present and alive.

The four dimensional state is by all means not uncommon, which many have tried to convey in art, music, poetry. The main point here I would like to elucidate is that this dimension, I believe, can strongly relate to the spiritual and mystical, and many of the characteristics of our human encounter with the Transcendent, which I outlined earlier on in the paper relates to this fourth dimension. Although the four dimensional state often occurs spontaneously, certain structured situations, such as *prayer, meditation and therapy* can facilitate it.

In the most favourable circumstances, these situations are characterised by *stillness, silence, a sense of presence and intense mutuality.* When the four dimensional state occurs in the one to one therapeutic setting, it carries the conviction that healing is taking place. I would like to stimulate your own reflection—what is your own sense, or experience, either in the consulting room or personally of the fourth dimensional state, or mode?

This dimension is also something to do with sensing, or knowing, however dimly or distantly, that reality where there is profound unity and interconnectedness of life. Somehow there is sense of being able to *see life* more and more clearly—a sense of being connected to, in a real and living way, the larger archetypal patterns, designs and meaning of our life. There is definitely a sense of becoming a part of a larger whole that is always there. I think it is beginning to apprehend, or touch, or taste the level of reality that Jung described as the *undus mundus*, or latent unitary reality.

Conclusion: What of the future

In an interview toward the end of his life, Jung was asked about the state of the world and the character of the age to come: "*What comes next? Aquarius, the Waterpourer, the falling of water from one place to another. And the little fish receiving the water from the pitcher. . .but there is danger in the water, on the banks.*"[8]

There is danger in the water because it is not normal water, but turbo-charged or numinous. As Jung puts it:

"...Spirit...has descended from its fiery heights; (it has) become heavy and turns to water. This water is no figure of speech, but a living symbol of the dark psyche. ....Since the stars have fallen from heaven and our highest symbols have paled, a secret life holds sway in the unconscious... our unconscious hides living water, spirit that has become nature, and that is why it is disturbed."[9]

Jung's sense of despair about the human situation is found throughout his career, especially in his later writings.

"Where are the answers to the spiritual needs and troubles of a new epoch? And where the knowledge to deal with the psychological problems raised by the development of modern consciousness."[10]

The general professions of psychiatry and psychology, for the most part, have little understanding of the numinous or spiritual, often because there is a more narrow and reductive view of the psyche, mind and soul. Some of the more helpfully trained specialists in this field are the Jungian analysts, where our depth psychological work is essential—we are trained to help ourselves, our clients and our community to learn to "see in the dark and to listen for traces of the spiritual and sacred forces, the numinous, living waters, within ourselves and our clients."

Traditional religion is now moving towards these new spiritual, contemplative understandings, through opening up further to movements of spiritualty, prayer, meditation and the longing and quest for deeper self-awareness and self-knowledge. There can never be an exact return to established structures and forms of the past, as they do not often speak to our present modern situation. So, we are seeing all these revolutionary changes in all the major traditions, as they attune themselves to what is happening within the mind, heart and soul of modern people today.[11]

All the traditional religious traditions are attempting to rediscover their lost, forgotten mystical sub-traditions, that have usually been kept out of orthodox teaching and relegated to the margins for centuries. It is these mystical sub-traditions that are so needed today because these traditions are equipped to deal with our present dilemma, that is, what to do with a psyche which has become activated, even contaminated, by sacred, numinous, spiritual sources.

Jung's pragmatic view appears to have been that a new religious dispensation was coming and, in our individual lives, to mainly focus upon our individuation journey, to become responsible for what is real, creative, true and fruitful within our heart, mind and soul and strive to serve and express our charism, gifts and talents to others, our communities and to the world. For Jung, anybody who has the privilege of individuation has to repay the debt to society because the individuated person takes so much from society.[12]

Teresa gives similar advice at the end of *The Interior Castle*, where she emphasises that the purpose of the contemplative journey is to be even more engaged in the world around us, in activities and works of service, charity and loving action, whilst simultaneously united with the Lord in the innermost dwelling places. In Christian understanding, the soul is united with God in order to imitate, and live, the life of Christ in the world and Teresa is emphatic about this:

> "*This is the aim and end of prayer, my daughters; this is the reason for the spiritual marriage, whose children are always good works. Works are the unmistakable sign that shows these favours come from God, as I told you. It will do*

me little good to be deeply recollected when alone, making acts of the virtues, planning and promising to do wonders in God's service, if afterwards, when occasion offers, I do just the opposite." (VII, 4/10)[13]

Jung was reluctant to make pronouncements about the future of religion—almost everything he said about the psychology of culture was based on the premise that secular humanism does not work, and as secularism is now in decline, people cannot live by bread alone, and spiritual nourishment is now in great demand. Jung accepted that we are living in liminal times, at the end of secularism and yet before a new civilisation that more fully retrieves the religious dimension.[14]

Endnotes

[1] C. G. Jung & S. Shamdasani (Ed), *The Red Book, Liber Novus.*

[2] C. G. Jung, *The Collected Works of C. G. Jung: Volume 9 pt. 2. Aion: Researches into the Phenomenology of the Self.*

[3] C. G. Jung, *The Collected Works of C. G. Jung Volume 10, Civilisation in Transition,* para 378-575.

[4] D. Tacey, *The Spirituality Revolution,* p. 11.

[5] C. G. Jung, *The Collected Works of C. G. Jung Volume 8, The Transcendent Function.*

[6] Ibid., para 68.

[7] C. G. Jung, *The Collected Works of C. G. Jung Volume 10,* para 856.

[8] C. G. Jung, "On the Frontiers of Knowledge." In William McGuire and RFC Hull (eds) *C. G. Jung Speaking,* pp. 370-72.

[9] C. G. Jung, *The Collected Works of C. G. Jung Volume 9, Archetypes of the Collective Unconscious,* para 50.

[10] C. G. Jung, *The Collected Works of C. G. Jung Volume 16,* para 396.

[11] J. McLean, *Towards Mystical Union.*

[12] G. Bright, "Where Did Jung's Red Book Come From and Why Does it Matter?" p. 19.

[13] J. McLean, *Towards Mystical Union,* p. 308.

[14] D. Tacey, *The Hell of Initiation: Jung's Ambivalence Toward Modernity,* pp. 18-19.

Section Two

REFLECTIONS
ON THE
CHRISTIAN MYSTICAL TRADITION

Chapter 10

INTRODUCTION TO THE CHRISTIAN MYSTICAL TRADITION

The Life of Saint Teresa

St Teresa, like other saints and masters of the Christian spiritual life, maintained that it is possible, in a real sense, for the human soul to attain union with God. She humbly claimed that she, like many others, had actually reached this state, and her teachings on these matters were an integral part of the tradition of Christian life and faith.

In her extraordinary autobiography, Teresa's pen flows spontaneously and creatively, expressing many of the most important experiences, meetings, situations, and spiritual transformations that God worked in her heart and soul in her journey towards divine union. Her detailed writings chronicle her long and blessed love affair with Jesus Christ, and the constant action of the Holy Spirit in her soul, that finally took her towards "the highest state of intimacy with God possible on this earth—the spiritual marriage."[1]

What does Teresa mean when she refers to mystical theology in her *Life,* and of the soul being in divine union in *The Interior Castle*? Why are these integral parts of the Christian tradition? Why is there now such a heightened interest in mysticism, particularly in Christian mysticism? Why is this subject of paramount interest, relevance and importance in present times? What does Teresa have to say to all those who are on the Christian contemplative path about the joy and perils of our journey towards divine union? What are the real difficulties and problems regarding mysticism and the contemplative life, and how can they be carefully discerned? How can we use the teaching and writings of our spiritual forebears to help us in our own spiritual journey today?

These and other related questions are the subject of the present book, which is primarily intended to be a modern commentary on one of the best-known texts of Christian mystical literature, St Teresa's *The Interior Castle*. There are several related aims of the book, which include exploring the interface between modern depth psychology, spirituality and mystical tradition, as well as providing a manual for spiritual direction designed to reflect a similar intention, atmosphere, flavour and approach as that of Teresa's original text, penned more than 400 years ago.

This commentary aims to be somewhat different from other books on, or about Teresa, as it is not primarily an intellectual or scholarly pursuit. Essentially, what I want to provide is an inspirational, instruction manual based on Teresa's original text, that will serve to encourage and assist seekers towards a more heart-centred, contemplative and intimate relationship with God, through the saint's own spiritual writings and guidance.

The book attempts to create a fusion, an "experientially shared space," between our heart and the writings and wisdom of the original text of the saint; insofar as it is possible to communicate mystical self consciousness, the text is trying to fuse feeling and knowing—*amore ipse intellectus est,* (to love is, in itself, understanding) as a well known expression of medieval Latin Christian mysticism puts it.[2]

Teresa of Avila was a truly remarkable woman. Born in the early sixteenth century into a noble Castilian family, with direct Jewish descent, she showed marked interest in spiritual matters as a child, and took up the religious vocation at the age of twenty-one. Teresa was popularly known during her lifetime as the "Holy Mother" and soon after as the doctor of mysticism, *doctora mistica*. She was canonized as a saint forty years after her death.

Teresa was an acknowledged mystic in her own lifetime, and underwent a staggering range of supernatural experiences. Everything she wrote is based on her own direct experience of God, and her writings were essentially intended to be used as spiritual direction manuals for her nuns, and have been used by many, many generations of spiritual pilgrims in their "journey in Christ" ever since.

So direct and penetrating is her insight, knowledge and understanding, so unpretentious and straightforward is her language, that we cannot but see our own spiritual yearnings and longings, our own progress, and our own "death and transfiguration" in the love of God mirrored in her writings. We can allow the life, writings and presence of the Holy Mother to assist our own soul towards divine union. Her writings reveal a powerful and penetrating honesty and intimacy, a complete integrity, an essential pragmatism and compassion, but above all, a deep humanity that have hardly been surpassed in the whole corpus of Christian mystical literature.

Teresa's life and her reform of the Carmelite tradition was a renewal of the fundamentals and essence of the ancient spiritual tradition of the Order of the Blessed Virgin Mary of Mt. Carmel, and she has been regarded as one of the greatest contributors to the Christian mystical tradition. Why this particular subject is so relevant and important is that a spiritual rebirth or awakening, strikingly similar to that in her lifetime, is underway in our own times.

Teresa's lifetime spanned most of the sixteenth century, when the European Renaissance and the Reformation were beginning. It is fairly obvious to observe that similar cultural, political, economic, ethnic, religious and spiritual convulsions and transitions are happening in our own times, and they appear to be even more urgent and global than those of the sixteenth century. What is striking is that there are so many parallels and similarities between the events and movements of today and those of the time when Teresa lived and wrote her most important and influential mystical literature.

In these early days of the new millennium, it can seem that the very foundations of what it means to be a civilized human being, living in an ordered and purposive universe are being attacked, undermined and destroyed more systematically than ever before in so many areas of our global society. We are living in most interesting and tumultuous times—witness the well-documented worldwide ecological crisis and the constant threats and rumours of increasing terrorism similar to the September 11th bombing catastrophe.

Additionally, the rise and proliferation of fundamentalism, in all its forms, religious or otherwise, in ever extreme, concrete, and even violent ways, is a particularly worrying trend. Our times appear to be characterized by increasing polarization and fragmentation within groups and institutions, within the very fabric of our society, and indeed, if we allow it, within our very own souls. There certainly does appear to be growing collective turmoil and chaos, no matter in which part of the world, or in what sphere of life you choose to look.

Historians have noted that there are certain periods which generally coincide with the beginning of the fall of cultures and civilizations, when part of the mass of humanity irretrievably lose their reason and begin to destroy what has been created by centuries of culture and civilisation. One wonders whether we are in such a time now, and whether we are witnessing the slow demise of certain religious structures and cosmologies that have been dominant in the collective over past millennia, in order to make way for something very new which is trying to emerge.

It is interesting to note that in the well known poem *The Second Coming*, by the Irish poet and writer at the turn of the last century, W.B. Yeats, appeared to refer prophetically to a time of impending collective turmoil and chaos, and the slow emergence of a new religious vision: *"And what rough beast, its hour come around at last, Slouches towards Bethlehem to be born?"*[3] What could Yeats possibly be referring to, and what is slouching towards Bethlehem trying to be born in our own time?

Alongside the global chaos and turmoil, I believe that our times are also experiencing a wider evolutionary shift, a significant change in direction, a true *metanoia*. A vast proportion of humanity are hungry to explore, experience and taste *for themselves*, in a modern contemplative way, the spiritual, and mystical dimension of life. They are seeking, by diverse means, to incorporate and integrate the spiritual into every aspect of living and life.

Striking features of our time include this rekindling of a deepening interest in mysticism, and in the ways of experiencing more direct knowledge of spiritual realities, and also the related areas of depth psychology, in its myriad forms. More and more people are becoming spiritually aware and are awakening to self-consciousness, to the great potentials of interior development and spiritual transformation and to the pressing need for a deeper relationship of themselves to the whole of creation, to God, to the Holy Spirit, to their fellow man and the global community.

There also appears to be a much wider recognition of the need for training and guidance; learning from those ancient traditions and paths of spiritual knowledge, understanding and love that facilitate and enable interior growth, development and surrender towards, and in, God. We are generally unable to achieve spiritual maturity, depth and integration on our own. For many, their religious experiences have awakened them to the mystical, contemplative core of their own religious tradition. Many people who have gained new understanding of their nature from using these methods are returning to Christian roots that they now understand more deeply.

Very large numbers of people are involved in the spiritual quest now, at the start of the new millennium, and life in the West is beginning to take a new direction now that such large numbers are rediscovering their essentially spiritual nature. Even fifty years ago, talking about the deeper spiritual realities so publicly was fairly taboo.

Already, virtually unnoticed, parts of our civilisation are becoming very different, so that today we are able to speak more openly of things that not so long ago had to be spoken of in whispers, particularly regarding the contemplative life and the Christian mystical tradition. In a civilization that has for so long forgotten that we are essentially spiritual beings, there now appears to be an evolutionary change in direction, a true metanoia of humanity turning towards the spiritual dimension of life.[4]

Some say that a new era of the Holy Spirit is rapidly approaching. It appears that the unprecedented accessibility of knowledge, from the secrets of science and space travel to the opening up and commonplace availability of many of the most important spiritual writings from every religious tradition, is designed to "feed" this tremendous spiritual awakening and deepening which is occurring globally. This encourages an increasing ability to perceive and sense and act from a living faith, through knowledge of the fundamental reality of our profound interconnectedness, and the interrelationship of all things within life and creation.

This new era is about the insistence of the reality of the spiritual and divine dimensions in life. It is about allowing these dimensions *to continually work within us* to enable ongoing spiritual and psychological transformation of our perception of ourselves, of others and of the wider world within larger design, order and meaning in life. This entails being able to live in awareness of the reality of the constant presence of God in, and all around us.

It also involves continually being in, and living out, a state of willingness, of openness of heart and selfless service and charity in our lives springing from our dedication to the reality of our underlying unity, within which all of life is so delicately held and balanced. These changes are now occurring on a global scale, irrespective of dogma, denominational creed, nationality or religious affiliation. The possibility of a great transformation within the heart of each soul is underway. We are on the cusp of new times, when the Heavenly Waters of the Holy Spirit are being poured upon humanity.

There has been much comment concerning the difficulty of the mainline Christian institutions to be able to sufficiently respond to, and connect with, this profound spiritual awakening of our time. It is an accepted historical phenomenon now that the traditional institutional Church has been on the decline for some time. People in the west are far less "outwardly" religious than previously; certainly if measured in terms of church attendance.

The number of people who regard themselves as Christians now seems to be a minority. Indeed, a recent article in a national newspaper reported the possibility of the Roman Catholic priesthood in Ireland "facing the prospect of extinction after the country' oldest seminary shut its doors last week because of its failure to attract a single new recruit. . . .Twenty-three years ago a third of Ireland's population welcomed Pope John Paul II and almost 90 percent attended Mass regularly. Attendance is now as low as 5% in some areas."[5]

Has the institutional church had its day? Are we moving into a post Christian civilization? Are the wonderful churches and cathedrals now simply becoming historical monuments to a bygone phase in western Christendom? As Lawrence Freeman, leader of the World Community for Christian Meditation, recently noted:

> "*The malaise of institutional Christianity has not gone away. It is puzzling and frustrating to try to understand how the mainline churches, despite all their determination and resources, still seem unable to connect with the profound spiritual needs of our time. For so many of the young, ready for idealistic and sacrificial commitment, hungry for inspiration, the church could give the sense of belonging that they seek as citizens of the global village.*
>
> *But instead of finding an inclusive vision, a comprehensive philosophy of life, a spirituality, they dismiss what they find as narrowness of mind, intolerant dogmatism, internal feuding, interdenominational sectarianism, medieval sexism and so on. It seems disloyal to reiterate it all. Perhaps the best way of dealing with it is to ask why—the unkindest cut of all—the most damning criticism is that Christianity lacks spiritual depth. Indeed, for many, it seems to lack spiritual depth, period.*"[6]

The unprecedented spiritual longing and emergency of our own times is certainly fueling an overwhelming need for this depth dimension of the Christian tradition to become much more widely known, understood and practised. The writings of the great Christian mystics and saints, such as St Teresa, have been ignored or concealed for so many years, particularly within the Protestant tradition. In many respects, the teachings of the mystics have been one of the best-kept secrets of the contemplative and enclosed religious orders of the Christian church over the centuries.

These orders, the Carmelites, Benedictines, Jesuits, Franciscans, Dominicans, and the Visitandines, which were founded in 17th century France, have kept the flame of their founders' inspiration very much alive, and have lovingly preserved their teachings and spiritual direction over many centuries. The mystical Christian tradition *is* certainly alive and well in modern times, as Freeman describes:

> "*I am fortunate to be in touch with another side of modern Christianity—the quiet but deepening and growing network of contemplative Christians, Christians with a practice of contemplative prayer. Their sincere, searching faith and the pressures of modern life have awakened in them a hunger for spiritual experience and for the depth dimension of their Christianity.*
>
> *Many have found with delight and relief the Christian tradition of contemplative prayer after exploring the spirituality of the East. While conducting regular lives and generally looking quite normal they, like the catechumens and Christians of the primitive church, follow a seriously faithful and daily contemplative practice. This does not isolate them in any ivory tower of private spirituality. Overall, and over time, their spiritual life integrates this contemplative dimension with other forms of communal prayer and activity in a church and in ministry to others.*"[7]

This depth contemplative dimension of Christianity has always existed, and continues to exist, in every Christian order or organization *genuinely* concerned with the conscious transformation and transfiguration of the soul towards union with God through prayer, contemplation and active service and

143

charity towards others and the world. This mystical dimension is, of course, only one element of the Christian tradition, and is inseparable from the many other parts that constitute the fullness of the whole, such as worship, service, community and interfaith dialogue.

The contemplative Christian tradition has flowered in particular places, times and individuals over the past 2000 years. It flourished in the Celtic Church during the 6-8th century in Anglo-Saxon Britain, through some of its most famous saints—St Columba and St Aiden of Iona, and St Cuthbert of Lindisfarne. The most obvious homes have been, and still are, in the ancient monasteries on Mt Athos, and throughout the Middle East.[8]

Some of the better known bearers of the Christian mystical tradition in the West have been Pseudo Dionysius, the Areopagite, in the early 6th century; Bernard of Clairvaux in the 11th century, one of the early spiritual fathers of the Cistercian order; Bonaventure; Meister Eckhart; Jan van Ruysbroec; Gregory Palamas in the 13th century; Catherine of Siena in the 14th century; the English anchoress, Julian of Norwich, authoress of *Revelations of Divine Love*; and the unknown author of the *Cloud of Unknowing*.

St Teresa and St John of the Cross continued the mystical tradition of Christianity in the 16th century as part of the major Reform of the Carmelite Order. Marie of the Incarnation, Jeanne-Marie Guyon as well as Pierre Caussade, author of *Abandonment to Divine Providence*, carried the tradition in the 17th and 18th century. More recent well known figures include Therese of Lisieux, Thomas Merton and Henri Le Saux. Probably the most famous collection of mystical writings is the Philokalia, containing texts on the ascetical life, prayer and the hesychast tradition, written by the ascetical Orthodox Christian fathers between the 4th and 15th centuries.

So, what is Christian mysticism, and what is mystical theology attempting to describe? Essentially, mysticism is describing the sort of knowledge of God that is obscure to the mind or the intellect. The meaning of "mystical" lies in the Greek root "*mu-*," which has to do with hiddenness, that which is closed or concealed. Words such as *mystikon, mysterion, mystes* are derived from this root, and were originally used in connection with the Greek mystery religions.[9]

As previously mentioned in his book *The Origins of the Christian Mystical Tradition*, Andrew Louth succinctly describes mysticism as:

> ". . . *characterized as a search for, and experience of, immediacy with God. The mystic is not content to know about God, he longs for union with God. 'Union with God' can mean different things, from literal identity, where the mystic loses all sense of himself and is absorbed into God, to the union that is experienced as the consummation of love, in which the lover and the beloved remain intensely aware both of themselves and of the other.*
>
> *How the mystics interpret the way and the goal of their quest depends on what they think about God, and that itself is influenced by what they experience: it is a mistake to try to make out that all mysticism is the same. Yet the search for God, or the ultimate, for His own sake, and an unwillingness to be satisfied with anything less than Him; the search for immediacy with this object of the soul's longing; this would seem to be the heart of mysticism.*"[10]

To explore the Christian use of such terminology we need to look at the meaning of the word, *mysterion*—mystery, in Christian vocabulary—as this is what the Greek Patristic writers refer to when they use *mystikos*, or mystic. *Mysterion* means a secret, but in its use in the New Testament it very specifically refers to the mystery of God's love for us revealed in Christ. It is a secret, or a mystery, not because it is kept secret, but because it is the revelation of something that *essentially remains hidden in its revealing*, being inexhaustible and inaccessible in the very event of its being made known and accessible to us in the life, death and resurrection of Christ. Contrary to being kept secret, it is something to be proclaimed and made known, since it is the revealing of God's love for us.[11]

For the early Christian Fathers, understanding the scriptures was not a simply academic matter. It was something for which one prepared through constant prayer, purification, humility and love. Through attention to the scriptures, and by the power of the Holy Spirit, it was possible to enter into a transforming relationship with God, through which, one could become conformed to the Image of God, the Son, enabling us to contemplate the Father. The Greek Fathers first conceived of the uncreated presence of God as an *image* of God in the soul, as an active participation in the divine life. Spiritual life, then, consists in this never ceasing process of assimilation to this divine presence in the soul, as a *"growing towards the image."*[12]

Thus, in Christian vocabulary *mystikos* refers to, and makes accessible to us, this mystery of God's love for us in Christ. It essentially has a three-fold meaning, referring to the "mystic" meaning of scripture, to the mystic significance of the Christian sacraments, or mysteries, and finally to mystical theology, which is knowing God as revealed in Christ, as belonging to the "fellowship of the mystery." This was summed up by the anonymous 5th century writer, Denys the Areopagite, whose writings gathered up the patristic mystical heritage and vastly influenced posterity.[13]

Denys elucidated the three ranges of meaning of *mystikos*, referring to the deeper meaning of scripture in which God reveals the mystery of His love, looking at the significance of the sacraments through which we are able to participate in this mystery, and exploring "mystical theology." He said that mystical theology was not something different, but looks less to the means than to the end, where the soul surrenders to God and, passing into the meaning of the signs and concepts it uses to grasp the mystery of love, is itself grasped and transfigured into that love. Denys established the regular use of the three ways of purification, illumination and union in the Christian tradition.[14]

When Denys wrote his treatise on "mystical theology," he was writing about the way in which Christian liturgy displays the "mysteries" of God's action in relation to the created order—the mystery of God going out from the depths of the divine nature to create, and then to become incarnate in, our nature—God binding creation together in communion and drawing creation back to its divine source. To understand this divine movement is to receive it into ourselves in such a way that we are taken beyond all words and signs. This openness or passivity to God's movement, "suffering divine things" is what "mystical theology" means.[15]

More specifically, the mystical life begins, as Teresa writes in her autobiography, when our self is surrendered, at a radical level, to the action, activity and purposes of God, so that it can no longer be thought of as acting from a centre that is essentially separated from God. The mystical is the "supernatural," as Teresa emphasizes in the fourth mansion of *The Interior Castle*, meaning the state in which what we are doing coincides, more or less, with what God is doing, or, in theological terms, the mystical is the formation of our created selfhood in the likeness of Christ.[16]

Bernard McGinn succinctly presents many of the essential difficulties in defining mysticism in his three-volume collection of works, *The Foundations of Mysticism*. He concludes that it is much more useful to present different ways of understanding the term under three main headings—as a part of a religious tradition, as a process or way of life, and as an attempt to express a direct consciousness of the Presence of God.

McGinn points out that, in his view, perhaps the greatest insight of von Hügel's book of the early 20th century, *The Mystical Element of Religion*, is that mysticism is actually only one element in a tradition or in any particular religious personality. No mystics (at least before the 20th century!) believed in or practised "mysticism." They believed in and practised Christianity (or Judaism, Islam, Hinduism or Buddhism)—that is, the mystical elements of religious traditions were always parts of a much wider historical and spiritual whole.[17]

McGinn has come to find that the term "presence" grasps the unifying note in the varieties of Christian mysticism most centrally. He summarises the mystical element in Christianity as those parts of the beliefs and practices that concern the preparation for, the consciousness of, and the reaction to, what can be described *as the immediate or direct presence of God*. However, the ways in which these special forms of encounter with God have been understood down the generations are multiple.[18]

One thing that all the Christian mystics have agreed on is that the experience in itself defies conceptualisation and verbalization, in part or in whole, and can only be presented indirectly, partially by a series of verbal strategies. Language in this dimension can only be used transformationally, not so much to convey information or content but to assist the seeker to hope, yearn, and to know that it is possible, to journey towards, and rest in, the same Unity of Being in Christ.[19]

From this perspective, there are a host of models, metaphors or symbols that mystics have employed in their accounts. Mystical union is one of the central ways of describing this mystical dimension, and of course, was primarily what St Teresa used. Among the other major mystical categories are those of contemplation and the vision of God, deification, the birth of the Word in the soul, ecstasy, or radical obedience to the present Divine Will.

So, one of the central claims of most mystical texts, and especially of *The Interior Castle,* is that it involves an immediate consciousness of the presence of God. Teresa's writings are a powerful witness to the possibility of entering into a sense of divine presence within the context of the ordinary religious observances, and, of course, in our everyday ordinary life. What differentiates mystical texts, and this particular text, from other forms of religious writings is that the presentation is both subjectively and objectively more direct and more immediate. This is certainly part of the intention in presenting much of Teresa's original text in this book.

So, what is all this for? As Teresa, and all the Christian saints have testified to in their lives and writings, the aim of the Christian life is to restore to splendour the corrupted, darkened image of God within ourselves, through our devotion, love and, ultimately, union with Christ. As an unchanged, uncorrupted icon of God, Christ reworks the corrupted image to reveal the original beauty within us, continually teaching and guiding us towards our divine archetype. Transfigured, Christ restores the radiance of a creation made dark by the Fall, and in our continually becoming "conformed to the image of Christ" we can slowly regain our divine inheritance and our own inmost spiritual nature.[20]

To recover the light of Christ within our soul is our task. It is because of this that the themes of incarnation, transfiguration and deification—or resurrection—are so crucial. The events in the life of Christ are not only, or even mainly, events that have happened once in the past. They are entirely and eternally present and are able to be experienced by everyone. Christ's life represents what we actually are and can become, as the incarnate symbol of each person's proper destiny in life.

Christ, or life, or light—the terms are interchangeable—was joined to the world, as St Simeon writes, *"as yeast, as a small offering in the dough of our nature, and He joined our nature with*

His own incomprehensible, unapproachable nature, and, to explain things better, He joined all the reality of His divinity substantially to our nature, and that human nature He mixed unmixably with His own substance, and He made it a holy temple to Himself."[21]

Thus, the idea of transfiguration is central to the Christian understanding of our destiny, as well as to the destiny of the whole created world—the one intimately involves the other. We must understand that what is exemplified in the life of Christ, as recorded in the New Testament, provides the standard according to which each individual can assess the radical and transformative spiritual possibilities that are continually open to them. Transfiguration signifies the most intimate and exalted experience of which we are capable; our whole physical being can be so irradiated with divine light that it can shine like the sun.[22] This is the spiritual marriage Teresa is referring to in the centre of the castle.

It has to be said that modern studies of mysticism have tended to separate and differentiate between mysticism and mystical theology, moving the field more towards the study of the phenomenology of mystical states of mind and experience. The essential problem with these modern, often academic studies, is that this approach artificially splits the people and their writings off from the whole religious tradition of which they were an integral part, leaving the mystery of faith and other elements that constitute the full expression and living of the spiritual life quite separate. The theological framework of the "mystics" is, I believe, absolutely critical to the study of their life and work.

How is it possible to ignore the whole context and milieu of their life, which is, of course, what nourished, fed, fuelled and gave expression to their particular unique spiritual flowering? It really is quite problematic to separate mysticism from mystical theology, particularly in the history and expression of the mystical life in the Christian tradition. The fact that the term mystical theology antedated the coining of the word mysticism by over a millennium points us in the right direction. We must appreciate the complex and unbreakable bonds between mysticism conceived of as a religious way of life and mystical theology.[23]

Teresa was an exemplar of the heart of the mystical life—the union of God in love—but it's probable that her analysing of states of prayer in accordance with their psychological characteristics has opened up an area of modern development that she would have hardly recognised, let alone approved of. Modern studies of mysticism have tended to define mystical experience, not in terms of the mystery of faith being worked out in the soul, but in terms of phenomenologically observed psychological states, leading to the possibility of cross cultural comparison between mystics of all faiths and none.[24]

This is precisely why, for the Church Fathers, and certainly in Teresa's own understanding, mysticism was never reduced:

> "...to the level of a psychological experience, considered merely, or primarily in its subjectivity.
> It is always the experience of an invisible objective world; the world whose coming the Scriptures reveal to us in Jesus Christ, the world into which we enter, ontologically, through the liturgy, through this same Jesus Christ ever present in the Church. For Denis, as for the Fathers who were contemporary with him, together with certain inseparable spiritual experiences, always represent the world to which they give access, this mystical world of which St John Chrysostom speaks, where all the angels sing to God a mystical melody."[25]

Of course, mysticism is certainly not a religious phenomenon peculiar to Christianity. Each religious tradition has its own mystical aspect and it is vitally important that the specific character of a particular mystical tradition be respected. As Rowan Williams has emphasised, the most useful generalisations regarding mysticism across different traditions concentrate on the comparability of the *function* of the lives of the mystics and the saints within their own tradition, rather than on comparability of the content of their mystical experience:

> "*These figures, [the mystics and saints in the Christian tradition] in written texts as well as the "text" of their lives, serve as points of orientation, touchstones of integrity, for the language and hopes of other believers precisely because they witness to so broad and comprehensive an access to the "sacred source" of Christian commitment, the action and passion of God in the whole event of Jesus Christ.*"[26]

Endnotes

[1] K. Kavanaugh, O. Rodriguez, (trans), *The Collected Works of St John of the Cross*, p. 20.

[2] B. McGinn, *The Language of Inner Experience in Christian Mysticism, Spiritis 1*, pp. 157-171.

[3] W.B. Yeats, *Collected Poems*, p. 211.

[4] R. Amis, *A Different Christianity*, p. 62.

[5] The Observer, 2 September 2002.

[6] L. Freeman, *The Grateful Church of the Future*, The Tablet.

[7] Ibid.

[8] See William Dalrymple, *From the Holy Mountain*, and Hieromonk Alexander (trans) *The Living Witness of the Holy Mountain: Contemporary Voices from Mt Athos*.

[9] G. Wakefield, (Ed) *Dictionary of Christian Spirituality*, p. 272.

[10] A. Louth, *The Origins of the Christian Mystical Tradition*, p. xv.

[11] G. Wakefield, (Ed) *Dictionary of Christian Spirituality*, pp. 272-273.

[12] L. Dupre, *The Deeper Life: An Introduction to Christian Mysticism*, p. 87.

[13] G. Wakefield, (Ed) *Dictionary of Christian Spirituality*, p 273.

[14] Ibid.

[15] R. Williams, *Teresa of Avila*, p. 143.

[16] Ibid., p. 144.

[17] B. McGinn, *Foundations of Mysticism, Volume 1*, p. xvi.

[18] Ibid., p. xvii.

[19] Ibid., p. xvii.

[20] R. Amis, *A Different Christianity*, p. 53.

[21] P. Sherrard, *The Sacred in Life and Art*, p. 99.

[22] Ibid., p. 86.

[23] B. McGinn, *Foundations of Mysticism, Volume 1*, p. xiv.

[24] G. Wakefield, (Ed) *Dictionary of Christian Spirituality*, p. 274.

[25] L. Bouyer, *Mysticism: An Essay on the History of the Word*, Richard Woods(ed), Understanding Mysticism, p. 52.

[26] R. Williams, *Teresa of Avila*, p. 158.

Chapter 11

THE THREEFOLD WAY

The spiritual path—the journey towards, and in, God—is, and always has been, fraught with manifold difficulties, delusions, battles and shadows. Without an accurate road map of the spiritual terrain and wise spiritual direction, which the great Christian saints and mystics have provided, it is certainly a dangerous and perilous journey. The writings of these spiritual titans are indispensable in our post-modern, secular, individualistic age, so that as much knowledge and understanding of the Christian mystical tradition as possible is made as available to as many pilgrims as possible.

It is for those seekers who have that insatiable longing, sincerity, passion, willingness and discipline to absorb and use the wisdom of our forebears in their journey towards, and in, God. This ancient classical map of the spiritual journey towards mystical union was slowly developed over years of inner experimentation by the early Christians and the Desert Fathers. It became crystallized through medieval mystics such as Hugh of St Victor, Blessed Jan van Ruysbroec and St Catherine of Siena, and reached a height of refinement with St Teresa and St John of the Cross. Variations and subdivisions multiplied, but the core of the doctrine remained the same.

One of the basic ideas in western mysticism is that spiritual life moves through stages in an ascending order. The classical division into purgative, illuminative and unitive stages was established in the early Christian centuries and has survived most of the transitional differences and school polemics in the following centuries. The first stage is known as the way of awakening, purgation and purification, *the via purgativa*, the second stage as illumination, *the via illuminativa*, and the third stage as mystical union, *the via unitiva*.

Each stage has clear characteristics and distinguishing signs, and each has an appropriate and different set of criteria for discernment. An experienced contemporary Jesuit spiritual director has written that:

> "*Though based on the inherited tradition of the Christian community, these stages have indeed been confirmed by my own personal experience as a spiritual director. I have found this general classical pattern to be very much a part of the individuated experience of most of the people I have directed.*"[1]

Awakening

The beginning of the stage of spiritual awakening, *metanoia* or turning towards God, is usually an intense form of conversion. This is sometimes a gradual process, but more often than not it can be an abrupt awakening to the reality of the spiritual dimension of life, which usually, in the initial stages, is in greater or lesser conflict with our ordinary everyday perception, attitudes, lifestyle and way of living and being. In some cases, the process of conversion can be quite sudden, experienced as being clearly imposed from without, rather than being slowly developed from within through faith. It can even have a mystical or supernatural character. One of the most famous examples from scripture is, of course, that of St Paul and his "road to Damascus" conversion: the sudden light, the voice, the ecstasy, and the complete alteration of life.

The varied ways and means of conversion towards the spiritual life, whether sudden or gradual, are well documented in the religious literature.[2] An experience of conversion can often develop as a result of a long period of restlessness, searching, uncertainty or trauma, or it can happen quite suddenly through a vivid, powerful or overwhelming experience of God's Love, Light or the Presence of Christ. The overall effect of any real conversion experience is that it breaks down, challenges and often completely overturns our habitual and normal conscious understanding and perception of ourselves, the world and our relationship to God.

These conversion experiences, or profound changes in the direction of our lives, normally begin to reveal the reality and existence of a very different spiritual dimension of life, and of ourselves, which had hitherto been hidden, unconscious, unknown and untouched. This is a familiar state for many young Christians at the beginning of their new relationship with God. Their initial prayer and worship are often enlivened by occasional moments, or tastes, of real and unmistakable awakening to the life changing touch, presence and love of God.

Indeed, Andre Dupre emphasizes the necessity of true spiritual awakening to the love of God as one of the primary conditions of any significant progress in the process of purification and purgation, noting that:

> "It is not sufficient for the novice to be full of spiritual desire. He or she must be 'awakened' to it in a manner over which he or she has no control. Many saints, as we know, have undergone rather abrupt conversions to spiritual life.

*It is generally assumed that mystics also experience a clear
'awakening' to a high state of spiritual awareness.*
*Yet in the 'Psychology of the Mystics,' the eminent philosopher
Joseph Marechal claims that for most people that awakening
occurs gradually in the course of ordinary prayer. It concludes
a process that has started with meditation, has then moved
into a more inward recollection which, in due time, has
turned into a state of habitual dwelling in the presence of
God. . . .Love must come first, with the soul becoming more
and more centred on God rather than on itself before any
real purgation can begin."*[3]

These fleeting spiritual illuminations are very common,
especially in our own times. Many pilgrims and seekers have
had wonderful "opening" experiences to the Holy Spirit and the
genuine taste of God's Presence and Love at some time in their
prayer and spiritual journey. However, this early stage of awakening
to the spiritual dimension is very much only the beginning. These
moments, phases, or experiences of awakening to God belong to
some of the most intimate and precious aspects of what it means
to be human. They are the beginning of our long journey home to
the heart of God.

What are the signs of our own awakening to the presence of
the Holy Spirit, to the spiritual dimension of life? These include
the sense of being absolutely alive, a tremendous vitality, a direct,
immediate knowing, or understanding, of our religious creeds, a
sense of great treasure, beauty and splendour. There can also be
an overwhelming sense of dread, of tremendous fear and anxiety,
of encountering the *mysterium tremendum* of God. There is a
sense of breaking through to something quite Other. Something
is shown to us that is very different, and it is not mediated by our
usual ideas, thoughts, or cognitive structures.

Some of these early types of awakening experiences powerfully challenge, and exceed, all the usual ways that we apprehend ordinary reality. There are many descriptions from the saints, mystics or wise spiritual directors that comprise the more sudden conversion experiences. With a more intense presence of the Holy Spirit in our lives, we can experience a fire beginning to burn from within, an immense calm, a sense of eternal or limitless peace, of profound well being and blessing, a sense of coming home or belonging, or waves of endless Love.

There can also be the sense of entering the nothingness from which all things come, of rhythmic surges of energy, or incredible, indescribable joy. We can have an experience of transcendent ecstasy, of water gushing as if "my breath is the breath of God." We might receive a touch or taste of absolute freedom and energy like electricity plugged into a Source of Life. There can be a markedly increased sense of the Presence of Christ, that life and existence seem to be in this very moment, now, alongside a real sense of the eternal. There can certainly be a change in our sense of time and space, and definitely a sense of the holy, or holiness.

In his famous text written nearly 100 years ago, *Varieties of Religious Experience,* William James explored some of the basic characteristics of encounters with the spiritual dimension.[4] Firstly, they have a quality of ineffability—they defy expression in logical rational terms, and are often only fully intelligible to those who have known some analogous experience.

Consider the smell of a rose, or the sensation of being in love, or the pleasure that comes while listening to a great symphony; none are amenable to adequate logical or intellectual description. Most utterances on such dimensions are really rather inadequate, except to those touched by a certainty of the reality of that dimension. The attempt to express the inexpressible is, of course, where psychology and theology go hand in hand.

Secondly, James pointed to the noetic *quality* of this dimension by defining these states as "states of insight into depths of truth unplumbed by the discursive intellect, insights which carry with them a tremendous sense of authority." We actually know something different in this dimension. It tends to break the subject/object dualism, and purely intellectual thinking, and introduces us into a transcendent reality.

Somehow, there can be a sense of insight, of knowing, touching, tasting, seeing the wholeness of things and life, of seeing and being within the profound interconnectedness of things which defies the mind, reason and the intellect alone. More importantly, our faculty for intuitively penetrating the veil of temporal reality seems to be activated by a source beyond ourselves. A consciousness can appear, a sense of unitive being, or non-duality. There can be a change in the sense of time and space, a sense of the eternal.

Thirdly, these states generally transcend our ordinary sense of ourselves, and can often be experienced as more real and awake than our ordinary waking consciousness. We feel much more alive. These experiences represent another level, or dimension, of reality that is deeper than the previous one. However, these transcendent states can seldom be sustained for long, and share the quality of transiency, requiring further inner work to make the state a lasting one. The following of a particular way of life can increase their frequency and make the states more permanent.

Fourthly, the sense of inner stillness, quietness, and surrender is vital. James called this passivity, which is a term that can be misunderstood. The implication of this characteristic is that ego-transcendent states almost always bring with them the feeling of something that is given. It is the preparation, the conscious surrender, in order to be receptive to the action of the Spirit—it is not possible to create or manipulate this state. There is a distinct quality of otherness.

The essential quality of stillness, of the body, mind, emotions, has the capacity to restore our ability to remember, to recollect, to remain ourselves and not be distracted or identified with influences from the outside. That is why prayer, meditation and contemplation are the essential pathways to connecting to, and living within, this deeper dimension.

The touch of the mystical is often spoken of in terms of the five interior senses of the soul when she is becoming betrothed to Christ, through the Holy Spirit. Teresa speaks about the sweet smell or perfume of the Holy Spirit in the fifth mansion when the bride is becoming betrothed to the Bridegroom.

Other saints and mystics have spoken about the sense of the interior taste of the Holy Spirit, as if we have been invited as special guests to a heavenly banquet, where there are the particular flavours, sounds, scents, textures and colours of Paradise. It is like nothing that we have ever tasted before, and is impossible to truly convey or describe to those who have not been to such a banquet.

The main psychological and spiritual changes of attitude that need to occur during these initial stages are the increasing recognition of how ignorant we are, of how little we actually know, of how much psychological work needs to be done in order to progress and deepen our spiritual life, of how open and vulnerable we are to be to the pressures and influences of the outside world, and of how powerful and insistent our self-love and egoism is.

The best way of beginning to develop our sense of self, or soul, is by increasingly devoting ourselves to prayer, meditation, the study of scripture and contemplative and mystical literature within a community, group or in solitude. We also would add the cultivation of compassion, patience, humility and generosity in as many practical choices and opportunities in life as possible.

In his spiritual autobiography, *the Golden String*, the twentieth century Catholic monk and mystic, Bede Griffiths described the nature of spiritual awakening:

"An experience of this kind (of spiritual awakening) is probably not at all uncommon, especially in early youth. Something breaks suddenly into our lives and upsets their normal pattern and we have to begin to adjust ourselves to a new kind of existence. This experience may come, as it came to me, through nature and poetry, or through art or music; or it may come through the adventure of flying or mountaineering, or of war; or it may come through simply falling in love, or through some apparent accident, an illness, the death of a friend, the sudden loss of fortune.

Anything that breaks through the routine of daily life may be the bearer of this message to the soul. But, however it may be, it is as though a veil has been lifted and we see for the first time behind the façade, which the world has built around us. Suddenly we know we belong to another world, that there is another dimension of existence. . .we see our life for a moment in its true perspective in relation to eternity. We are freed from all the flux of time and see something of the eternal order that underlies it. We are no longer isolated individuals in conflict with our surroundings; we are parts of whole, elements in a universal harmony."[5]

The beginning of awakening to the spiritual dimension of life often has its roots in the earliest memories of childhood, where it is not uncommon to have spontaneous experiences, or moments, of a different spiritual reality to ordinary, everyday life, experiences pregnant with a depth of meaning, vitality, richness and significance far beyond the actual physical situation. Such moments of awakening are unforgettable and indescribable, as they are moments of recollection and remembrance of ourselves, and of our relationship to spiritual realities.

As a child, my own relationship to nature and the local community was central to my spiritual awakening. Much of my childhood and adolescence centred on my interest in religion and activities in the local Christian community. . .from a young age I always felt a particular connection and fascination with the religious life and spirituality. There were many moments as a child—either in church, on retreat, or in "the bush" which I would now describe as religious or numinous experience, where a presence of something quite beyond me, which I recognized as a sense or touch of God, or something quite Other, had been unquestionably real and strong.

Purification and Purgation

"*Purification is a perpetual process. That which mystical writers mean, however, when they speak of the way of purgation, is rather the slow and painful completion of conversion. It is the drastic turning of the self from the unreal to the real life: a setting of her house in order, an orientation of the mind to (spiritual) truth. Its business is the getting rid, first of self-love; and secondly of all those foolish interests in which the surface consciousness is steeped. The essence of purgation, says Richard of St Victor, 'is self simplification.'*"[6]

This stage has to do with what is traditionally called ascesis, the ongoing work on, and purification of, oneself in order to overcome the effects of the past, and to heal our psyche and soul. In all religious traditions, ascetical practices have been deemed to be necessary in order to purify ourselves, so as to "enter and taste the delights of the garden of Paradise."

There are different kinds of ascesis—physical ascetical practices, such as particular prayer postures, and psychological and spiritual ascetical practices, of which prayer, meditation and contemplation usually form the core. Psychotherapy, psychoanalysis and the many therapeutic endeavours that are now available are also potent tools to help individuals successfully work through childhood trauma, and all kinds of psychological and emotional difficulties and obstacles.

This stage usually becomes more serious and necessary when the initial awakening phase has slowed down, or stopped happening. For many people, the beginning of purification stage can bring on growing disappointment and disillusionment. It is only if the pilgrim seriously engages in, and commits themselves to undergoing the real difficulties and rigors of their internal purification process that such "spiritual" disappointment can be overcome by a change of heart. This intense emotional purification of the heart can then lead on to the deeper phase of illumination.

This ongoing and ever-present process of self-purification entails a tremendous inner analysis; a continual commitment to uncover and take full responsibility for our unconscious patterns and games; a constant facing of our past wounds and traumas and their continuing effects on us, and an ongoing confrontation with all the forms of subtle betrayal and sabotage of self and others. Only through a developed and stable practice and rhythm of prayer, meditation and service, and only if we have truly aroused devotion in our heart towards God, is it possible to endure and travel through the tremendous rigors and difficulties of this period.

The primary aim of the purification stage is the production of real repentance, of a deepening *metanoia*, the essential "change of mind" away from ourselves and towards God; to become ever more deeply engaged in that fundamental transformation of our heart and outlook towards new, spiritual ways of looking at ourselves, at others and at God.

For some, the deeper conversion towards the reality of the spiritual life will be from the motivation of the fear and wrath of God. However, fear, that anxious and negative state, can, given generosity and openness towards it, give way before long to the deepening realization of the love of God, and the turning away from a selfish, ego-centred life and attitudes. This change comes not from fear of punishment, but through recognising the rebellion against His love that the old life essentially is—a state that we long to change and have transformed within our heart.[7]

Of course, at this stage, deeper engagement in self-knowledge and rigorous self-examination is indispensable, as Teresa emphasizes in the first mansion. The purpose is not to undermine or to destructively criticise oneself, but to enter the process of self enquiry, of ruthless openness, self honesty and personal integrity so as to arrive at a real knowledge of oneself in the sight of God, becoming naked, open, receptive, surrendered, ready in His Sight.

There is no substitute for the patient, slow psychological and psychotherapeutic work of exploring, understanding and learning to accept ourselves the way we are. In this regard, knowledge of God presupposes, and is intimately connected to, knowledge of self.

The depth and progress of our spiritual life does not necessarily depend on our mental health or capacities. A deepening union with God is generally accompanied by an increasingly more integrated personality and a greater focus of energy in the service of God. Knowledge of God presupposes, and is intimately connected to, knowledge of self.

The yearning and desire to move towards deepening states of contemplative prayer and meditation must be complemented and augmented by the ongoing struggle to develop an in-depth understanding of ourselves, and by an increasing ability to reflect on, sense, articulate and adequately respond to what is going on within our psyche, both from the conscious and the unconscious levels.

Spiritual transformation today is not only a matter of moving towards the innermost dwelling places, but also of ever more precise and technical self-knowledge, which begins at the earliest stages on the path and continues at all times, at all points and at all stages toward the mystery of union, as Teresa so clearly states.

There is a constant re-evaluation of our life, where the attachments, identifications and projections onto exterior life are waning. As the seeker's senses, passions and spiritual perception are steadily able to become more emptied of an emphasis on our own personal gratifications, and able to become more refined, purified and objective through the action of the Holy Spirit in our heart, what were previously visionary "glimpses" can become a more permanent recognition of, and being in, the presence, mystery and mercy of God.

Slowly, as we are able to more fully face what is untransformed, addicted and still desperate inside, and are able more and more to expose ourselves to God's beauty and mercy, then His Presence and Love is able to infuse or install itself in increasingly steady ways in our heart and lives.

Essentially, in this purification stage, we are continually being placed, face to face, with our life, both conscious and unconscious, with all our soluble and insoluble problems, and one of the major tests of spiritual discrimination and discernment is the objective distinguishing between the permanent, eternal influences, and the personal, temporary influences.

As soon as we turn towards the interior world in prayer and reflection, we usually encounter whole dimensions of ourselves that have previously been unconscious, hidden and unknown. In modern psychological parlance, these refer to the shadow parts of the psyche, which describe all the psychic contents that have been driven back into the unconscious, including all the neglected, undeveloped, unacknowledged parts of ourselves.

At these early stages, rigorous self-knowledge and humility need to be growing. Humility is one of the most powerful forces of spiritual growth and development. No effort, and no teaching, is true and transformative that does not lead to increasing humility, which does not turn us around and, closing us off from the pressures of the world, begin to open us to the constant pressure of the Love of God.

We cannot hope to achieve right and true relationship with others, the world or with God unless we have such a sense of that reality, which alone enables us to see and understand ourselves and our real condition in these outer edges of the castle in their true spiritual perspective, which can only grow in the soil of deepening humility.

The purgative way is fraught with difficulties, blocks, distractions and obstacles, often seemingly overwhelming, that seem to constantly pull us away from God. In the active purgative stage, our efforts need to be marshalled to overcome the major obstacles that obstruct our spiritual progress.

In her classic book, *Mysticism,* Evelyn Underhill describes the two main forms of active purgation: the slow process of *detachment,* which is intended to sever the existing ties of desire, and *mortification,* the deliberate choice of what is disagreeable, painful or humiliating which is intended to reverse habitual patterns of affection and behaviour.[8] The Christian monastic tradition has institutionalised the active pursuit of spiritual detachment through the vows of poverty, chastity and obedience that every nun and monk has to take on fully entering the religious life.

St John of the Cross describes the purgative process in terms of the active and passive night of the senses in his writings entitled the *Ascent of Mount Carmel* and the *Dark Night of the Soul,* which I discuss in more detail in the third mansion.[9] In this stage, John focuses on the importance of detachment from our desires and passions, which enables us to more deeply enter into the relationship with God through stillness and silence.

John insists that it is the inner detachment that matters, not the physical privation:

"John explicitly warns against excessive mortification, which focuses undue attention on bodily desires. Not the pleasure, but the desire of pleasure, its self-contracting aspect by which I turn back into myself, must be renounced. Pleasure is a necessary component of physical life. For one who is hungry, not to enjoy eating is neither natural nor desirable. But to eat merely for the sake of pleasure deflects the soul from its upward moment.

Significantly John posits the love of Christ, not the pursuit of personal perfection as the main motive of all mortification. . .the renunciation of desire must, from the beginning, be motivated by what lies beyond man, rather than by an egocentric concern with moral progress. An ascetic pursuit of virtue for its own sake has no part in Christian mysticism. Even the desire of spiritual perfection must be God centred from the start."[10]

So, we can have all the best of intentions at this stage, but we are not yet stabilized in virtue, and the attraction of the world, the flesh and the devil is commonly very strong—our love for God is weak and fitful, alternating with periods of weariness and tepidity, and from time to time we are often severely tempted to give up the hardness of this increasingly narrow way:

"The Slough of Despond, the Hill of Difficulty, the Valley of Humiliation, and Vanity Fair are all met in this way, and the soul needs much encouragement if it is to persevere valiantly. A large part of ministry and spiritual direction with the cure of souls is spent sitting on a stone near the top of the Hill of Difficulty encouraging pilgrims.

For the Hill of Difficulty is the grind of the whole thing which none of us can escape, the grind of resisting sin, of turning a deaf ear to temptation, of sticking to the necessary rules, the grind of the early morning alarum, of monotonous days, the grind of helping people about their weaknesses, of seeing their suffering, a grind disfigured by the failure of losing one's passport through sins of infirmity and sins of surprise, and of having to climb down to find it in penitence and to climb back again forgiven once more."[11]

If these ascetical efforts are intense enough, the process of purification of the heart can lead to a reawakening of the presence of the Holy Spirit at a deeper level in our being. The essential attitudes at this stage, of patience and perseverance, and being grounded in self – knowledge, enable us to hold on, in deepening faith, through the very difficult and often harrowing chasm of the dark night of the senses in order to make more and more purgative efforts, so that the rare and fleeting awakening spiritual experiences will eventually begin to *catch fire in the heart* and turn into illumination.

The stage of purgation, or purification relates to the second and third mansion of Teresa's Interior Castle. Her emphasis on the prayer of recollection, or active remembrance, at this stage relates to all forms of contemplative prayer that involve some active technique, such as specifically focusing on a holy image, or sacred literature, or focusing on recollection with imagination on Scripture, such as Ignatius's Spiritual Exercises.

Illumination

"Though He has frequently entered into my soul, I have never at any time been sensible of the precise moment of His coming. I have felt that He was present, I remember that He has been with me; I have sometimes been able even to have a presentiment that He would come: but never to feel His coming nor His departure. . . .It is not by the eyes that

He enters, for He is without form or colour that they can discern; nor by the ears, for His coming is without sound; nor by the nostrils, for it is not with the air but with the mind that He is blended. . .

By what avenue then has He entered? Or perhaps that fact may be that He has not entered at all, nor indeed come at all from outside: for not one of these things belongs to outside. Yet it has not come from within me, for it is good, and I know that in me dwelleth no good thing. I have ascended higher than myself, and lo! I have found the Word above me still. My curiosity has led me to descend below myself also, and yet I have found Him still at a lower depth. If I have looked without myself, I have found that He is beyond that which is outside of me; and if within, He was at an inner depth still."

St Bernard of Clairvaux[12]

This is the way for those who have made some progress in the spiritual life, where our faith, loyalty and longing for God is deepening into love, where we are spiritually moving towards becoming His friend, towards a deeper, more intimate friendship with Jesus. This is now the beginning of the truly interior life where we are assured of His Friendship: "*I do not call you servants any longer because the servant does not know what the master is doing; but I have called you friends, because I have made known to you everything that I have heard from my Father.*" (John 15:15)

We have been preparing for this by becoming so stripped away, naked, vulnerable and open, becoming small, humble and transparent enough, waiting in expectation, quietly, passively, being as receptive as possible to the movement of the Holy Spirit so that when He begins to touch, to enter into and ultimately transform our soul, we are able to respond to His call, His touch, His hand of Friendship, in order to be able to be created afresh in

His ineffable peace and silence.

Now, in this cyclical rhythm of the spiritual journey, the purgative phase is giving way, at different times with different intensities, to the perception of a new spiritual, transcendent reality, a new expanded consciousness of the reality, and love, of God, alongside a definite sense of His Presence in our soul. The increasing awareness of divine presence at this stage is now becoming impressed and infused on the soul so directly, so firmly, and so clearly that there is no mistaking that something quite new is beginning to enter and transform our heart, mind and perception. Spiritual guidance and discernment are becoming even more important at this stage in order understand and accept these new and wonderful graces that God is beginning to bestow.

The intensive experience of a divine presence is considered the most characteristic mystical phenomenon of this part of the way. This can have a distinctive, almost physical quality. The term "physical" may be misleading, since the highest, exclusively mystical visions are not physical at all. However, it conveys an even more intense feeling of presence. The ordinary feeling of God's presence occurs at a lower degree of intensity than the awareness of a physical presence, while the mystical occurs at the same or at a higher degree (indeed it frequently has all the characteristics of an awareness of physical presence).[13]

Closely connected with the sense of the presence of God is the definite sense of moving into a different dimension of life, of time, of perception, of knowing, of understanding. It is as if we begin to move into eternal time, where we are intimately touched by, and begin to truly know, with different interior senses, with the centre of our heart and soul, so to speak, the reality of the unity of God and His creation. We begin to live within, breathe, exist, see and understand the paradox of how all of life and creation is simultaneously in constant dynamic movement, and absolutely still, silent, at peace, stationary, all at the same time.

This sense of eternity, of His time, is quite real and tangible, and we realise that this dimension of eternity, God's time, has always been, is, and will always be intersecting our own human ordinary time. Yet, up until this stage, we have been asleep to its living existence. We have not as yet been able to fully live, breathe, and participate in both, simultaneously, until we have been graced to receive the touch, the illumination of the Holy Spirit in this stage of the path.

George Fox describes this beautifully:

"Now, I was come up in spirit through the flaming sword into the Paradise of God. All things were new; and all the creation gave another smell unto me than before, beyond what words can utter...The creation was opened to me; and it was showed me how all things had their names given them, according to their nature and virtue. And I was at a stand in my mind whether I should practise physic for the good of mankind, seeing the nature and virtue of the creatures were so opened to me by the Lord... Great things did the Lord lead me unto, and wonderful depths were opened unto me beyond what can by words be declared; but as people come into subjection to the Spirit of God, and grow up in the image and power of the Almighty, they may receive the word of wisdom that opens all things, and come to know the hidden unity in the Eternal being."[14]

It is important to note that illuminative experiences can occur in many different ways in many different circumstances. Such a revealing of divine presence and the eternal life may go side by side with daily life and normal mental activities, without any ecstatic or visionary expressions. It does not usually occur in a sudden flash. However, one of the defining characteristics of this way is that a deeper love of, and need for, prayer and silence is developing. As we are becoming more wholehearted in our desire for, and our need to be with, Him, we now strive after more time and space in prayer, solitude and peace in order to enter the intimate chambers of the heart with Him.

Through time, discourse in prayer will become less necessary and finally impossible, and we will pass to affective prayer, pure and simple, which is the normal prayer of souls in this way. This should be a natural spiritual interior development, and this deepening movement of prayer should not be pressed for before we are truly ready for it. It is possible, though uncommon, for a soul to reach contemplation by discursive meditation or vocal prayer alone, and these ways must not be regarded as too elementary for this stage.[15]

With the deepening practice of prayer goes increased love of it. A deeper desire for silence and solitude slowly develops. Thus, in the illuminative way, we begin to love being with Him more than anything else, and consequently want to be alone with Him all the time. This interior aloneness with Christ is becoming a primary necessity of life.

Our aim is not, of course, to become anti-worldly, reclusive, or to retire into seclusion away from life or society. Quite the reverse – the challenge is to become contemplatives in the world, truly in the world but "not of it" in our heart and soul, as non-attached and non-identified as is psychologically and spiritually possible.

Our usual preoccupations, perceptions, thoughts, ideas, affects and anxieties about the world in this stage are profoundly changing, as our sense and perception of life and of ourselves begin to open up to a strange new fullness of the spiritual life, in this dimension of His Presence and His Eternal Time.

This stage is often characterised by an increased intensity of infused contemplation. A sense of the passive prayer of recollection is deepening towards what Teresa describes in the fourth and fifth mansions as the prayer of quiet—a greater sense of interior stillness and silence. As prayer and contemplation deepen and the gradual process of interiorisation stabilises, a more or less permanent state of interior quiet is beginning to slowly develop.

We are entering into an increasingly more passive state of consciousness, a "self forgetting attentiveness, a profound concentration, a self merging, which operates a real communion between the seer and the seen."[16] We begin to love recollection and interior silence and we will want to be with Christ not only in prayer, but also in every part of our life.

Thus, at this stage of illumination, intense love for God is slowly becoming a wholehearted commitment for all of us, our conscious and unconscious parts, in an increasingly deepening transformation in God. Our ordinary rhythm of life and our personality, of course remain, but are slowly becoming subordinate to the sense of increasing openness to Love and Presence and to the expression of His Love in all aspects of our life and living, in body, mind and soul.

So, in the illuminative way, there is a deeper sacrifice of our personal self, wishes and desires. The way of love is essentially the way of sacrifice and surrender, and our interior purification uncovers from subtly hidden places, our selfishness and egotism. In the earlier stages, our willfulness and selfish desires have been fought directly, but here they are put in their proper place by the deliberate exercise of humility. Now that God is becoming the centre of our being, our self is being quietly dissolved and transfigured, since both cannot occupy centre stage in our soul.[17]

In the eastern Orthodox tradition, this stage is known as magnetization, or gravitation, to God. St Theophan, a well-known Russian ascetic, described this as the beginning of an inner realignment that changes the strength and quality of everything that comes from our being. Our life's centre of gravity begins to change and revolve around God much more wholeheartedly.

We are able to do this through the formation of what is called a magnetic centre. The reality of the spiritual impulse within us is now becoming much more formed. We are able to dwell more deeply within our interior castle, this ark that separates us from the influence and distractions of the world, and leads to the flowering of a life of spontaneous prayer of the heart.[18]

St Theophan describes this spiritual progress from one stage to the next:

> "When iron clings to a magnet it is because the power of the magnet draws it. In spiritual matters the same thing is true; it is only clear that God is touching us when we experience this living aspiration; when our spirit turns its back on everything else and is fixed on Him and carried away.
>
> At first this will not happen; the zealous person is still turned wholly on himself. Even though he has "decided" for God this is only in his mind. The Lord does not yet let Himself be tasted, nor is the man yet capable of it, being impure. All he can do is to serve God without tasting Him, so to speak.
>
> Then as his heart begins to be purified and set right, he begins to feel the sweetness of a life pleasing to God; so that he begins to walk in His ways gladly and with love. It becomes his natural element, in which he delights. Then the soul starts to withdraw from everything else as from the cold, and to gravitate towards God, Who warms it. This principle of gravitation is implanted in the fervent soul by divine Grace."[19]

In *The Interior Castle*, Teresa describes the fourth mansion as this critical transition between the stages of purification and illumination. Here, as she describes so eloquently and passionately, mystical experiences often increase instead of dwindling, and their meaning starts to become clearer. The many small illuminations begin to take "fire in the heart," and can lead, in time, to a permanent union with Christ, our Beloved, in the innermost mansion.

With the illuminative phase, there is also a growing sense of being increasingly more transparent. We are able to become more immediately open, honest and direct as we have less that is unconscious, hidden from view and based on our own personal agenda. Basically, we are surrendering in order to become more God-centred and less 'I'-centred. This is the fulfilment of John's words: "*He who has the bride is the Bridegroom. The friend of the Bridegroom, who stands and hears him, rejoices greatly at the Bridegroom's voice. For this reason my joy has been fulfilled. He must increase, but I must decrease.*" *(John 3: 29-30)*

What is the nature of this mysterious illumination? Apart from the certitude it imparts, what form does it usually assume in the consciousness of the self? The saints and mystics assure us that its apparently symbolic name is really descriptive; that they do experience a kind of radiance, a flooding of the personality with new light. A new sun rises above the horizon and transfigures their twilit world. Over and over again they return to light imagery in this connection.

Frequently, as in their first conversion, they report an actual and overpowering consciousness of radiant light, ineffable in its splendour, accompanying their inward adjustment. Underhill summarises different descriptions of illumination:

> "*Light rare, untellable!*" *said Whitman.* "*The flowing light of the Godhead,*" *said Mechthild of Magdeburg, trying to describe what it was that made the difference between her universe and that of normal men.* "*Lux vivens dicit*" *said St Hildegarde in her revelations, which she described as appearing in a special light, more brilliant than the brightness around the sun. It is an 'infused brightness,' said Teresa 'a light which knows no night; but rather, as it is always light, nothing ever disturbs it.*"[20]

In this quite mysterious divine embrace of the soul by His Presence and Light, the enjoyment of God is beginning to fill the spirit, as well as the body. It is penetrating and awakening the depths of our habitually unconscious existence. Between sleep and wakefulness, when the frontier that separates the conscious from the unconscious can be crossed, and when the body within the body is exposed, ecstasy and joy, which can be humanly overwhelming and unbearable, begin to seize hold of the whole personality.[21]

John Cassian explains:

"It is not easy to know how and in what respects spiritual tenderness overwhelms the soul. Often it is by an ineffable joy and by vehement aspirations that its presence is revealed. So much so that the joy is rendered unbearable by its very intensity, and breaks out into cries that carry tidings of your inebriation as far as a neighbouring cell.

Sometimes on the contrary the whole soul descends and lies hidden in abysses of silence. The suddenness of the light stupefies it and robs it of speech. All its senses remain withdrawn in its inmost depths or completely suspended. And it is by inarticulate groans that it tells God of its desire. Sometimes, finally, it is so swollen with a sorrowful tenderness that only tears can give it consolations."[22]

The main characteristics of the illuminative way are the deepening of the infused virtues of faith, hope and charity. The power of spiritual insight into the workings of the Holy Spirit and a real knowledge of the things of God are developing in the soul through the graces our Lord is beginning to bestow. This infused virtue of faith in God enables us to experience the very real sense of God, by means of which He begins to enlighten and guide us in His ways. Our life begins to be more and more genuinely irradiated by faith and joy. The spiritual insight that comes by love is not a substitute for intellectual effort to those who are intellectual, but are its guide and completion; for them the two works must go on simultaneously and harmoniously.[23]

In the purgative way, hope is usually not very strong. There will be many times when the interior work against our resistance and negativity is very difficult, when the odds seem overwhelmingly against the soul and we come perilously near to despair. Now, in the illuminative way, hope begins to become a reality to the soul. Love and knowledge of God are beginning to issue in that certain trust in Him which is Hope. Our life is becoming centred on Christ. We have an increasing desire to become like Him.[24]

Mystic illumination takes place on several levels. It may be a perception, a vision of the senses, a physical awareness that *is not provoked* by an ordinary sense stimulus. The saints and the mystics actually see with their eyes what other people cannot see. The illumination stage can also be characterized by an often bewildering series of visions, ecstasies and illuminations that can tremendously expand the pilgrim's self-knowledge, through the action of the Holy Spirit.[25]

Teresa's name and reputation are associated with the more extreme and unusual mystical experiences that she had herself. She writes about these in the latter sections of *The Interior Castle*, particularly in the sixth mansion, detailing the means that God uses to waken the soul—through different sorts of visions, locutions, wordless prayer, "flight of the spirit" and even levitations. It is obviously difficult for those with no experience of such mystical states to make sense of these, but her text is essentially a spiritual discernment manual with specific guidance on how to understand, interpret and integrate such phenomena.

It is important to note that sensory illumination need not necessarily be mystical in the strictest sense. In the exercises called "application of the senses," Ignatius Loyola invites the spiritual pilgrim to see with his eyes what is happening in the stable at Bethlehem, to hear the words that are spoken, to smell and taste the sweetness of God, to kiss the holy places where God is present. Yet, these exercises are not intended for mystics only and continue a long, mainly Franciscan, tradition. Here the mystic builds firmly on the foundation of ordinary Christian piety.[26]

At the level of the imagination, other forms of illumination take place. St John refers to infused, passive states that affect the imagination as visions, revelations, voices and spiritual feelings. In these clearly mystical states, the person sees visions or hears words while remaining fully conscious of their "imaginary," that is, their non-sensuous character. Teresa clearly distinguishes between sensory visions and those visions that she "sees" without eyes. In general though, mystics do not rank visions, imaginary or sensory, among the higher forms of divine illumination.

Long before our present knowledge of the unconscious, these more dramatic phenomena of altered consciousness were easily suspected as allusions to the devil and were hence confronted with a critical mind. Only their practical effects would reveal whether they came from God or not. Our more advanced knowledge of the unconscious has rendered us even more hesitant to accept visions and voices as direct expressions of God. Not surprisingly, when the soul is shaken to its depths by mystical alteration, certain archaic forms and types, barely veiled in the accepted symbols of the mystic's faith, can often rise to the surface.[27]

There are good reasons to distrust any religious visions—hallucinatory or imaginary—that are not solidly anchored in an overall religious context. Even to visions that illuminate, rather than deceive, St John of the Cross advises that we should not attach any importance. In all circumstances it remains difficult to distinguish the epiphenomena of an unconscious transformation from an authentic divine illumination. At best, sensory and imaginary visions or voices play a supporting role in the mystical development.

They may strengthen or concretise a mystical insight.[28]

However, with these expansions and enhancements come a new set of difficulties and temptations, which need careful and wise discernment. One of the greatest dangers to the seeker is the tendency to inflation and grandiosity. Unless there is ever more humility, surrender, letting go, detachment and disidentification from the spiritual experiences and ecstasies, this stage can be very destructive.

It is important that our intentions and motivations for the journey towards God have been thoroughly tested for their sincerity, through constant purification, so that essentially we do not want anything for ourselves. Our desire is for God alone, above and beyond anything He can give us or do for us.

The deeper we go on the spiritual path, the more subtle, invisible and powerful the tests and temptations can become. Our safety lies in remaining self-aware, humble, awestruck before the indescribable and boundless glory of God, and as detached and unidentified as possible by all the new insights and revelations that are being given by Him.

The highest form of mystical illumination is that dark contemplation which, often in an instant, transforms the soul and fills it with lasting insight. Here we are confronted with the kind of intellectual vision where even the cautious John of the Cross says no illusions can deceive the visionary. We are in the realm of what John calls "dark contemplation," dark because no distinct vision occurs.

There is nothing to be seen, smelled or heard. Purely, senseless, imaginationless illuminations of this nature have been called "intellectual" visions, yet they are neither visions nor "intellectual." Here the term stands for the purely mental, as opposed to the sensory or imaginary. It implies no kind of discursive understanding.

This transition to a more unitive state of consciousness, towards mystical union or the sacred marriage, involves nothing less than what the Christian mystics described as the "dark night of the spirit," or, in more modern language, dismemberment of the false self. This annihilation is at once the greatest grace and the most protracted agony on our spiritual journey.

St John of the Cross is the great expert on this stage. He speaks of the active and passive night of the spirit in the second book of the *Dark night of the Soul.* Teresa focuses on this stage of illumination in the fifth and sixth mansions of *The Interior Castle.*

St John analyses these deeper states of infused contemplation and refers to them as an inflowing of God into the soul. At this height of awareness, the mind's normal powers of cognition no longer function. In the *night* of the active powers of the mind, illumination means utter darkness. Teresa refers to the "ligature of the faculties" while God makes his presence felt "in the most secret region of the soul, that has but a slight knowledge of it."[29]

Union

Teresa described mystical union in the innermost mansion or chamber:

"In the spiritual marriage with our Lord. . .the soul always remains in its centre with its God. Union may be symbolized by two wax candles, the tips of which touch each other so closely that there is but one light: or again, the wick, the wax, and the light become one, but the one candle can again be separated from the other, and the two candles remain distinct; or the wick may be withdrawn from the wax.

Spiritual marriage is like rain falling from heaven into a river or stream, becoming one and the same liquid, so that the river and the rainwater cannot be divided. Or it resembles a streamlet flowing into the ocean, which cannot afterwards be disunited from it. This marriage may also be likened to a room into which a bright light enters through two windows—though divided when it enters; the light becomes one and the same." (Seventh Mansion, Chapter 2,5)[30]

This is the way of Christ's lovers, and represents, in its highest manifestations, the climax of Christian perfection and wholeness. It is seen in its fullness in the selfless charity and complete union of the saints. However, there is considerable variation between souls in this way, and, and even the saints, like the stars, differ from one another in Glory.[31]

In the illuminative way, the soul has learned to walk with Christ as Friend, and in process of time this has become more and more interior, until we are in continual communion with Christ within the depths of our heart and soul. This mysterious knowledge of "union with God" in the deepest part of the soul is now being made clearer and clearer, and an ever-steadier understanding of it is progressively deepening.

This knowledge, understanding and unitive state is nothing less that a new birth, or the second birth. It is the place where the Betrothed, or Brides of Christ are ready to meet their Heavenly Bridegroom, where the soul is beginning to be transfigured in God's Light and Love. The "old man/woman" has truly died, for the "new man/woman" to be raised up by the grace of God.

The pilgrim now knows and realizes that the lover, the soul, and Christ, the Beloved and His Love, which is all encompassing, are "not two," are not separate any longer, but are now conjoined, "two becoming one," united in marriage, are now of one being and essence, and nothing can ever separate them, in essence, again.

The external, transcendent Christ is not lost, but as we now dwell in continual interiorisation, Christ is known and worshipped as immanent within the soul itself, who is "clothed in the wedding garment of Light," where "the wick, the wax and the light become one" in the seventh dwelling place of our interior castle. There is habitual interior union with Him, and with the Holy Trinity through Him.

This knowing, experience, understanding is lived and breathed in every conceivable way and from every conceivable angle. There is the definite sense of a Unity of Being, which is like nothing that has gone before, as if all the small parts of life and creation have somehow been profoundly restored and reconnected into One Whole, through a power of Love which is at the same time, utterly transcendent and immanent.

In the illuminative way, the soul has become more recollected and has deliberately striven to become so. Now we are conscious of a fundamental habitual recollection, which, though not always conscious, is yet always there. We desire to possess God always, and never to depart from His presence; there are no bits of life that we want to keep for ourselves, for we live our whole life in God's sight.[32]

The most defining characteristic of sacred marriage are not raptures, visions, or any supernatural phenomena, but a steady possession of awareness of God's Love and His Light which is beginning to radiate from, and transfigure, the centre of our being, wherever "I" am and in whatever "I" may be doing, as a stable indwelling of the presence of God.

Once this highest mystical awareness has been reached, the distinction between ordinary states of consciousness and transitory, mystical states, so clear in the earlier dwelling places, recedes without vanishing completely. There can still occur flashes of special illumination, but the general condition has become "illuminated."[33] Even while occupying ourselves with all demands and expectations that the world makes on, we retain the persistent awareness of God's presence.

Our consciousness has become transformed and transfigured so as to dwell in the constant awareness of His Presence, in the midst of ordinary life, work and service, neither distracting from the other. Both John and Teresa lived their later years in this state of union and became more and more efficient as their work became infused with a mystical inspiration. Because of the permanent character of the highest state of contemplation, Teresa and other saints and mystics refer to it as a "marriage," that is, a state of being, rather than a singular experience.[34]

In the eleventh century, one of the most famous mystical theologians of the Orthodox tradition, St Simeon the new Theologian, wrote about mystical union as being clothed in the wedding garment of the Light of Christ:

> *"Blessed are those who are clothed in light,*
> *For they are wearing the wedding garment,*
> *Their hands and feet shall not be bound,*
> *Nor shall they be thrown into everlasting fire.*
>
> *Blessed are those who have kindled the light*
> *In their hearts, who keep it unquenched,*
> *For as they joyfully depart from this life,*
> *They will meet the bridegroom, torch in hand,*
> *As he leads them into the bridal chamber.*
>
> *Blessed are those who have approached the divine light,*
> *Who have entered it and been absorbed by it,*
> *Mingled in its brightness, sin has no more power,*
> *They will weep bitter tears no more.*
>
> *Blessed is the monk, offering his prayers to God,*
> *Who sees Him, and is seen near to Him,*
> *Who feels himself out of time and space,*
> *For he is in God alone, knowing not*
> *If he is in or out of the body;*
> *He hears ineffable words, not to be spoken;*

He sees what no eye has seen or ear heard,
Nor has it entered the heart of man.

Blessed is he who has seen the Light of the world
Formed in himself, for he has conceived Christ
Within himself; he will be counted as his mother,
As Christ, in Whom there is no lie, has said."[35]

The purpose of the contemplative journey, and the blessings of His wedding gifts in the bridal chamber, is certainly not for our own personal use. Very much on the contrary, *the water is for the flowers*, and the whole purpose of our contemplative journey is to be able us to go back to the world around us, able to engage in the struggle of God's creation, confident that in our innermost selves we are united with Christ, our Lord, in his bridal chamber.[36]

There is the abandonment of our will to the will of God, the purified yearning that the will of God be done in all things, as Teresa emphases so strongly in the latter mansions. There is a fundamental simplification in life and prayer; the soul becomes unable to practise any virtue separately, for that virtue is simply a manifestation of charity, while in prayer we are not really capable of making forced acts of the virtues because they all become acts of love.

We are able to express the constant deepening of our love and charity to others and the world. The virtues are now no longer actively sought and practised; we have entered upon the intuitive possession of the gifts of the Spirit, and willing to love God in all things, the gifts find expression in action, and everything is seen and done in God.

So, in these final stages of the contemplative journey, we are able to rest in the presence of God and simultaneously be engaged in the activities and works of loving action, charity and service to our neighbour. Even more wonderfully, we are able to deepen our activities in new ways now that our heart and mind are completely centred in God. The constant blessings of resting and being in divine union overflows and penetrates other's lives, through the union of our being and action.

Endnotes

[1] F. Houdek, *Guided by the Spirit: A Jesuit Perspective on Spiritual Direction*, p. 37.

[2] Ibid., pp. 78-88.

[3] L. Dupre, *The Deeper Life: An Introduction to Christian Mysticism*, p. 69.

[4] W. James, *Varieties of Religious Experience*.

[5] B. Griffiths, *The Golden String*, p. 11.

[6] E. Underhill, *Mysticism: the Nature and Development of Spiritual Consciousness*, p. 202.

[7] F.P. Harton, *The Elements of the Spiritual Life: A Study in Ascetical Theology*, p. 307.

[8] E. Underhill, *Mysticism: the Nature and Development of Spiritual Consciousness*, p. 220.

[9] K. Kavanaugh & O. Rodriguez, *The Collected Works of St John of the Cross*.

[10] L. Dupre, *The Deeper Life: An Introduction to Christian Mysticism*, p. 71.

[11] F.P. Harton, *The Elements of the Spiritual Life: A Study in Ascetical Theology*, p. 309.

[12] E. Underhill, *Mysticism: the Nature and Development of Spiritual Consciousness*, p. 244.

[13] L. Dupre, *The Deeper Life: An Introduction to Christian Mysticism*, p. 77.

[14] E. Underhill, *Mysticism: the Nature and Development of Spiritual Consciousness*, p. 258.

[15] F.P. Harton, *The Elements of the Spiritual Life: A Study in Ascetical Theology*, p. 318.

[16] L. Dupre, *The Deeper Life: An Introduction to Christian Mysticism*, p. 76.

[17] F.P Harton, *The Elements of the Spiritual Life: A Study in Ascetical Theology*, p. 321.

[18] R. Amis, *A Different Christianity*, pp. 285-294.

[19] Ibid., p. 293.

[20] E. Underhill, *Mysticism: the Nature and Development of Spiritual Consciousness*, p. 249.

[21] O. Clement, *The Roots of the Christian Mysticism*, p. 235.

[22] Ibid., p. 255.

[23] F.P Harton, *The Elements of the Spiritual Life: A Study in Ascetical Theology*, p. 315.

[24] Ibid., p. 316.

[25] L. Dupre, *The Deeper Life: An Introduction to Christian Mysticism*, p. 77.

[26] Ibid., p. 78.

[27] Ibid., p. 78.

[28] Ibid., p. 79.

[29] Ibid., p. 82.

[30] St Teresa of Avila, *The Interior Castle*, p. 176.

[31] F.P. Harton, *The Elements of the Spiritual Life: A Study in Ascetical Theology*, p. 323.

[32] Ibid., p. 327. See also *The Mystical Space of Carmel: A Commentary on the Carmelite Rule*, by Kees Waaijman.

[33] L. Dupre, *The Deeper Life: An Introduction to Christian Mysticism*, p. 84.

[34] Ibid.

[35] Bishop of Nafpaktos Hierotheos, *A Night in the Desert of the Holy Mountain*, p. 137.

[36] P. Tyler, *The Way of Ecstasy*, p. 123.

Chapter 12

THE THIRD SPIRITUAL ALPHABET, GUIDE OF ST TERESA: A LEARNING HIDDEN DEEP IN THE HEART

A movement of renewal

The flowering of the Christian contemplative tradition in the fifteenth and sixteenth centuries, which flowed so powerfully and creatively through the lives and writings of St Teresa of Avila and St John of the Cross, was part of a general movement of religious reform and renewal throughout Europe. From the mid-fifteenth century in Spain, there had been a great flowering of Franciscan mystical writing, and a form of prayer entitled *recogimiento*, or "recollection," was being practised by groups of Franciscans across Spain from at least 1480. These groups of the reform movement of *recogimiento* had certain central characteristics in common, which were: the universal call to Christian perfection; the affirmation of external works, rites and ceremonies; the importance of interiority; the following of Christ in his humanity and divinity; the interrelatedness of the active and contemplative life (and the relative importance of the latter); annihilation and quietude; the importance of *consolaciónes* and *gustos* ("spiritual delights"); the role of love; the role of the will; love derived from contact with God, without prior study; and a focus on prayer of the heart.[1]

No other guide

One of the major texts of this new religious movement of renewal was Francisco de Osuna's *Third Spiritual Alphabet*, which enjoyed great popularity in Spain at the time and was published in several editions.[2] This work describes in detail the complex psychological processes of the prayer of recollection and offers advice and signs of progress along the way. His language is warm and simple, using original and often charming symbols from ordinary life. Throughout the golden years of the Spanish Renaissance, his writings were circulated and treasured by countless spiritual seekers—most famously, by the young Teresa of Avila.

Teresa spoke clearly of her reliance on the *Third Spiritual Alphabet* as a guide for the practice of prayer from an early stage of her life as a religious. She was given the book to read by an uncle sympathetic to her need; it was a timely gift, and Teresa spoke of how she began to follow the path of the prayer of recollection. She describes Osuna as her "master" in prayer for twenty years, in this passage from her *Life*:

> "*I was very happy with this book and resolved to follow that path [the prayer of recollection] with all my strength. Since the Lord had already given me the gift of tears and I enjoyed reading, I began to take time out for solitude, to confess frequently, and to follow that path, taking the book for my master. For during the twenty years after this period of which I am speaking, I did not find a master, I mean a confessor, who understood me, even though I looked for one.*"[3]

Osuna was her master in prayer, speaking to her at a critical period of her spiritual formation through his *Third Spiritual Alphabet*. This was also her guide through the intensities of her religious experience and, at a later stage, a resource for her when teaching others the practice of recollection.

Who was Francisco de Osuna?

The author of this important work was born in about 1492 to a family serving under the powerful patronage of the counts of Ureña, and named after his birthplace, the town of Osuna in the province of Seville in southern Spain. As an Observant Franciscan, he belonged to the main branch of the Order and lived a communal life dedicated to prayer and meditation; he was passionate about the practice of poverty and charity. Osuna was a prolific writer on prayer, and he formulated maxims as memorable and pithy guides for meditation which he arranged alphabetically. His six *Spiritual Alphabets*—of which the famous one, discussed here, is the third—created the structure for his series of Treatises within them; and each *Alphabet* follows a different spiritual theme, such as: the Passion; prayer and ascetical practices; and, most notably, the practice of recollection.

Osuna's spirituality was eclectic, combining elements of Franciscan spirituality, such as the affective way of the heart, with the Augustinian philosophy of love. The Augustinian way stresses that oneness between God and humanity is the essential starting point for the spiritual life, and that this communion or friendship is possible for everyone. In his synthesis, Osuna saw mystical theology and prayer as a harmony of love and understanding, of the will and the intellect. He anticipated Carmelite teaching with its emphasis on going beyond dependence on sensory awareness, and the inner work of emptying the heart so as to become free from limiting compulsions and over-attachment.

Osuna saw the practice of recollection as a participation in the way of prayer exercised and taught by Jesus. He also acknowledges the other forms of spiritual exercises common in his time, including penance, meditations on the Passion, acts of mercy, fasting, and pilgrimages. However, he then goes on to say: "if you wish to advance further and imitate loftier things, our letter advises you to frequent recollection and become an expert in it, thus emulating Our Lord, who used to go out into the desert where, apart and recollected, he could more secretly and spiritually pray in concealment to his and our heavenly Father."[4]

A distinctive approach

The movement of *recogimiento*, or recollection, placed the heart and *oración afectiva* ("affective prayer") at the centre of its concerns, as it did also the concept of "unknowing," and the importance of the body—which should not be seen as divorced from the soul, as had been the case with the suspect spiritual movement of the *alumbrados*. The prayer of recollection is primarily a way of *contemplativa afectiva* centred on love, and which may reach a degree where the understanding, for a while, ceases to function altogether—a contemplation where there is no thinking of anything (*no pensar nada*).

However, outside these particular times of special grace—when God unites the soul with himself, and the understanding sleeps—the person must continue to exercise the understanding. This brings us to the distinctive position of the *Third Spiritual Alphabet*. Osuna lived and wrote at the time of the *alumbrados* controversy: a movement of pseudo-mystics whose spiritual approach was quietist and who practised "abandon" (*dejamiento*). By contrast, "recollection" (*recogimiento*) was practised by the opposing school—which is the position held by Osuna. This spiritual controversy, then, is the specific context in which the *Third*

Spiritual Alphabet—and its central teaching on recollection—can be situated.

In this work, Osuna uses many symbols and images from Scripture and everyday life, in an intentional way, to open and awaken our attention to our experience of prayer. Worthy of note— and here, he is a true precursor of Teresa—is his advice never to lose sight of the Sacred Humanity of Christ. Osuna's distinctive approach lies in the way he uses pithy wisdom sayings as the focus for each individual Treatise within the work, which provides the structure of the whole *Alphabet*. Each saying is a distillation of a complex truth, and in each of the twenty-three Treatises[5] he meditates on the meaning of the saying in question—much of the time in the spirit of *lectio divina*.

"Walking together"

In the First Treatise, Osuna writes about the psychology and experience of our fragmented self, and the constant need for healing; and he introduces his first wise saying: "Which Speaks of the Constant Vigilance We Need to Strive [for] in Purity of Spirit to Attain to God, Saying: May the Person and Spirit Always Walk Together."[6] Right from the start, then, he gives us the foundation principle for recollection, which is the harmony that comes from our body, mind and spirit "walking together"—a powerful symbol that speaks of the possibility of inner harmony of the whole person who is seeking to "attain to" or know God.

Two meditations are offered on what hinders, and what helps, this harmonious walking (or working) together of the capacities and potentialities of the sensual nature and those of the spiritual mind: "wherever you go carry your mind along, for no one should go divided unto himself. Do not allow the body to travel one path, the heart another."[7] Osuna also has important psychological and spiritual reflections on the importance of harmonising the powers of our mind and our emotional energies, of harmonising the powers of body and mind in prayer, and of maintaining harmony in our conscience.

"Taste and see"

Central to Osuna's affective, mystical, theology in the *Third Spiritual Alphabet* is the notion of "taste" of God, rather than knowledge. In many passages he plays on the word *saber* ("know") and *sabor* ("taste"), much as Teresa does in her writings. In Osuna's words, "mystical theology" is a *sabroso saber*—literally, a "tasty knowledge."[8] In the Sixth Treatise, he expands on this theme in a wonderful discourse about the difference between speculative theology and mystical theology. For Osuna, *theologia speculativa* "has recourse to reasoning, argumentation, discourse, and probability, as do other sciences." And he continues: "It is called scholastic theology, which means it is of learned people, and if someone wishes to excel in it, he needs the learning tools of any science: a good mind, continual exercise, books, attentiveness, and a learned teacher to study under."[9]

A hidden theology

The other theology, *theologia mystica*, he says, differs from other sciences or learning as it is a "hidden" (*escondida*) theology that is totally unlike any other branch of learning: "[mystical theology] pertains to the will, which is enamoured with the highest good, and this is the theology of God's just lovers. . .this theology will be perfected by adding love and it will no longer remain hidden, but be manifest to all, from the youngest to the oldest."[10] *Theologia mystica* is pursued not through learning, books and teachers, and Osuna emphasises that it is not possible to "teach" this theology: "I do not presume to teach it in the alphabet, nor can any mortal do so, for Christ reserves to himself the ministry of secretly teaching the hearts where that theology lives hidden like a divine science."[11]

In the depths of the heart

Osuna calls the tradition of *theologia mystica* the path or tradition of *wisdom*—because,, he writes, "it is delectable knowing. Such wisdom, according to Saint Paul, is found only among the perfect, for the imperfect are not given to eat of such sublime teaching. It is called wisdom because it allows us to know how God tastes, and the wise man says of it when he speaks of God: 'He gave wisdom to those who worked mercifully.'"[12] Osuna also calls it the art of love: "because only through love is it realised,. . . and also because Christ, the God of love, teaches it to those with a loving heart."[13] He describes it, too, as the path of *profundity* —"with respect to the depth and darkness of the devotion, for it originates in the depths of man's heart, which are dark because human understanding has been deprived of light. Seeing the heart plunged into shadows, the spirit of God comes over the heart on the waters of desire to proclaim his divine light."[14]

The "lady of learning"

Osuna writes that the whole subject of his *Third Spiritual Alphabet* is a continuation of the ancient lineage of Christian *theologia mystica*, the "tasty knowledge" of God—"because the good teacher Jesus imparts it in the secret hiding place of the heart." And he continues: "As our principal teacher, [Jesus] kept for himself this principal doctrine, for among all disciplines theology is the queen and lady of learning."[15] Thus, the tradition of *theologia mystica* essentially describes knowledge of God that is imparted "in the secret hiding place of the heart" and is obscure to the human mind or intellect. As we can see from this, and as will become clear in the next article, Osuna's *Third Spiritual Alphabet* had a powerful and decisive effect on St Teresa—she who is herself a "lady of learning" in the secret hiding place of the heart.

Endnotes

1 See the discussion in P. Tyler, *The Return to the Mystical: Ludwig Wittgenstein, Teresa of Avila and the Christian Mystical Tradition*, p. 109.

2 M. E. Giles, *Francisco de Osuna -The Third Spiritual Alphabet*.

3 K. Kavanaugh & O. Rodriguez, (trans), *Teresa of Avila: The Book of Her Life*, in *The Collected Works of St Teresa of Avila*, pp. 66-67.

4 M. E. Giles, *Francisco De Osuna: The Third Spiritual Alphabet*, Chapter 6:1, p. 159.

5 Ibid., see Introduction, pp. 1-34.

6 Ibid., p. 45.

7 Ibid., Chapter 1:2, p. 50.

8 See P. Tyler, *Teresa of Avila: Doctor of the Soul*, p. 49.

9 M. E. Giles, *Francisco De Osuna: The Third Spiritual Alphabet*, Chapter 6:2, p. 162.

10 Ibid.

11 Ibid., Chapter 6:2, p. 161.

12 Ibid., Chapter 6:2, p. 164.

13 Ibid.

14 Ibid., Chapter 6:2, p. 165.

15 Ibid., Chapter 6:2, p. 161.

Chapter 13

THE THIRD SPIRITUAL ALPHABET, GUIDE OF ST TERESA: EXPLORING THE PATH OF RECOLLECTION

Subtle spiritual movements

In the previous article, I introduced the *Third Spiritual Alphabet* of Francisco de Osuna—a work which the young Teresa, at the beginning of her religious life, took as her guide. As previously mentioned, when she came to write her autobiography, she looked back on the impact his book had had on her, and one theme stood out for her in particular, as she writes in her *Life*:

> "*I was very happy with this book and resolved to follow that path [the prayer of recollection] with all my strength. . .I began". . .to follow that path, taking the book for my master.*"[1]

Teresa herself would be a great teacher of the prayer of recollection, so the impact on her of the *Third Spiritual Alphabet*, in her formative years, cannot be underestimated. Among the sections (called "Treatises") in that work, the sixth is devoted in a special way to the prayer of recollection, which will be the main theme of the current article.

In this Sixth Treatise of his work, Osuna outlines ten interrelated spiritual movements in the heart—or ten interior acts of prayer—which it is possible to practise, through the prayer of recollection, in order to "train yourself,"[2] as he expresses it. His aim was to bring greater clarity to how we can direct our awareness and intention in the subtle spiritual movements which are already going on within us: movements, we shall see, that may be described in such ways as a "reconciling," a "gathering together" or a "collecting what is dispersed."[3] Osuna gives us a general overview or blueprint of the whole inner movement of transformation, which may help us recognise where we are and what may be changing within us.

Recognising presence and communion in the heart

The first of these essential interior movements is that of gathering together, in the sense of a relationship of reconciliation between people. He writes that recollection "gathers together those who practise it and, by erasing all dissension and discord, makes them of one heart and love."[4] The prayer of recollection is not conducted in isolation: primarily, it is a shared experience. Spiritual recognition is not based on the idea of external criteria of belonging, but is experienced as something inward, intensely visceral and strengthening—as a profound stirring, a joyful astonishment, and a sense of coming home.

Bringing awareness inwards to let go of concerns

The second movement of recollection is a "drawing in" of our awareness, away from an exterior orientation. When we are constantly over-preoccupied with outer roles and concerns, the soul can be very vulnerable. In this second movement, then, the exterior person is now being gathered within himself or herself. This turning inwards is not an avoidance of the world, but is about changing the way in which we engage with outer roles and responsibilities. It is about creating a free and realistic relationship with the world, and drawing nourishment from spiritual resources within us.

Reconciling body and mind

The third movement is to reconcile sensuality and reason. In this movement the sensual nature, "which previously had run about in a disorderly and unsubmissive way," is given "welcome" and placed "under the jurisdiction of reason"[5]—an essential working together of body and mind towards recollection of the whole person. Here, Osuna offers the Old Testament story of the angel's advice to Hagar to be reconciled with her former mistress, Sarah, as a symbol of this restored relationship (cf. Genesis 16:9).

Anchoring the mind in the heart

The fourth movement of recollection is one that inclines us towards solitude, and away from many outer stimulations and distracting relationships. We find ourselves wanting to "retire from the traffic of people and noisy places to dwell in more secluded regions and to go out only now and then."[6] We find we have an increasing desire to go back to that single-minded, undivided, simple attention in silence. Osuna offers an image to convey the eagerness of this return: the urgency of an eel that wants to escape from "the fisherman's hands so it can wriggle back into the water."[7]

Quietening sense to guard the heart

The fifth movement of recollection quietens or calms the senses. What is being noticed here is a change in appetite: "Recollected people also look away promptly and humble their eyes, taking no pleasure in seeing anything, for their only wish is to see God with their hearts."[8] What was previously attractive and stimulating now loses appeal and, in fact, may seem wearisome. This is a deepening of detachment: not only detachment from what occupies our hearts and minds, but a change in the very patterns of knowing and wanting. The structured practice of silent prayer offers an effective way of training us to do this. In silence, we move beyond our thoughts to rest within spiritual presence in our heart.

Tempering and redirecting physical energies

In the sixth movement of recollection, our physical energies are gathered into spiritual life. What Osuna describes is a gathering in of the energies of the body, so that they become "calmed, tempered, corrected."[9] The powerful energies of instincts—sexual, aggressive and protective—are being gradually gathered up and harnessed in the work of recollection.

Emptying the heart to receive virtues

In the seventh movement, there is a gathering up of the strength of the virtues in those who "give themselves over to the devotion [of recollection]"[10]; this holds all the meaning of self-emptying surrendering to the presence of God in the heart. To the extent that emptying is an art, Osuna uses the phrase "self-forgetting" or "pouring out the self" to describe it. The virtues and graces that fill the soul in emptiness can only be received, and he eloquently describes the manner of receiving: to receive without analysing, and without giving into fear. We are, in fact, training ourselves in the art of radical gratitude, which is the art of giving wholehearted loving attention to what is received—sinking our awareness in it, relishing it, feeding it.

Surrendering and finding spiritual identity

Recollection is a movement of fulfilling the true spiritual identity of the self. The devotion of recollection is to "gather together man's senses in his heart's interior where the glory of the king's daughter [our soul]" is found.[11] The radical surrender of our need to know God through the senses, and our need to be in control of prayer, sinks us into the darkness of the interior of the heart, which is creative and not destructive. Here, discussing the eighth movement of recollection, Osuna uses the image of a hedgehog: *"Compare the recollected person with the hedgehog who contracts his body and retreats into himself without concern for anything outside. Like a very heavy stone concealing the hedgehog, this devotion. . .is refuge for the recollected person who has everything he needs within and does not think ill of those without who may inflict harm on him."*[12] The art and exercise of recollection is living, over time, within the tension of deep paradoxes— experiencing simultaneously the abyss of the heart's interior, and the safe grounding of the "hedgehog"; or, to express it another way, experiencing both the majesty of the soul and its utter hedgehog-like humility.

Surrendering and transforming the powers of the soul

The ninth moment of recollection transforms the powers of the soul in the heart: namely the will, the intellect and the memory. Here, these inner faculties are transfigured "with the soul's highest part where the image of God is imprinted"[13] and operate in a way that transcends their usual mode of functioning. This is traditionally called their "perfection" or "completion." And it is what Osuna also calls "the spirit of the just, which spirit seeks God in groaning"[14]—an inarticulate movement of the will towards God.

Joining God in the soul and the soul in God

Recollection is complete in the dynamic centre of union in the heart which unites "God with the soul and the soul with God."[15] Here, in the tenth movement of recollection, the whole personality is illuminated and radiates love and truth from this centre outwards, in the way that transparent crystal refracts light. From this dynamic centre, the wholly recollected person participates fully in the powerful acts of God within: the "mighty deeds"[16] of transformation that take place in the soul.

Radical gratitude – the essential attitude for healing

In the discussion, above, of the seventh movement of recollection, mention was made of gratitude. This is an important aspect of recollection and deserves to be looked at here. In the Second Treatise of his work, Osuna introduces another wise, pithy saying: "Let All Your Works Abound in Fervent Thanks."[17] He offers helpful reflections on the necessity for, and powerful healing power of, gratitude; and he emphasises, drawing on St Gregory, that "the greater the gifts, the greater our debt, and the more we need to have a carefully tallied receipt. What can benefit us most with respect to this is gratitude, so let us begin the journey to repay little by little all we owe to the One who has provided us every good thing, and in a single act of thanks our accomplishment will be twofold: to repay our debt and make ourselves worthy of greater gifts."[18]

The spiritual wisdom, here, is that the greater the gifts we have received, the greater must be our gratitude, thankfulness and obligation to share with others all that we have received—to give something back. From the perspective of gratitude, everything we have received is gifts of grace and goodness—given by God "in trust," so to speak, as potentialities and possibilities. The transformative wisdom Osuna is highlighting is that the growth of radical gratitude in our lives can be a key to our spiritual growth, and that it guides, helps and brings to birth what would otherwise remain unformed and unborn in life. Whatever this spark of consciousness is at the heart of our being, radical gratitude, then, is the key to bringing it to birth, form and fullness in our lives.

St Teresa – reader of the *Third Spiritual Alphabet*

In one of the few references, in *The Interior Castle*, to the author of the *Third Spiritual Alphabet*, Teresa refers to the importance of *recogimiento*, or "recollection," and the tradition of *theologia mystica*:

> "*I don't know in what way or how [those who are recollected deep within] heard their shepherd's whistle. It wasn't through the ears because nothing is heard. But one noticeably senses a gentle drawing inward, as anyone who goes through this will observe, for I don't know how to make it clearer. It seems to me I have read where it was compared to a hedgehog curling up or a turtle drawing into its shell." (The one who wrote this example [Osuna] must have understood the experience well.)*[19]

We can begin to understand why Osuna's writings, and the *recogimiento* movement, which placed the heart and affective prayer at the centre of its concerns, would have appealed so strongly to the young Teresa. As we have said, Osuna explores, in many passages throughout the book, *sabroso saber*—literally, the "tasty knowledge" of God—much as Teresa explores and develops it in her own writings. He also develops his notion of "spiritual delights" (from the Spanish *gustos*), or the "taste" or "delight" of God, which is a key term later used extensively by Teresa. Thus, knowledge of God, for Osuna, is derived not from knowing (*saber*) but from taste (*sabor*), in particular from tasting the *gustos espiratuales*, the "spiritual delights."

Teresa emphasises the importance of spiritual delights in the fourth mansion of *The Interior Castle*, which is understood as the mansion of "transformation and transition"[20]—where, by metaphor, disorientation and simple language, she demonstrates her transformative strategies.[21] Here, she differentiates between consolations and spiritual delights. Consolations are experiences of joy, peace, satisfaction, happiness, similar to those experienced in ordinary, everyday life, which are naturally acquired experiences and sensations evolving from prayer, meditation, leading a God-centred life, and doing good works for others. Spiritual delights are "infused mystical gifts" that come directly from God, and human nature or events cannot initiate them. Spiritual delights can only be present when God is acting on the individual in a special and blessed way—they belong to infused, supernatural, mystical prayer.

Water from the source

Teresa shows us the effects of "spiritual delights" through helpful symbols and metaphors in her text. She finds it helpful to speak in this connection of "expansion": "the dilation begun by the celestial waters in the depth of our being. . .appear to dilate and enlarge us internally, and benefit us in an inexplicable manner, nor does even the soul itself understand what it receives."[22] She also refers to this in terms of a beautiful fragrance: "It is conscious of what may be described as a certain fragrance, as if within its inmost depths were a brazier sprinkled with sweet perfumes."[23]

To describe and understand the effect of receiving "spiritual delights" in prayer, Teresa famously uses the symbol of two different water fountains filling a basin, each of these fountains being supplied with water from a source. The first type of water basin is analogous to active, discursive prayer where a lot of effort is required in getting the waters to the fountain from a distant source; this corresponds, Teresa says, to the consolations we receive in prayer through our own efforts of meditation, for example.

But the other basin is quite different, where the water flowing into this fountain comes from a source directly below the basin: direct from God himself, dwelling within our heart. Teresa tells us that this is analogous to infused, or supernatural, prayer—where no energy, labour or technology is used to bring the water to the fountain. And she describes it in this way:

> "*The other fountain, like divine consolations, receives the water from the source itself, which signifies God; as usual, when His Majesty wills to bestow on us any supernatural favours, we experience the greatest peace, calm and sweetness in the inmost depths of our being; I know neither where, nor how. This joy is not, like earthly happiness, at once felt by the heart; after gradually filling to the brim, the delight overflows throughout all the mansions and faculties, until at last it reaches the body. Therefore, I say it arises from God and ends in ourselves, for whoever experiences it will find the whole physical part of our nature shares in the delight and sweetness.*"[24]

Endnotes

[1] K. Kavanaugh & O. Rodriguez, (trans), *Teresa of Avila: The Book of Her Life, in The Collected Works of St Teresa of Avila*, p. 67.

[2] M. E. Giles & K. Kavanaugh, *Francisco De Osuna: The Third Spiritual Alphabet*, Chapter 6:1, p. 158.

[3] Ibid., Chapter 6:3, pp. 165-170.

[4] Ibid., p. 170.

[5] Ibid., Chapter 6:4, p. 171.

[6] Ibid.

[7] Ibid.

[8] Ibid.

[9] Ibid., p. 172.

[10] Ibid.

[11] Ibid p. 173.

[12] Ibid.

[13] Ibid.

[14] Ibid.

[15] Ibid.

[16] Ibid., p. 174.

[17] Ibid., p. 68.

[18] Ibid., Chapter 2:1, p. 69.

[19] St Teresa of Avila, *The Interior Castle*, IV:3.

[20] J. McLean, *Towards Mystical Union*, p. 201.

[21] P. Tyler, *Teresa of Avila: Doctor of the Soul*, p. 146.

[22] St Teresa of Avila, *The Interior Castle*, p. 54.

[23] Ibid.

[24] Ibid., p. 53.

Chapter 14

INTRODUCING THE MYSTICAL TEXT
"THE INTERIOR CASTLE"

Teresa wrote *The Interior Castle* in 1577, five years before she died. It was to become one of the best-known treatises of Christian contemplative literature and is the product of mature reflection on her journey towards God, and of a lifetime of observing and directing her spiritual daughters—the nuns of Carmel. In this work, she speaks with a degree of assurance and maturity not found in her other writings. After the Inquisition had seized her autobiography, her confessor suggested that she "write a fresh book, and expound the teaching in a general way, without saying to whom the things that you describe have happened."

Teresa describes a vision in which she saw the soul as *"resembling a castle, formed of a single diamond or very transparent crystal, and containing many rooms, just as in heaven there are many mansions."*[1] The text is essentially a description of and guide to spiritual change, progress, surrender and transformation throughout seven mansions, which represent three main stages in the life of interiorisation and prayer.

In the first three mansions, she tells of what the soul can do to move towards the inner mansions where God dwells. The fourth mansion is the transitional stage where the soul begins to undergo interior transformation, and God begins to take over. The most interior mansions are where Teresa describes God as increasingly purifying the soul towards His Likeness, leading to a state of spiritual marriage in the seventh, and innermost, mansion.

Teresa's experience and expression of spirituality, her description of the stages of the spiritual life and, indeed, many of her contemplative writings are suffused with the language of symbols and imagery. In the text, she says that certain experiences and descriptions of the important stages in the spiritual life could only be expressed in image, metaphor or allegory.

Her symbolism is a living, dynamic mix of a variety of images that arose within her in response to her own direct spiritual progress and surrender to God. For her, the soul was, at different times, a garden, a tree, a castle, a butterfly—in addition to a whole range of other imagery throughout the text e.g. water, fountains.

The Seven Mansions

In *The Interior Castle*, St Teresa maps out the contemplative path towards union with God. Much preliminary preparation must occur before the seeker is ready to fully surrender to the Love and the will of God for their life.

In the initial stages, the journey entails the growth and nurturing of a sense of soul, or the Self in the modern Jungian sense. This sense of individuation is called the "journey towards God." Often tremendous pain and suffering over a long period of time accompany the disintegration of our false, outmoded conditioning as we move towards the innermost dwelling places and our surrender to the Love and Light of God.

The purpose of the psychological journey is to bring our soul to a place of relative balance in ordinary life. This place lies just outside an unknown interior castle inside which another journey can begin. All mystical tradition speaks about that "other journey," the "journey in God" that begins at the place of the soul. It is as if we arrive at the outer court of a magnificent castle.

The interior castle symbolises our soul. Teresa gives an account of the mystical journey of the soul through each of the mansions until the centremost mansion is surrendered to, where, she tells us, *"the most secret things pass between God and the soul. In the seventh and innermost mansion is the King of Glory in the greatest splendour, illumining and beautifying all the mansions."*[2]

As previously mentioned, in the first mansion, she describes the castle as *"containing many mansions, some above, others below, others at each side, and in the centre and midst of them all is the chiefest mansion where the most secret things pass between God and the soul."*[3] She says that each mansion is inside the other—*"Think of a palmito, (which is a tree indigenous to that area of Spain) which has many outer rinds surrounding the savoury pith within, all of which must be taken away before the centre can be eaten."*[4]

It is important to emphasise that Teresa is not advocating a strictly hierarchical model of different stages of the spiritual life. The scheme of the three ways, or stages, of progress in the spiritual life—purification, illumination and union—dates back to the influential writings of the fifth century monk Pseudo Denys the Areopagite, author of *Divine Names, Mystical Theology and Celestial Hierarchy.*

Two medieval theologians, St Bonaventure and Hugh of Balma, took up the Dionysian triad and wrote famous mystical treatises on the interior life. Each took opposing views as to whether the stages are primarily hierarchical or are mainly different ways to access God.[5]

Bonaventure wrote the mystical treatise *On the Three Ways* in the thirteenth century. He saw the three stages as different types of contemplative exercises to be put into practice as ways of access to the experience of God:

> *"There are three forms of exercise in these three ways: meditation (with reading), prayer and contemplation. In each one of these three forms of prayer, the soul is purified, illumined and perfected."*[6]

However, Hugh of Balma, writing in *Theologia Mystica* in the second half of the thirteenth century, conceived of the three ways as successive stages of the spiritual life, where each stage is consolidated before moving on to the next:

> *"Three ways must be followed if a person is to possess this excellent wisdom; the first cleanses the heart, the second enlightens it, and the third unites it with God."*[7]

Teresa's perspective was certainly a blend of these views of the mystical life, and she guided her "daughters of Carmel" with particular discernment, according to the different dispositions and needs of the individuals in her spiritual care. Doubtless she would have been fully conversant with differing perspectives, having had John of the Cross and Peter of Alcantara to guide her, two of the greatest mystical saints and ascetics of the era.

For Teresa, God is the Beloved—the Spouse within the innermost chamber of the heart. The contemplative journey inward is the journey to a place where God's Love fuses, melts, and dissolves into the life of the soul. She is also very careful to describe this castle as having an abundance of rooms. She does not want us to be deceived and think that we have encountered the Love and Presence of God when we have not.

Outside the castle are those who feel no attraction to God or the spiritual life, who are entirely caught up in the life of physical ambition, pursuit and gratification. She says that the first dwelling place represents the awakening of our spiritual life through devotion and the longing for God, and that prayer, meditation and reflection are the gateways into this castle.

In these early stages of the spiritual life, Teresa counsels perseverance, humility and self knowledge in equal measure, the spiritual task here being how to learn to *"enter itself."* Knowing ourselves, in this context, is about being able to be increasingly familiar with, and accepting of, our own fallibility, our needs, vulnerabilities, our blocks, pain, limitations, and ultimately our complete dependence on God.

She discusses the difficulties in turning away from worldly appearances and outward life towards the spiritual life and a relationship to God. It begins the loosening of thousands of attachments and identifications—who we think we are; our image of ourselves; our perceived status; our need to achieve and be seen in a particular way, in whatever form that may take.

In order to penetrate more deeply into our interior castle, she advises us to examine traps of *"possessions, honour or business affairs, and give up unnecessary things, each one in conformity with their state in life."*[8] She emphasises that the issue is not about any particular type of worldly action, but against those that stand between us and the love of God and neighbour.

She advises that it is essential to keep close to spiritual teachers and mentors in the outer mansions. The soul is not strong enough to defend herself alone where she needs protection, guidance, and the nurturing of hope and faith in God. Teresa constantly emphasises the importance of humility, which, of course, is the antidote to inflation, grandiosity, pride, arrogance and egoism.

In the second dwelling place, Teresa concentrates on the role of prayer as the doorway into our interior castle, and on the importance of perseverance. She says that God reaches us here mainly through objective means, such as literature, sermons and inspiring friendships. It is the beginning of the painful and arduous process of interior spiritual transformation in God.

She warns that we will feel uncomfortable and vulnerable in this dangerous dwelling place. We can be making great efforts to turn around towards God, and may be beginning to taste moments of God's Presence, but the longing for God and the sense of exile and separation from Him can begin to feel much more acute and painful.

She seems to be referring to the teasing and perilous state of the inner world, of the transparent walls in the castle, where we can see the deceptively visible centre but do not know how to reach it: where it is impossible to orientate ourselves without spiritual guidance and discernment.

Teresa says that here the soul is actually in less danger than in the first mansion, as there is a growing understanding of our progress in our journey towards, and in, God, and we can increasingly expect to penetrate more deeply into our interior castle. We suffer more at this second dwelling place simply because we have fewer defences. The more our soul is turning towards Him and reaching out to the Divine Spouse, the more He is reaching out and eagerly beckoning us towards Him.

She writes about the cacophony of temptations, distractions and conflicts that can occur when our spiritual life deepens. In this place, we are less able to deceive ourselves. We become more aware of our evasions and self-delusions and our interior and exterior conflicts can seem, paradoxically, to intensify.

It is important to understand that the increased conflict is a sign of increasing clarity of understanding. As we see more of what our peace and wholeness *could be*, we sense and see more plainly our own lack of it. A fuller consciousness begins to dawn of what our efforts can and, more importantly, cannot achieve. The heart of Teresa's call to prayer is a radical spiritual transformation, nothing less than the alignment of our will with God's Will.

For Teresa, spiritual life means active life in the world, using ongoing discernment about our spiritual work and destiny. It means an awakening of charity; a deepening capacity for suffering in the performance of deeds of charity, and an enkindling spiritual fire to sustain these actions. Advice from a spiritual director can be a great help.

The third mansion is an extended meditation on Matthew 19—the story where a (rich) man asks Jesus what he must do to possess eternal life, in addition to keeping all the commandments, and Jesus responds by commanding total surrender *"If you wish to be perfect, go and sell what you own, and give money to the poor, and you will have treasure in heaven; then come, follow me."*[9]

Here we are called to a life of deeper spirituality and love for, and in, Christ, and surrender to His will. In this dwelling place, the human personality and will are very much still in control This is what is being so severely tested—our psychological and spiritual maturity, our spiritual sincerity and increasing willingness to surrender, let go and trust to God's Will. Teresa talks about the increasing need for spiritual discernment and discrimination at this stage, as it is not possible to judge from outward appearances what is happening deeper within the soul.

Like Jesus admonishing the young man, Teresa directly challenges those times in our lives when we might be feeling complacent, or safe, or content that we are doing "all the right things." It is a call to more radical change, awakening and transformation in the love of God. The problem she is emphasising here is that the soul has not yet fully surrendered to God—our own will and efforts have brought us to this place.

Although we might be doing all the right and virtuous things in the eyes of the world, internally we might still be maintaining a fearful and anxious regard about ourselves; we can still be locked, to some extent, within ourselves. She says tartly that this stage is very characteristic of persons who are so extremely correct that they are often shocked at everything they see!

Here, we are called to give up, however reluctantly, those things and aspects of our lives which are the nearest and dearest, particularly those with which we are the most identified The giving up may be what is necessary to bring us closer to God. The loss of things we are close to, and the enormous pain and suffering this can cause are themes that Teresa returns to time and again, particularly at the dark night of the soul in the latter mansions. She emphasises that there is a need to understand and to proceed from a deeper humility, a humility that now possesses a kind of holy abandonment of ourselves into the possibilities of a deeper spiritual life.

The fourth dwelling place is the place of spiritual transition and transformation, where the inner landscape begins to qualitatively change. Up to this point all we have done is prepare ourselves for surrender in our readiness and ability to accept our inner incompleteness and total dependency on God. From here on infused grace begins to operate more fully—our progress is up to God alone.

This is the place where *the natural and the supernatural combine.*[10] In prayer we are beginning to experience something very different, as if being more and more effortlessly absorbed into a state of grace. It is a deeper level of conversion and abandonment of our own will. Teresa says the rational faculties must be decreasing as our capacity to love and be loved is increasing.

Some of Teresa's most sublime descriptions of deep prayer are here, and some of the subtle experiences of deep silence. In this dwelling place she writes of consolations and spiritual delights, of two particular spiritual experiences. The Spanish *contentos* is translated as consolations, which are experiences of "joy, peace, and satisfaction, happiness. . .similar to those derived from ordinary everyday events."

The Spanish *gustos* are experiences, described as spiritual delights of "infused," "supernatural" or "mystical prayer." Often there is a sense of deep joy and ecstasy, which is more powerful than anything experienced before, or a sense of intoxication and total and complete awe in contemplating the grandeur and mysteries of God.

In this dwelling place, there is a deeper and more profound level of surrender to God. We are being asked to let go even more of our own agenda, and when these moments of infused prayer or gusto or spiritual delight come, our task is to surrender to them. Teresa speaks here about an increasing sense of deep joy, of an intense ecstasy, of the gradual indwelling of an indescribable Love. In this place of deeper quiet, the human will and the divine will are in stages of deeper absorption, in preparation for the more permanent and established state of union.

Teresa is always mindful of the constant need to test the sincerity and genuineness of all spiritual development and experiences. Her spiritual guidance as to the wise discernment of these different states of prayer and absorption shows how to distinguish between genuine absorption in the divine, and states of stupor.

From the fifth dwelling place to the end of the text she is concerned with describing the perils and delights of the union of the soul with God. She stresses time after time that "the devil," or our own destructive powers, can be as active as ever. Humility, which has been essential throughout, from now on becomes imperative, and she shows how to be on guard against false spiritual pride. The soul is beginning to undergo a deeper state of interior spiritual transformation, where the heart is surrendering even more to being infused and penetrated by the Holy Spirit and God's Love.

215

She describes a deepening prayer of quiet that becomes a prayer of union. There can be a sense of such stillness that the body scarcely moves and that distractions of ordinary consciousness—thoughts, memories and imagination—cannot disturb the profound inner silence. The distinctive prayer of the fifth mansion is a brief spell, lasting up to half an hour, of increasing absorption in God, and often very little identifiable awareness of our physical state and surroundings.

This is the beginning of the union of human and divine will and she emphasises that it is not possible to enter these more interior dwelling places by personal effort alone, but only by the grace of God. The fifth mansion is explicitly associated by Teresa with the text from Colossians 3:3: *"You have died and your life is hid with Christ in God,"* hiddenness being the keynote.

The metamorphosis of a silkworm into a butterfly is her main symbol to describe the transformation of the soul towards union with God. This also echoes the central feature of hiddenness. The soul at this stage is akin to a silkworm. The dark cocoon that is being spun around us is our prayer, waiting and stillness. By emptying the self we build Christ around us, for the emergence of the butterfly, the transformed soul, fragile and restless, but beautiful.

Teresa's description of the cocoon-like stage—"becoming dead to the world," "enveloped in its cocoon"—is a description of the stage of the "dark night of the soul." Her symbolic representation refers to experiences and states of pain, suffering, often intense alienation and sense of loss, despair, darkness and depression, which, for Teresa, were essential preludes to the more unitive spiritual states of the most interior mansions. Teresa seems to accept this type of suffering as an inevitable consequence of deepening surrender.

Our spiritual development and transformation in God is about the re-enactment, over and over again, of this story of the death of the worm and the birth of a butterfly. It describes our passages, crises, depressions, difficulties, our transitions and turning points. They nearly always, in large or small measure, entail a process of dying and rebirth into a different sense or experience of who we are, of our relationship to God and others, in our service and vocation in the world.

In this dwelling place, Teresa writes that the Beloved is giving the grace of the Holy Spirit as a token of the impending betrothal to the soul, in preparation for becoming His Bride. The soul cannot understand the mystery of spiritual union—it is inexplicable and paradoxical to the rational faculties. Teresa, being such a practical woman, emphasizes the importance of weaving this focus of deep prayer and mystical silence into the praxis of daily life, and noted that the test of the authenticity of our prayer life is whether our love for our neighbour is growing in response.

The sixth mansion occupies nearly a third of the text, and deals with interior states of prayer and the intensification of the spiritual life, covering both the nature of the suffering and in the various ecstasies of prayer that can occur. She emphasises the importance of the ongoing process of spiritual discernment since this is the stage of the greatest disorientation of the soul. She discusses the increasing strength and subtlety of internal and external tests, trials, obstacles and opposition that can develop in response to a deepening spiritual life in this dwelling place.

This can be exacerbated by the tender and exquisite love that the soul is experiencing in times of intimacy with God—a type of oscillation between a sense of Divine presence and Divine absence. The butterfly, which has come to birth in the preceding stage, is vulnerable, restless and confused. There are acute trials ahead, including an intensification of the "dark night," the onset of illness as well as persecution.

In this dwelling place, Teresa introduces the new experiences that the soul receives, and gives guidelines to help discern whether the soul is on the right path. Teresa speaks at length, passionately, of the Divine Love of God for the soul, and of the need for renunciation by the soul into that great Love that God has for his Bride. The soul is betrothed to her Beloved, Christ, and this shows in many different ways. His Divine Love is awakening the soul through the interior senses, either by interior vision or sight. Or the soul may begin to hear His Divine call, or smell the sweet perfume of the Holy Spirit.

Teresa is famous for her unusual and intense spiritual experiences, but in the text her instructions and guidelines for dealing with such interior states are particularly down to earth, full of common sense and extremely wise. The main events that she concentrates on in this mansion are locutions or interior words that seem to be spoken by God, wordless prayer, "the flight of the spirit," interior visions, raptures and ecstasies.

She emphasizes the importance of looking at the effects of such experiences and how they have been integrated into life, advising prudence and patience until time reveals their fruits. All true spiritual phenomena will lead to a greater awareness of God and His Love, to a greater sense of humility, and a deepening awareness and compassion for others and their suffering.

The seventh and innermost mansion, Teresa writes, is different from all the others. For her, the interior marriage occurred through a vision of the Holy Trinity, and her inward conviction that the union of her will with God's will had taken place. She describes the seventh mansion as where "*this secret union takes place in the deepest centre of the soul, which must be where God Himself dwells,*" quite independent of the physical senses or faculties. In this interior state, in the core of our heart, there is no separation between soul and God.

Teresa says that spiritual marriage "*might also be compared to water falling from the sky into a river or fountain, where the waters are united, and it would be no longer possible to divide them, or to separate the water of the river from that which has fallen from the heavens. Or it may be likened to a tiny stream, which falls into the sea; there is no possibility of separating them."*[11]

She emphasizes that this union has nothing to do with the sensory world or the physical senses—that it takes place deep, deep within the heart. Although this union is happening in the centre of the heart, in the outer mansions there can still be difficulties, conflicts and pain. Mystical union is totally effortless and occurs in the Silence *"the understanding need not stir nor seek for anything more; the Lord who created it, wishes it now to be at rest, and only through a little chink to survey what is passing in the soul."*[12]

In this innermost mansion, it is interesting that Teresa gives little attention to interior experiences, looking instead to the effects of this union in our relationship to others and the world. The purpose is the *"birth always of good works, good works"* and a call to action and a life of active love in the world, with the confidence that it is possible to maintain an indwelling Presence of God in the innermost recesses of our heart.

St Teresa today

Teresa's life and Reform responded to a spiritual need of her times to turn away from material living and to return to the essence of our ancient spiritual tradition. A similar rebirth has begun in our own time in response to a need even more urgent than before. The possibility of a great transformation within the heart of each soul is underway.

We are on the cusp of new times, when the Heavenly Waters are being poured upon humanity, where conscious individuals will become the incarnating vessels of the Holy Spirit on an ongoing basis.[13] As I have said earlier, a new era is rapidly approaching, and the unprecedented availability of spiritual knowledge is feeding the tremendous spiritual awakening that is occurring globally.

Perhaps we are in the final preparatory stages of the Parousia, the coming of the celestial Jerusalem on earth. Perhaps we are anticipating the definitive victory over death and the transfiguration of the cosmos that will happen at the Parousia.[14] For those with dawning awareness of this, who see the tiny "window open to Eternity" slowly widening, the wisdom and teaching of the Christian contemplative journey provided by St Teresa, and others among our spiritual forebears, are vitally necessary.

Endnotes

[1] St Teresa of Avila, *The Interior Castle*, p. 5.

[2] J. McLean, *Towards Mystical Union*, p 89.

[3] St Teresa of Avila, *The Interior Castle*, p. 6.

[4] Ibid., p. 13.

[5] J. Melloni, *The Exercises of St Ignatius Loyola in the Western Tradition*, p. 38.

[6] Ibid., p. 38.

[7] Ibid., pp 40-41.

[8] St Teresa of Avila, *The Interior Castle*, p. 16.

[9] Matthew 19:21, New Revised Standard Version Bible.

[10] J. McLean, *Towards Mystical Union*, p. 205.

[11] St Teresa of Avila, *The Interior Castle*, p. 109.

[12] Ibid., page 114.

[13] E. Edinger, *The Aion Lectures*, p. 193.

[14] O. Clement, *The Roots of the Christian Mysticism*, p. 266.

Chapter 15

MYSTICAL THEOLOGY AND THE RENEWAL OF CONTEMPLATIVE SPIRITUAL PRACTICE

Mystical theology, like all theology, is not primarily theoretical; it is concerned rather with the living of life, and especially with a life lived in the context of an experience of the Divine. Mystical experience may come unexpectedly, and it is not necessarily the case that it is a reward for those who have lived pious and holy lives, but often it does come in the context of a life of prayer and spiritual practice. If it does so, we need not understand this as cause and effect in some predictable way, but rather as a part of a dialogue between the human being and God. We might say that mystical experience is in some way experienced as God's response to prayer. Mystical theology is also concerned with the human response to God; with praxis as prayer. Mystical theology is thus intimately concerned with spiritual practice, in the sense that such practices are a part of a dialogue between God and human beings, a part of the way in which human beings express themselves towards God.

Spiritual practices are easily viewed as something additional, as something that spiritual people do, but which other people do not do. They are thus a kind of optional extra in life, for those who want them. Such a view suggests a narrow definition of spiritual practice, rather like a peculiar hobby, without which most people can manage quite well. This perspective fails to recognise both the inherent spirituality of all human life—and thus all praxis—and the immanence of God in all things. Moreover, it fails to recognise the integral relationship between praxis and wellbeing. Mystical theology does not overlook this link between the way in which we live our lives and the extent to which we flourish as human beings.

In the present chapter we will consider some of the spiritual practices that have been addressed or alluded to by other authors who have contributed to this volume. We will also draw on some other resources from the Christian mystical tradition from which we have each benefited. In each case, we are only offering some examples, and we hope that the reader will explore more widely some of the implications that arise within their own practice, drawing on the rich and diverse resources of other Christian traditions. But, first, we must consider briefly the nature of wellbeing.

Well-being

There have been many definitions of the nature of "well-being" over the past few decades, and it has tended to be a rather vague, generalised concept that reflects values, philosophies, influences and theologies of various, and often differing, individuals and groups. Dictionary definitions refer to a condition of contentment, health, success or welfare, and modern academic notions of "well-being" have usually been explored from subjective, psychological, physical health and economic perspectives. These perspectives are somewhat limited, and reductionist, compared to the traditional

Christian spiritual understanding of a more holistic view of human well-being, which links "well-being" to happiness, virtue or the "good life."[1]

We would like to explore a fuller vision of human well-being, from a Christian perspective, which is the focus of the chapters of this book. Human well-being includes all parts of the human being which are so closely connected and intertwined—spiritual, mental, emotional physical and social/community aspects. Ancient Christian understanding has looked beyond limited, instrumental, or reductionist, approaches to ask, "What is it that makes a good life of the whole human person, a life that is flourishing, rather than simply struggling along?" One central feature to emerge from Christian texts, especially from the early Desert tradition, the *Philokalia* and the writings of the Spanish mystics in the sixteenth century, is a view, perspective and understanding that human well-being is contingent upon the only non-contingent source of wellbeing, which is God. Wellbeing is thus about being able to participate, as fully as possible, in the life of God, in Christ.[2]

In this tradition, human well-being is ultimately concerned with an orientation to the Divine, to God, and that the primary and ultimate source of our well-being is found in our journey and relationship towards, and in, God. So, we could understand that full human well-being is concerned, fundamentally, with experience of the Divine, which is the focus of Andrew Louth's chapter. He comments on Vladimir Lossky's book *The Mystical Theology of the Eastern Church,* and explores the shift in the modern understanding of mysticism, and mystical theology, in the early/mid twentieth century, in terms of coming less to mean strange experiences such as visions and levitations, to more of a defined sense of the "mystical," or an experience of the Divine, through a deepening of a life of prayer within the sacramental life of the Church community.

Louth quotes the following passage from *The Mystical Theology of the Eastern Church*, in which Lossky elucidates his understanding of the "mystical":

> *"The eastern tradition has never made a sharp distinction between the mystical and theology; between personal experience of the divine mysteries and the dogma affirmed by the Church. . . . To put it another way, we must live the dogma expressing a revealed truth, which appears to us as an unfathomable mystery, in such a fashion that instead of assimilating the mystery to our mode of understanding, we should, on the contrary, look for a profound change, an inner transformation of the spirit, enabling us to experience it mystically. . . . For the Christian, therefore, the mystical cannot exist without theology, but, above all, there is no theology without the mystical. . . . The mystical is accordingly treated in the present work as the perfecting and crown of all theology: as theology par excellence."*[3]

The "mystical" is thus integrally related both to experience of the Divine and to the task of theology. Indeed, theology *is*, necessarily, both mystical and experiential. Louth explores further what Lossky meant by "mystical theology," suggesting that he starts from an understanding of the mystical as bound up with some kind of inward, personal experience, beyond conceptualisation, which ultimately becomes identical with participating in the sacramental life of the Church community, as the human mind and heart becomes conformed to God and his revelation of Love through the Son and the Spirit.

Peter Tyler also explores the nature of inner experience in his chapter in relation to the works of Wittgenstein and Merton. Here, the inwardness of the experience of prayer is recognised as a problem—it is delusional, illusory, elusive and distracting. Rather than being consummated in sacrament or in conformity to God, it is resolved rather in an unknowing that overcomes the subject-object dualism. Here, Christ is found within, but is unknown, unseen. Paradoxically, this subverts the very possibility of spiritual practice. God is found not as a reward or result following something that we "do," but rather as an astonishment, a sudden change of perspective, a gracious response to what we cannot do. Prayer leads us to God when we realise "what a mess we are in." We are thus most in a state of well-being when we least have confidence in, or awareness of, ourselves.

Many other Christian saints and mystics down the centuries have explored the importance of mystical theology in relationship to a vision of the fullness and wholeness of human well-being as experienced in relationship with God. An example of this that has been very influential upon each of us is that of the great Spanish mystics and saints of the sixteenth century. Francisco de Osuna, Teresa of Avila and John of the Cross wrote extensively on the journey of prayer and the spiritual life, within the context of mystical theology.[4]

One of the most important spiritual teachers and writers of the time, Francisco de Osuna, whose *Third Spiritual Alphabet* was a significant influence upon Teresa of Avila, wrote about mystical theology as a "hidden" theology, which differs from other branches of learning. For Osuna, mystical theology is concerned with the will. It is the theology "of God's just lovers."

"this theology will be perfected by adding love and it will no longer remain hidden, but be manifest to all, for the youngest to the oldest."[5]

This theology is not to be learned in the same way as the "speculative" theology with which Osuna contrasts it. Speculative theology is learned most easily by those who are intelligent, and

227

requires the reading of books, careful attention, practice, and a good teacher. In contrast:

> "*The hidden theology we are describing, however, is not attained by those tools as much as through pious love and exercising moral virtues to prepare and purge the soul. The soul also needs other theological virtues to enlighten it: the gifts of the Holy Spirit and the evangelical beatitudes in accordance with the three hierarchal acts of purgation, illumination and perfection.*"[6]

Mystical theology is thus concerned with a life lived in love of God and others, and according to the spiritual disciplines (the life of "purgation" as Osuna knew it). This is not pursued through learning, books and teachers; indeed De Osuna emphasized that it is not possible to "*teach*" this theology:

> "*I do not presume to teach it in the alphabet, nor can any mortal can do so, for Christ reserves to himself the ministry of secretly teaching the hearts where that theology lives hidden like a divine science.*"[7]

Osuna employs a variety of names for this tradition of mystical theology. It is the way of wisdom, profundity, and the "art of love."

> "*It is also called union because the person who attains to God in this prayer is made one spirit with him by an interchange of wills whereby he wants only what God wants and God remains with man's will and together they are like one in everything, similar to two things that are so perfectly united that they almost cease to be themselves and become totally conformed into a third being.*"[8]

If mystical theology is concerned with well-being, then in this tradition (as in other Christian traditions), it is certainly not about an easy or comfortable understanding of what it means to be in a state of wellness. It is concerned with what the later depth psychologists would refer to as the subconscious, and thus with things which human beings tend to repress and avoid because, when exposed to the light of consciousness, they make us uncomfortable:

> *"This exercise is known as profundity with respect to the depth and darkness of the devotion, for it originates in the depths of man's heart, which is dark because human understanding has been deprived of light. Seeing the heart plunged into shadows, the spirit of God comes over the heart on the waters of desire to proclaim his divine light."*[9]

Osuna clearly states that the whole subject of his *Third Spiritual Alphabet* was a continuation of the ancient lineage of Christian mystical theology in his time:

> *"Some call it mystical theology, which means hidden, because the good teacher Jesus imparts it in the secret hiding place of the heart. Wishing to reserve this teaching for himself, he gave his followers a smaller role and less authority to instruct in this than in any other learning. As our principal teacher, he kept for himself this principal doctrine, for among all disciplines theology is the queen and lady of learning who, according to the wise man, calls her ladies, meaning the other sciences, to the castle of faith where they are to serve their mistress, theology."*[10]

Thus, the tradition of mystical theology is essentially describing knowledge of God that is imparted *"in the secret hiding place of the heart"* and is obscure to the human mind or intellect[11]. We thus return to the paradox that Tyler elucidates in relation to Wittgenstein and Merton. Prayer is a finding of Christ within us, but we find only in losing, we know only in unknowing. We encounter God in prayer, yet prayer is not something that we can "do." Prayer as a spiritual practice is—in this sense—impossible.

Expressing the inexpressible

Corrine Saunders, in her chapter, looks at Margery Kempe's experiences, as recorded in the *Book of Margery Kempe.* She explores an approach foregrounding mystical theology, with its emphasis on an individual spiritual life. This coincides with a new interest in Margery's inner voices and visionary experiences in recent scholarship. Margery's theology can be seen as mystical, as her book recounts her experiences of mystical phenomena across her life; experiences of what she clearly believed to be a supernatural kind in which she believed that she directly, and personally, gained immediate knowledge of God.

In writing of Margery's experiences of the Divine, Saunders refers to her attempt to "express the inexpressible." How can we express the ineffable, the "many secret things" that we experience, Margery asks herself? Words can gesture towards, but never entirely capture feeling, always being removed from experience. The book returns again and again to the gap between earthly and celestial, the impossibility of articulating the sublime. Margery's spiritual joy and comfort are *"so marvellous that she could never tell of it as she felt it."*[12] Her holy thoughts are *"so subtle and heavenly that she could never describe them afterwards, as she had them in feeling."*[13]

Saunders' demonstrates that Margery's words mark the attempt of an uneducated, in some ways simple, woman to convey complex philosophical and theological concepts. Her *Book* is, in a way, itself a spiritual practice devised to this end. It describes a variety of Margery's other spiritual practices, such as visualisation and meditation, pilgrimage, participation in the Eucharist, and ascetic discipline. *The Book* attempts to articulate that which cannot be articulated but, rather than doing this in complex verbal ways (as other, more sophisticated and highly educated, authors have done), Margery does it in simple concrete and highly visual ways. She articulates very forcefully and unambiguously the emotion behind the images—the strange invasion of the body in her cryings becomes at once a physical sign sent by God, a spiritual test, and the means to illumination of the soul. These wordless sounds also capture the unknowability, the impossibility of articulating in language, the nature of our experience of, and relationship to, the Divine.

Saunders highlights that Margery's noise—in all its senses— made her both remarkable and distrusted, yet it was precisely through that noise that she left her mark on society. Through the writing of her *Book*, through the medium of scribes and through the conventions of devotional writing as a spiritual practice, Margery's extraordinary voice takes on a new authority, with her "inner eye and ear" open to rich imaginative landscapes. Her homely yet profound narrative, over half a millennium on, can still speak to us today of deep and immediate spiritual experiences and revelation, as a specifically and idiosyncratically female *imitatio Christi*, which is the model offered by many contemplative texts over the centuries.

Contemplation as "The Praying Cure"

Spiritual practices, if viewed as essential for the well-being of the whole person, may be understood as offering a kind of therapy, or healing, for the soul, mind and body. Healing of the soul is brought about through many ways, primarily through meditation and prayer, pain and suffering, the compassion of God, wisdom and reproof.[14] It is thus a result of both active spiritual practices and passive receipt of that which God bestows—often in experiences of darkness or adversity. Similarly, the modern practice of counselling/psychotherapy, and the understanding of the psyche from a Jungian perspective[15] can be very helpful *as a part of* the journey toward healing, wholeness and wellbeing. For example, Jungian analytical psychology is generally open to the spiritual dimension of human personhood, and is both something at which the patient must actively work, at the same time as they are passively in receipt of analysis by a therapist. Within the "shadow" experiences of the human psyche, conferred by life and interpreted in therapy, the soul is able to grow and flourish.

For healing of the whole person, we would argue, a telos is ultimately required which is firmly located in, and towards, the Divine. A telos of this kind is essential if progress is to be made in moving towards a contemplative "unknowing," transcending human rational thought and ideas. This is the traditional distinction in mystical theology between two ways of knowing, two ways of being or different forms of awareness, which has been described by Christian saints and mystics throughout the centuries. Augustine of Hippo speaks of a higher part of the mind reserved for the contemplation of God and a lower part of the mind that reasons.

Evagrius of Pontus, the fourth century monk and writer, is one of a host of contemplative writers to make an important distinction between the calculating, reasoning mind that makes use of concepts in a process we call discursive thought and that dimension of mind that comes to knowledge directly without the mediation of concepts, which he called *nous,* an intuitive spiritual intelligence. When Evagrius defined prayer as *"communion of the mind with God"* he meant a dimension of our consciousness that runs deeper than discursive thought. Thomas Aquinas took up this same distinction and, speaking for virtually the entire tradition, called the aspect of the mind that thinks and calculates "lower reason" and the aspect of the mind that communes directly with God in contemplation "higher reason."[16]

The mystical tradition, particularly as emphasised in the writings of the Carmelite saints and mystics, Teresa of Avila and John of the Cross, asserts that there is a form of consciousness which goes beyond sense impressions, beyond the knowledge we can get from touching, smelling, seeing, hearing, and tasting, which has to do with essences and the inner being of things. This knowledge has to do with the core of our existence, where we confront the silent core of our being. Ultimately, it is divine knowledge, and we can participate in it if we are prepared to embark on the journey into stillness, into quiet, through entering an ascetical process of interior detachment and purification from attachments and identifications with sense impressions. In personal terms, the fruit of this deeper journey is that we come to know our self in new ways, this knowledge coming from the Divine, and not from our ego-centric, perspective.[17]

Spiritual Direction

Most of us need help in this journey towards wellness and spiritual growth. In his chapter on Baron von Hügel (1852-1925), a well-known spiritual director, Kallistos Ware explores some of the important elements in offering spiritual guidance. Ware emphasises three key elements in the practice of spiritual direction from the writings of von Hügel: his understanding of truth as a bright light, surrounded by darkness, his dialectical approach, insisting on the "friction" of opposites, and his interpretation of religion as a combination of external fact and inner experience.

In his appreciation of God's unknowability and of the value of silence, von Hügel shows himself to be a truly apophatic theologian. But an apophatic spirituality does not deny the importance of speech—either in prayer or in conversation with others. And talking to a spiritual director can help us to better understand what it is that we do not understand, better delineate those frictions in life that cause us pain, and better delineate both the external truths of religious faith and also our inner experiences.

All of these things can be difficult to articulate, but the spiritual practice of attempting to articulate them, as best we can, in conversation with a spiritual director, as well as attempting to articulate them in solitude and in prayer, is important. It is not at all the same thing to have tried to put mystical experience into words, only to fail, as it is not to have attempted to do this at all. (Neither is it the same to attempt this task alone as it is to attempt it with another person—such as a spiritual director.) And the attempt is important as a spiritual practice which takes us deeper into the mystery that is God.

Of the three elements of religion as he understood them, the historical, the rational and the mystical, it was to the mystical that von Hügel was most attracted, and he saw it as the most important of the three. Speaking of God, he writes:

> "He it is Who, however dimly yet directly, touches our souls and awakens them. . .to that noblest, incurable discontent with our own petty self and to that sense of and thirst for the Infinitive and Abiding, which articulates man's deepest requirement and characteristic."[18]

Von Hügel saw the human being's "deepest requirement and characteristic" as the potential for direct communion with the living God. Such a communion, expressed in mystical experience, is not something strange and peculiar, but an expression of "the innermost *normal* consciousness of mankind," which is possible for all without exception. Yet, whilst possible for all, this experience is not easily found or understood. It is paradoxical, elusive and encountered through "friction" and "darkness." To this end, spiritual direction provides invaluable assistance. It orientates us when there are no landmarks, encourages us to carry on even when we think we are lost, and reassures us when we find no assurance from either within or without.

Prayer and Daily Life

In Bernadette Flanagan's chapter on Quotidian practices, she shows the importance of the daily practice of prayer, especially within new monastic communities. These communities are bearing witness to the many ways in which it is possible to embrace classic monastic ideas and practices (contemplative prayer, ways of living in community and embodied spiritual practices such as fasting and silence) while also reimagining and recasting them to give shape to a new, authentic and sometimes prophetic life practice in quotidian circumstances. This contrasts with the daily practices of Margery Kemp, undertaken firmly outside of monastic community discipline. However, the new monasticism and Margery's *Book* share a common concern with the trials and tribulations of daily life, with the oppositions and reassurances provided by others, and with the importance for spiritual growth of the wider communities in which we live.

The early desert communities, from which the monastic tradition emerged, emphasised a life apart. Ironically, it was in the context of solitude that the importance of community and relationship were most emphasised. Thus, the importance of hospitality to visitors becomes more acute when visitors are encountered infrequently and only in such an inhospitable environment as that of the north African desert. Amma Syncletica, (as Flanagan describes) in moving to the outskirts of Alexandria, encountered and cared for those who were themselves marginalised from mainstream society. Similarly new monastic communities, in setting themselves apart, paradoxically offer a practice of spirituality which both highlights and more effectively responds to the stresses, clamour and noise of contemporary life.

Daily spiritual practices, such as for example a pattern of daily prayer, create a paradox. On the one hand, incorporation of prayer into a daily routine makes prayer more pervasive. In this sense, it becomes important, it is emphasised and underlined. On the other hand, the familiarity of daily prayer causes it to merge into the background. It can become over-familiar, habitual—almost invisible. Those who pray infrequently are more aware of the difference of prayer—of its contrast with the quotidian order— but only at the expense of making it less frequent, less a part of the fabric of life. Those who pray daily have less sense of what life might look like without prayer. They become more at risk of taking it for granted. But in "doing" prayer on a daily basis, they thus potentially become more aware of their own poverty in prayer— more aware of the paradox that it is God who "does" prayer, and not we ourselves.

Pilgrimage

Rosalind Brown's chapter on Durham cathedral emphasises the importance of pilgrimage to important spiritual and sacred sites. The cathedral attracts around 700,000 people every year, and she emphasises how pilgrimage can be a transformative experience because *in the mystery of God, there is encounter with the divine while they are here, whether or not they can express it as such.*[19]

In the words of the former Dean of the Cathedral:

"We should not make easy assumptions about God nor think we can ever fully know him or understand his purposes. Perhaps that is what has drawn me into cathedrals for most of my ministry, for these are places where the "idea of the holy," numinous buildings, beautiful liturgy and profound

music reach into the soul to help us do justice to the great
mysteries of faith."[20]

Great places of pilgrimages, such as Durham Cathedral, can offer a threshold of something awesome, a place where people encounter a living tradition that has been lived faithfully for centuries and which challenges our contemporary lifestyles and priorities. Brown suggests that pilgrimage can act as a portal to an experience of the Divine, and to an understanding of mystical theology. Pilgrimage sites are liminal places, where it is safe to ask questions and listen for unexpected answers.

Elsewhere, one of us has suggested that as we visit and enquire about holy places, such as Durham Cathedral, they in turn pose questions to us.[21] The historical and spiritual narrative of faith that they provide invites us to locate our story within their story. They offer narratives within which we can find meaning for our own hopes and fears. Exactly how they do this might be open to question, but they offer a kind of scale—symbolic, physical, and temporal—against which we can measure our own experiences. They invite us to join the community of faith which they both represent and (at least in places such as Durham Cathedral) continue to provide a home to. They humble us, challenge us and inspire us. They draw us in to a place of prayer and mystery. Perhaps more importantly, they provide us with a kind of spiritual practice which may then be extrapolated to other places, including those which are decidedly not holy. They help us to appreciate the whole of life as pilgrimage, and find God in ordinary and profane, as well as holy, places.

Mystical Theology and Spiritual Practice

In a variety of ways we have explored here the paradox that spiritual practices are both important and unimportant. Ultimately, we cannot "do" anything that brings us closer to God, and we are dependent entirely upon grace for any experience that we might have of God. Only in unknowing do we draw closer to God, and that which we usually count as knowledge or reason cannot take us far in the life of prayer and spiritual well-being. However, this is not to say that pilgrimages are not worthwhile, or that daily prayer is of no value. The wise counsel of a good spiritual director, or a good therapist, can help us to see things that we could not see on our own, and within the mysteries of contemplative prayer lay the possibilities for our healing.

In this chapter we have only begun to scratch the surface of the wide range of spiritual practices on offer in the Christian tradition. We have given little or no consideration to the sacraments, to fasting, confession, penance, retreats, the Ignatian exercises, lectio divina, social action, mindfulness of mortality, the Jesus prayer, psalmody, or many other spiritual practices. Were we to examine these other practices also, we might broaden our repertoire in some way, and gain a deeper awareness of the diversity of ways in which human beings have sought to engage in practice with mystical theology, spiritual well-being, and the quest for God. However, it is probably also the case that we would find ourselves further repeating our key themes of the inherent paradox and impossibility of the quest. Mystical theology is both inherently something that must be lived, and not only thought or talked about, and also something that can never be "done" but only received. God can only be found "within," and yet in the finding is always elusive. Furthermore, in the course of the quest, distinctions between inner and outer seem to be lost and to become only less comprehensible.

Ultimately, spiritual well-being is found only when it is made both our telos and goal, and also that which we are willing to lose. As Jesus is recorded as saying:

For those who want to save their life will lose it, and those who lose their life for my sake will save it.[22]

Conclusion

In conclusion, we would like to propose that mystical theology and spiritual practice, as outlined in this book, is essential for the full growth, and flourishing, of human health and well-being, in all its aspects. However, we would also caution against the placing of undue emphasis on particular methods or practices, and against any view of spiritual practices which might make us too reliant on ourselves or neglectful of our enduring dependence upon the grace of God. Prayer is something that God does, into which we are graciously invited.

We would like to leave the last word to Thomas Merton:

"we should not look for a 'method' or 'system' but cultivate an 'attitude,' an 'outlook': faith, openness, attention, reverence, expectation, supplication, trust, joy. All these finally permeate our being with love in so far as our living faith tells us we are in the presence of God, that we live in Christ, that in the Spirit of God we 'see' God our Father without 'seeing.' We know him in 'unknowing.'" [23]

Endnotes

[1] C. Cook, *The Philokalia and the Inner Life: On Passions and Prayer*, p. 153.

[2] Ibid., p. 201.

[3] V. Lossky, *The Mystical Theology of the Eastern Church*, pp. 27-28.

[4] See J. McLean, *Towards Mystical Union*, and P. Tyler, T*he Return to the Mystical: Ludwig Wittgenstein, Teresa of Avila and the Christian Mystical Tradition*.

[5] M. E. Giles & K. Kavanaugh, *Francisco De Osuna: The Third Spiritual Alphabet*, p. 162.

[6] Ibid., p. 162.

[7] Ibid., p. 161.

[8] Ibid., p. 164.

[9] Ibid., p. 165.

[10] Ibid., p. 161.

[11] See J. McLean, *Towards Mystical Union*, p. xvii and P. Tyler, *The Return to the Mystical: Ludwig Wittgenstein, Teresa of Avila and the Christian Mystical Tradition*, Chapter 5.

[12] C. Saunders, *The Mystical Theology of Margery Kempe*, chapter in *Mystical Theology and Contemporary Spiritual Practice*, p. 52.

[13] Ibid., p. 52.

[14] C. Cook, *Healing, Psychotherapy, and the Philokalia*. In Bingaman, B. & Nassif, B. (Eds.) *The Philokalia: A Classic Text of Orthodox Spirituality*, p. 231.

[15] J. McLean, *Towards Mystical Union*, pp. 87-146.

[16] J. McLean, *Teresa of Avila and Depth Psychology*, p. 16.

[17] J. McLean, *Teresa of Avila and Depth Psychology*, p. 18.

[18] F. von Hügel, *The Mystical Element of Religion, Volume 1*, p. 4.

[19] R. Brown, *Unlikely Mystics: Durham Cathedral as Mystical Space for Ordinary People*, chapter in *Mystical Theology and Contemporary Spiritual Practice*, Cook, McLean and Tyler, pp. 58-79.

[20] Ibid.

[21] See C. Cook, *Finding God in a Holy Place*.

[22] Luke 9:24, New Revised Standard Version.

[23] T. Merton, *Contemplative Prayer*, p. 34.

APPENDIX

(See Chapter Nine)

Spiritual and Religious beliefs/practice amongst AJA members survey

This is a brief, confidential survey (based on the above survey) about the spiritual and religious beliefs/ practice amongst AJA members.

****

"In using the word religion, we mean the actual practice of a faith e.g. going to a church, synagogue, temple or mosque. Some people do not follow a specific religion but do have spiritual beliefs or experiences. For example, they may believe that there is some power or forces other than themselves that might influence their life. Some people think of this as God or gods, others do not. Some people make sense of the lives without any religious or spiritual belief."

1. ***Would you say that you have a religious, or spiritual understanding of your life (please underline one or more)***
   Religious/ Spiritual/ Religious and spiritual/ Neither religious nor spiritual

(If you have never had a religious or spiritual belief or practice, there is no need to continue…thank you for responding)

2. **Can you explain briefly what form your religious/spiritual belief has taken?**

3. **Some people hold strongly to their views and others do not. How strongly do you hold onto your religious/ spiritual view of Life? Please circle the number that best describes your view?**

   0   1   2   3   4   5   6   7   8   9   10

   Weakly   *Strongly*
   held view   *held view*

4. **Do you have a specific religion? If so, can you give more detail?**

   1. *I do not observe a religion*
   2. *Roman Catholic*
   3. *Church of England/Anglican*
   4. *Other Protestant*
   5. *Moslem*
   6. *Jewish*
   7. *Hindu*
   8. *Buddhist*
   9. *Other*

5. **Do any of the following play a part in your belief? For example, you might pray or meditate, alone or with other people (tick as many as apply to you and please give more detail)**

   - *Prayer - alone or with other people* _____
   - *Ceremony, (e.g. religious service) - alone or with other people_____*
   - *Meditation, - alone or with other people_____*

- *Reading and study - alone or with other people* _____

_____

- *Contact with religious leader - alone or with other people*_____
- *None of the above* _____

6. **What role, and importance, is the practice of your belief(e.g. private meditation, prayer, study, religious services) in your:**
- **personal life –**

Not necessary **0 1 2 3 4 5 6 7 8 9 0** *Essential*

*Could you explain further the role/importance of your spiritual practice in your personal life*_____

_____

- **professional life –**

Not necessary **0 1 2 3 4 5 6 7 8 9 0** *Essential*

*Could you explain further the role/importance of your spiritual practice in your professional life*_____

_____

Written Responses to Survey

Q2. Can you explain briefly what form your religious/spiritual belief has taken?

- Used to practise daily church, daily prayers at home, and daily meditation. Now a deep awareness and respect for the miracle of life

- Until my 40's, regular church attendance, active in the church. Regular prayer and bible reading plus other writings. Since then, inward searching, certainty and uncertainty, about a spiritual dimension through reading, conferences, contemplation, music poetry discussions, silence.
- Christian, Anglican, contemplative and charismatic
- Buddhist practice
- I believe there is a greater power than we are aware of consciously, however this may be understood or define (for example, the Self, in Jung's sense of the term)
- Specifically, Christianity initially from my mid-30's but now, many years later, I would say that I am more interested in the transcendent mystery of the divine without any institutional encumbrances, if that were possible.
- Thinking about religious concepts, following Richard Rohr whom I find more helpful and attending Anglican services.
- Belief in the existence of the other world/unconscious (includes personal, cultural, collective unconscious)
- Sense that there is something, some power or force in the universe larger than myself. Perhaps love, perhaps it is something else. The world is bigger and larger than man-made and nature is to be respected.
- Meditation. Numinous experience. Daily practice.
- Being kind, thoughtful and making space for thinking and feeling in sacred spaces.
- Consistent prayer practice and long term study
- I was brought up by a very religious mother, and had a religious education throughout the school years. I have moved away from formalised religion, whilst still having a strong sense of spiritual.
- Daily meditation and yoga for many years. Exploration of many religious/spiritual writings and imagery. Deep

knowledge of God/Goddess from personal numinous experiences.

- Originally guidance from the Jewish and Christian traditions. More recently through engaging with Jungian analysis and studies. A knowing that my life (and the life of others) us influenced by forces greater than myself. This knowing arising out of experiences of awe and wonder, amongst many others.
- Contemplative prayer, recognition of God in all of the universe, etc.
- Personal prayer and meditation; participation in the life of a local church community, silent retreat
- Private introverted contemplation around some Christian wisdom
- Quaker, becoming Buddhist
- I attend a Christian church and enjoy the traditions and belief in a higher spirit that it offers. I also think about our relationship with nature and allow myself to touch stones, plants, shells and be with whatever that evokes within me.
- It's more of a "knowing" than a belief, and I don't have an explicit practice. I have moments of profound connection, often brought on by music. I am aware of the sense of responsibility and curiosity that wants me to be more disciplined in developing a practice.

Q3 *Could you explain further the role/importance of your spiritual practice in your personal life?*

- Difficult, it is to do with purpose, the journey from birth to death, meaning a higher power.
- My rock and foundation – what makes sense of everything, my sense of identity, my values, my inspiration, my strength

- I meditate daily, I subscribe to Buddhist principles in my daily life, I attend a Buddhist class weekly and I go on 10 day silent retreats annually.
- It is a core aspect to my life. Without it, my life would have no meaning.
- To me, it is the foundation of all my thinking, ethical and in my work – though the patients would not know. It is the basis of life.
- Maintaining a connection to my inner world, which in turn is connected to the whole other world, which extends to the cosmos.
- Grounds me, keeps me feeling there is a bigger purpose to thinks than the day to day nonsense, helps me through difficult times, allows me to slow down and wonder at life and nature.
- It is central to everything I do.
- Allows me to bear and try to tolerate difference
- I pray regularly on my own, and in groups
- Something deeply personal and internal
- Underpins how I live my life
- Provides sense of community and joining in sacred music is uplifting. I am a member of church choir.
- It offers a sense of being sustained and held; and that there is a purpose to my life which is unfolding
- It is the ground on which and out of which I live – embodying this is important too i.e. incarnating this
- I would describe it as the rock on which I build the rest of my life.
- It's a soft, subtle sense of the mysterious.
- I feel that to exist more fully in this world, I need to have a relationship with nature and spiritualty. It provides a sense of belonging and wholeness.
- Provides space for reflection, I am aware of being part of a bigger whole, I feel connected and joyful.

Q4. *Could you explain further the role/importance of your spiritual practice in your professional life.*

- I wish there was space to talk about ethics, morals, integrity, respect.
- It helps to ground and centre me, especially when work is difficult
- It informs how I see people i.e. made in the image of God, it means I pray for each person I see and seek wisdom and discernment as I work with them.
- I meditate and send metta to my patients and supervisees. The Buddhist ethical principles provide a container for my professional life.
- A fundamental attitude of mind, rather than actual practice is what is important in my professional practice.
- I feel that we work in the territory of the unknown, which includes the metaphysical, although of course, I can never actually know this, but I feel it is important to ground myself in a meditative framework of life. Listening to the cosmos, nature, the angels of God, whatever you want to call them.
- AS above, have put 70% because I fail to do all I would like to do. Life intervenes.
- It is essential to hold a religious attitude in my work as a Jungian analyst and psychotherapist.
- It helps me to stay centred. I offer the suggestion to others to meditate when it seems appropriate. It also helps me appreciate that others have their own beliefs and practices.
- Its central to everything I do/think/feel
- Helps to understand faith and bear difference
- Prayer is very important to me, to keep me centred, interior and connected to the Holy Spirit
- A core, underpins my professional practice

- I have several people struggling with the place of faith and the spiritual in their lives. I hope my return to church and willingness to tolerate doubts again helps me to be with them. Anyway, I have always needed a sense on the spiritual e.g. in the natural world.

- I can see that the practice associated with my religious and spiritual beliefs makes a (sometimes subtle) difference to my life experience; I cherish the differences I experience; which usually takes the form of a greater positivity.

- I do not impose any particular practice or belief on my patients, but my own experience is foundational to who I am and from which the whole of my life springs.

- How I regard my patients and myself. Has helped in understanding addicted people and those close to them.

- Helps me to centre-and to realise I facilitate and do not bring about transformation.

- It helps to have some familiarity with many wisdom traditions – openness and curiosity. I think to engage suffering deeply requires some sense of faith – whatever this means. Some knowledge of psychology of fundamentalism and closed systems comes in handy.

- My patients often speak about searching for something more than the immediate and concrete and I feel that my spiritual practice allows me to hear them for fully and explore their meanings and the depths.

- An anchor for the rest of the work.

BIBLIOGRAPHY

Adler, G. (1961). *The Living Symbol.* Bollingen Foundation.

Adler, G. (1979). *Dynamics of the Self.* Coventure.

Alexander, H. (Trans.) (1995). *The Living Witness of the Holy Mountain: Contemporary Voices from Mt Athos.* St Tikhon's Seminary Press.

Amis, R. (1995). *A Different Christianity.* SUNY Press.

Antier, Jean-Jacques (2007). *Teresa of Avila: God Alone Suffices.* Pauline Books.

Association of Jungian Analysts Feschrift, 1977-1998 (1998). Limited edition, private circulation.

Bishop of Nafpaktos Hierotheos (2003). *A Night in the Desert of the Holy Mountain.* (E. Mavromichali, Trans.) Birth of the Theotokos Monastery Greece.

Bouyer, L. (1980). *Mysticism: An Essay on the History of the* Word, Richard Woods(ed), Understanding Mysticism. Image Books, New York.

Bright, G. (2019). Where Did Jung's Red Book Come From and Why Does it Matter? *Guild of Pastoral Psychology* (Lecture/Pamphlet 333).

Caussade, P. (2018). *Abandonment to Divine Providence.* (E.J. Strickland, Trans.). Digireads.com Publishing.

Chariton, I. (1966). *The Art of Prayer: An orthodox anthology*. (E. Kadloubovsky and E Palmer, Trans). Faber and Faber.

Clement, O. (2013). *The Roots of the Christian Mysticism*. (2nd Ed.) New City Press.

Cook, C. (2010). *Finding God in a Holy Place*. Continuum.

Cook, C. (2011). *The Philokalia and the Inner Life: On Passions and Prayer*. James Clarke.

Cook, C. (2012). *Healing, Psychotherapy, and the Philokalia*. (B. Bingaman & B. Nassif, Eds.) *The Philokalia: A Classic Text of Orthodox Spirituality*. Oxford University Press.

Cook, C., McLean, J., & Tyler, P. (2018). *Mystical Theology and Contemporary Spiritual Practice*. Routledge.

Dalrymple, W. (1998). *From the Holy Mountain: A Journey Among the Christians of the Middle East*. Henry Holt & Co.

Dupre, L. (1981). *The Deeper Life: An Introduction to Christian Mysticism*. Crossroad Publishing.

Edinger E. (1996). *The Aion Lectures*, Inner City Books.

Field, N. (1996). *Breakdown and Breakthrough: Psychotherapy in a New Dimension*, Routledge.

Freeman, L. (2000). *The Grateful Church of the Future*. The Tablet.

Fry, T. OSB (trans). (1998). *Rule of St Benedict*. Vintage Spiritual Classics.

Giles, M. E. (trans) (1981). *Francisco de Osuna -The Third Spiritual Alphabet*. Classics of Western Spirituality, Paulist Press.

Griffiths, B. (1954). *The Golden String*. Templegate.

Harton, F.P. (1957). *The Elements of the Spiritual Life: A Study in Ascetical Theology*. SPCK.

Hieromonk Alexander (Golitzin) (1995). *The Living Witness of the Holy Mountain: Contemporary Voices from Mt Athos*. St Tikhon's Seminary Press.

Houdek, F. (1996). *Guided by the Spirit: A Jesuit Perspective on Spiritual Direction*. Loyola Press.

Howells, E. (2002). *John of the Cross and Teresa of Avila: Mystical Knowing and Selfhood.* Crossroad Publishing.

Jacobi, J. (1967). *The Way of Individuation.* Harcourt, Brace and World Inc.

James, W. (1902). *The Varieties of Religious Experience.* Longman, Green and Co.

Julian of Norwich. (2015). *Revelations of Divine Love.* (B. Windeatt, Trans.) Oxford University Press. (Original work published ca 14th century).

Jung, C. G. (August 20, 1945) in a Letter to P.W. Martin.

Jung, C. G. (1964). *Man and His Symbols.* Dell Publishing.

Jung, C. G. (1966a). On the Psychology of the Unconscious (R. F. C. Hull, Trans.). In H. Read et al. (Eds.), *The Collected Works of C. G. Jung: Volume 7. Two Essays on Analytical Psychology.* Princeton University Press. (Original work published 1943)

Jung, C. G. (1966b). The Relations Between the Ego and the Unconscious (R. F. C. Hull, Trans.). In H. Read et al. (Eds.), *The Collected Works of C. G. Jung: Volume 7. Two Essays on Analytical Psychology.* Princeton University Press. (Original work published 1928)

Jung, C. G. (1966c). The Psychology of the Transference (R. F. C. Hull, Trans.). In H. Read et al. (Eds.), *The Collected Works of C. G. Jung: Volume 16. Practice of Psychotherapy.* Princeton University Press. (Original work published 1946)

Jung, C. G. (1967a). Freud and Jung: Contrasts (R. F. C. Hull, Trans.). In H. Read et al. (Eds.), *The Collected Works of C. G. Jung: Volume 4. Freud and Psychoanalysis.* Princeton University Press. (Original work published 1931)

Jung, C. G. (1967b). *The Collected Works of C. G. Jung: Volume 5. Symbols of Transformation* (R. F. C. Hull, Trans.) (H. Read et al., Eds.). Princeton University Press. (Original work published 1952)

Jung, C. G. (1967c). Commentary on "The Secret of the Golden Flower" (R. F. C. Hull, Trans.). In H. Read et al. (Eds.), *The Collected Works of C. G. Jung: Volume 13. Alchemical Studies.* Princeton University Press. (Original work published 1929)

Jung, C. G. (1968a). *The Collected Works of C. G. Jung: Volume 9 pt. 2. Aion: Researches into the Phenomenology of the Self* (R. F. C. Hull, Trans.) (H. Read et al., Eds.). Princeton University Press. (Original work published 1951)

Jung, C. G. (1968b). Introduction to the Religious and Psychological Problems of Alchemy (R. F. C. Hull, Trans.). In H. Read et al. (Eds.), *The Collected Works of C. G. Jung: Volume 12. Psychology and Alchemy.* Princeton University Press. (Original work published 1943)

Jung, C. G. (1969a). The transcendent function (R. F. C. Hull, Trans.). In H. Read et al. (Eds.), *The Collected Works of C. G. Jung: Volume 8. Structure and Dynamics of the Psyche.* Princeton University Press. (Original work published 1958)

Jung, C. G. (1969b). Psychology and Religion. In H. Read et al. (Eds.), *The Collected Works of C. G. Jung: Volume 11. Psychology and Religion.* Princeton University Press. (Original work published 1940)

Jung, C. G. (1969c). Foreword to Suzuki's "Introduction to Zen Buddhism" (R. F. C. Hull, Trans.). In H. Read et al. (Eds.), *The Collected Works of C. G. Jung: Volume 11. Psychology and Religion.* Princeton University Press. (Original work published 1939)

Jung, C. G. (1969d). Archetypes of the Collective Unconscious (R. F. C. Hull, Trans.). In H. Read et al. (Eds.), *The Collected Works of C. G. Jung: Volume 9 pt. 1. Archetypes and the Collective Unconscious.* Princeton University Press. (Original work published 1954)

Jung, C. G. (1970a). *The Collected Works of C. G. Jung: Volume 14. Mysterium Coniunctionis* (R. F. C. Hull, Trans.) (H. Read et al., Eds.). Princeton University Press. (Original work published 1955-56)

Jung, C. G. (1970b). A Psychological View of Conscience (R. F. C. Hull, Trans.). In H. Read et al. (Eds.). *The Collected Works of C. G. Jung: Volume 10. Civilization in Transition.* Princeton University Press. (Original work published 1958)

Jung, C. G. (1971). *The Collected Works of C. G. Jung: Volume 6. Psychological Types* (R. F. C. Hull, Trans.) (H. Read et al., Eds.). Princeton University Press. (Original work published 1921)

Jung, C. G., & Riklin, F. (1973a). The Associations of Normal Subjects (D. Riviere & L. Stein, Trans.). In H. Read et al. (Eds.), *The Collected Works of C. G. Jung: Volume 2. Experimental Researches.* Princeton University Press. (Original work published 1904)

Jung, C. G., Adler, G., & Jaffé, A. (Eds.); R. F. C. Hull (Trans.) (1973b). *C. G. Jung letters, Volume 1.* Princeton University Press.

Jung, C. G., Adler, G., & Jaffé, A. (Eds.); R. F. C. Hull (Trans.) (1975). *C. G. Jung letters, Volume 2.* Princeton University Press.

Jung, C. G. (1980). On the Frontiers of Knowledge. In William McGuire and RFC Hull (Eds.) *C. G. Jung Speaking.* Picador.

Jung, C. G. (1983). *Memories, Dreams, Reflections.* Fontana.

Jung, C. G. & Shamdasani, S. (Ed) (2009). *The Red Book, Liber Novus.* M. Kyburz and J Peck, (Trans.) W.W. Norton and Co.

Kavanaugh, K. & Rodriguez, O. (Trans.) (1979). *The Collected Works of St John of the Cross.* ICS Publications.

Kavanagh, K and Rodriguez, O. (Trans.) (1980-1987). *The Collected Works of St Teresa of Avila,* 3 Volumes. ICS Publications.

Laird, M. (2006). *Into the Silent Land: The Practice of Contemplation*. Darton, Longmen, and Todd.

Lossky, V. (1991). *The Mystical Theology of the Eastern Church*. Clarke and Co.

Louth, A. (1981). *The Origins of the Christian Mystical Tradition*. Clarendon Press.

May, G. (1992). *Care of Mind, Care of Spirit*. HarperCollins.

McGinn, B. (1990). *Foundations of Mysticism (Volume 1)*. SCM Press.

McGinn, B. (2001). *The Language of Inner Experience in Christian Mysticism*. Spiritis 1.

McLean, J. (1997). *Toward Sacred Union – The Mystical Journey of the Soul*, Vol 34. Sufi.

McLean, J. (2003, 2013, 2017). *Towards Mystical Union*. St Pauls.

McLean, J. (2005). St Teresa of Avila and Self-Knowledge: Psychology and the Spiritual Journey. *Mount Carmel Journal*. *53*(1).

McLean, J. (2005). God Enters Through Our Wounds: St Teresa and the 'Shadow'. *Mount Carmel Journal*. *53*(4).

McLean, J. (2007). *Teresa of Avila and Depth Psychology*. The Guild of Pastoral Psychology. (Lecture/Pamphlet 299).

McLean, J. (2014). The Third Spiritual Alphabet, Guide of St Teresa: A Learning Hidden Deep in the Heart. *Mount Carmel Journal*. *62*(4).

McLean, J. (2015). The Third Spiritual Alphabet, Guide of St Teresa: Exploring the Path of Recollection. *Mount Carmel Journal*. *63*(1).

Melloni, J. (2000). *The Exercises of St Ignatius Loyola in the Western Tradition*. Gracewing.

Meltzer, D. (1975). Explorations in Autism. Roland Harris Educational Trust.

Merton, T. (1996). *Contemplative Prayer.* Image/Doubleday, New York.

Merton, T. (1972). *New Seeds of Contemplation.* New Directions Paperback.

Miller, J. (2004). *The Transcendent Function: Jung's Model of Psychological Growth Through Dialogue with the Unconscious.* SUNY Press.

Ogden, T. (1989). *The Primitive Edge of Experience.* Jason Aronson Inc.

Peers, E. A. (Trans.) (1946). *The Complete Works of Saint Teresa of Jesus:* 3 Volumes. Sheed and Ward.

Samuels, A. (1985). *Jung and the Post Jungians.* Routledge.

Saunders, C. (2018). *The Mystical Theology of Margery Kempe,* chapter in *Mystical Theology and Contemporary Spiritual Practice.* Cook, McLean and Tyler, Routledge.

Sherrard, P. (1990). *The Sacred in Life and Art.* Golgonooza Press.

Solomon, H.M. (1998). The Self in Transformation: The Passage from a Two to a Three-Dimensional Internal World. *Journal of Analytical Psychology. 43(2).*

Spearing, C. (2001). *The Cloud of Unknowing and Other Works.* Penguin Classics, New York.

St Teresa of Avila. (1957). *The Life of Saint Teresa by Herself.* (J.M. Cohen, Trans.). Penguin Classics. (Original work published 1611)

St Teresa of Avila. (1995). *The Interior Castle.* Fount/HarperCollins Religious. (Original work published 1588)

Tacey, D. (2004). *The Spirituality Revolution.* Taylor and Francis.

Tacey, D. (2007). After Tradition: Closer Encounters with the Sacred. *Guild of Pastoral Psychology.* (Lecture/Pamphlet 300).

Tacey, D. (2009). *The Hell of Initiation: Jung's Ambivalence Toward of Modernity.* Guild of Pastoral Psychology. (Lecture/Pamphlet 302).

The Observer, 2 September 2002.

Tyler, P. (1997). *The Way of Ecstasy*. Canterbury Press.

Tyler, P. (2011). *The Return to the Mystical: Ludwig Wittgenstein, Teresa of Avila and the Christian Mystical Tradition*. Continuum.

Tyler, P. (2013). *Teresa of Avila: Doctor of the Soul*. Bloomsbury.

Ulanov, A.B. & Dueck, A. (2008). *The Living God and the Living Psyche*. William Eerdmans, Cambridge.

Ulanov, A. (1988). *The Wisdom of the Psyche*. Daimon.

Underhill, E. (1996). *Mysticism: the Nature and Development of Spiritual Consciousness*. Oneworld.

von Hügel, F. (2018). *The Mystical Element of Religion*. (Classic reprint). Forgotten Books.

Waaijman, K. (1999). *The Mystical Space of Carmel: A Commentary on the Carmelite Rule*. Peeters.

Wakefield, G. (Ed.) (1983). *Dictionary of Christian Spirituality*. SCM.

Ware, K. (2000). *The Inner Kingdom*. St Vladimirs Seminary Press.

Welch, J. (1982). *Spiritual Pilgrims: Carl Jung and Teresa of Avila*. Paulist Press.

Williams, R. (1991). *Teresa of Avila*. Geoffrey Chapman.

Yeats, W.B. (1990). *Collected Poems*. Picador.

Young-Eisendrath, P. & Miller, M. (Eds). (2000). *The Psychology of Mature Spirituality*. Routledge.

INDEX